Hello Chris

I hope the book gives you a flavour of the extraordinary that it is to follow a Lions Tour.

Perhaps it might tempt you to South Africa in 2021...

My very best wishes

Kev

FOCUS ON THE FANS: Lions Tour 2017

Fan Names

Nearly 600 Lions and All Blacks fans are name-checked individually or collectively in the narrative of this book and its picture captions. We thank you all for taking the trouble to talk to us and for allowing us to tell your stories of your tours, interwoven with our own. We appreciate just as much the many more fans we encountered who appear unnamed in pictures in the book, and those with whom we had conversations in New Zealand that didn't result in a story being included.

In the order of where we first encountered you on tour, individuals or the groups they were part of who are in the book are listed here. If there are spelling errors, omissions or incomplete names we hope these are few and far between, but apologise for them. These may have occurred for a number of reasons:

i.   Inaccurate written recording of names by me (for which I cite my partial deafness as a defence) or by my glamorous assistant, aka my wife, Val (who you'll all excuse anyway just because it was Val)

ii. Difficulty with transcribing voice recordings because of background noise (chiefly other Lions fans in bars)

iii. Your handwriting if you wrote your name down yourself

iv. Your friend's handwriting if someone else wrote down your name

Where we haven't been able to contact people to verify identities, you remain either incorrectly or only partially identified. Please forgive.

AUCKLAND AIRPORT ARRIVALS
Andy Palmer (1)
Gudrun Palmer

WHANGAREI
Michael Holland
Sue Holland
David Holland
Jan (with friend David Holland)
Phil Moore
Clive Lucking
Al Pearce
Bill Dunlop
Cathy Goddard
Steve Goddard
Pauline McDermott
Mark O'Connell
Jack Tully
Alex Scott
Sally Scott
Shani Brough
Ian Brough

Julian Evans
Liz Evans
Peter Taylor
Howard McKenzie
Taz
Ron Wills
Steve Hanratty
Bill Armstrong
Bryan Hodgson
Ginnene Harvey-Lovell
Ben Harvey-Lovell
Michael Lovell
Natasha Finlay
Steve Finlay
Leon Finlay
Melissa Brake
Kerry Stevenson
Eric Sprigg
Maurice Arnold
Les Barclay
Lloyd Matthews
Lauren Barclay

Margaret Matthews
George Moore
Nicola Moore
John Moore
Dave Dumelow
Val Ager
Leigh Fitzgerald
Lizzie Carroll-Thom
Michael Byrne
Paula Whelan
Steve Bosworth
Andrew White
Andi Ttofa
Nine of Britain's finest young doctors and nurses (all working in New Zealand)

AUCKLAND – BLUES MATCH
Max Leighton
Maria Leighton
Xander Leighton
Scarlett Leighton
Blues fan Grant

Simon, John (the bar owner), Leila and Shanie from 'Outside Obie'
George Pritchard
Sandy Geddes
Norrie Flowers
Paul Thomson

CHRISTCHURCH

Justin Davies
Anthony Flynn
Clodagh Toomey
Damien Meere
Sarah Hayes
Tim Bird
Henry Bird
Mal Morgan
Isabel Morgan
Jackie Teeling
Kieran Teeling
Paul Coleman
Jude Coleman
Luca Coleman
Izzy Coleman
Dylan Coleman
Ted Williams
Nicola Williams
Nicholas Price
Dick Jones
Diana Jones
Jamie Little
Gavin Campbell
Michelle Chung
Sam Chung
Jo Thomas
Rob Thomas
Peter Beatty
David (Dai) Lloyd
Mark Davies
Chris Moore
Toby ?
Jeremy Stevens
Nicolas Casely-Parker
Gabriel Schondent

Jay Rogers
Stu James
Andy Walton
David Johnston
Jodie Davies
Chris Davies
Annie and Adam (from Bude)

DUNEDIN

Taff (Kevin), Phil and Gareth
Trudi Gatland and dad Terry, mum Margaret and
Auntie Noelene
Johnny Morris
Karl Hendry
Elaine Hughes
Matt Hanly
Elliot White
Simon Foot
Olly Maxwell
Alex Fenton
Jack Westenra
Chris McNamee
Terri-Anne Busbridge
Sapphire De-la-haye
Ben Bacon
Rachel Bacon
Jack Surcouf
Calum Fraser
Oliver Beaumont
Sen Dhayalan
Rob Gill
Paul Heatley
Felix Goodone
A N Other (with the six above)
Tim O'Donnell
Tina O'Donnell
Calum Auld
Gordon Ferrier
Brian Leary
Brendan Leary
Simon Leary
Haydn Leary
The crew of 'HMS Gatland'

Barry O'Neil
Michael Silke
Lance Robinson
Mark Robinson
Andrew Hearne and Kiwi friends Neil and Anthony
Anthony McGladdery
Emily Acton
Jake Bristow
Jane Bentley
Steve Bentley
James Reeves
Katie Phillips
Liam Black
James Kelly
Justin Roberts
Cath Hawbrook
Pete Bleddyn-Jones
Alun Owen
Paul Roser
Christina Jackson

ARROWTOWN/QUEENSTOWN

Stephen Jack
Thomas Buckley
Jonny Murray
Gavin Murray
Julie Murray
Charlie Murray
Sinead Ryan
Charles Kelly
Emma Walsh
Alan Cremin

ROTORUA

Andrew Pollock
Jhuan Roux
Peter Lindsley
Ian Lindsley
Mike Hollister
Geri Thomas/Hollister
Brian Thomas
Nick Smith
Mairead McGinley

Sophie Starr
Nigel Starr
Simon Chadwick
Aifric O'Malley
Lesley Warne
Reg Warne
James Broomer
Brett Crowton
Will Caspari
Nigel Bellamy
Glyn Jenkins
Wendy Jenkins
Paul Roles
Yvonne Morgan
'G' Morgan
Peter Wren-Hilton
Jacquie Wren-Hilton
Paul Percival
Kyla Bourne
The Thirsty Fencers

HAMILTON
Marc van de Peer
Jo Mallard
Ian (Ducky) Mallard
David Coates
Jim Hughes
Huw Jenkins
Maria Nordstrom
Mark - Maria's partner
Simon Elliot
Caroline Theobald
Sue Woolford
Bob Woolford
David Williams
Rhys Williams
Andrew Long
Elle Long
Julia Oaten
Paul Oaten
Caryn Snell
John Snell
Ethan Bates

Simon Bates
Sarah Bates
Colm Murphy
Conor Murphy
Ronan Boylan
Rolo James
James Lambert
Frank Skinner
Gareth Price
Andrew Bell
Anne-Maria Bell
Doug Price
Daniel Trick
Rachel Trick
Katie Dooley
Rhys Beddow
Robert Samuel
Desert Island Dave
Stuart Knox
Andy Morley
Richie Jermyn
Iain McGannand
Rob Anderson
Neil Wilkinson
Bertie Burleigh
Lloyd Williams
Max Bray
Ian Harris
Elwyn Owens
Dylan Owens
James Dare
Kevin McIntosh
Jordan Howes
Tony - Jordan's Grandad
Dominique Forrest
Dan Westerby
Chris Ward
Andrew Richards
Fiona Williams
Jessica Talbot
Alex Gammon
Charlie Leddy

Mark Leddy
Barry Smith
Mark Thorrington
James Whelan
Michael Bryon

WAITOMO CAVES
Sonia Clark
Colin Davidson
Kathy, Colin's daughter
Jeremy Ankers
Rachel Parkes
Josie, Jeremy and Rachel's baby daughter

AUCKLAND – 1ST TEST
Graham Newling
Judith Williams
'Brisbane Rob'
Gary O'Brien
Jonny O'Brien
Mike Cutt
Frasier Cutt
Toby Cutt
Simon Clarke
Amanda Clarke
Paul Matthews
John Tidy
Lizzie Tidy
Sarah Melvin
Sinead Healy
Emer O'Leary
Birlyn Greenough
Bechan Jones
Alison Butler
Deirdre Reilly
Iain Douglas
Mal Douglas
Ann and Brian Jones
Nicci Hyman
Leanne Collins
Ollie Stuchbury
Josh Skinner
Joff Jennings

Tim Harrison
The Knutsford Boys
Ross Preston
Finlay Preston
Tony Campbell
Kevin Bowers
Antony Bowers
Jon Jenner
Annelise Kerr

WELLINGTON
The Ginvalids
Tim Manning
Neil MacGregor
Tony Wilson-Spratt
Trevor Barker
Jon Everest
Jane Shaw
Derek Lockett
Keith Duffy (and the memory of Martin Duffy)
Pauline Baxter
Darren Vicat
Gary Marriner
Harry Hoard
Margaret-Anne Tuke
Simon Tuke
Boys from Dunvant RFC
Matt Lambourne
John Gilfillan
Kevin Manning
Graham Hill
Gary Evans
Warren Blakestock
Julien Daniel
Mike King
Charlie Ives
Keith Leadbetter
James Della-Porta
James' mate Trev
Will Uzzell
Simon Flanagan
Jordan Phipps
Daniel Leworthy

Mathew Leworthy
Andy Spencer
Berry Hill Rugby Club
Hayley Pynsent
Jonny Peel
Paul Whitham
David Haller
Kevin Morgan
Geoff Aspinall
Ronnie Hunter
David Murphy
Andy Frewin
Rob Edwards
John Greatrex
Ray Mills
Kim Mills
Euan Mills
Maria Elias
Nigel Elias
Will Vander Gucht
Jack Cooper
Simon Gateley
Colleen Rowlands
Adrian Rowlands
Sian Thomas
Paul Thomas
Scott Gregory
Gary Miller
Colin Picton
Lee Miller
Sean Grundy
Mark Kenny
Kim Scott
Peter Longmore
Phil Birch
Walter Todd
Tom Birch
Alex Todd
Sean Ahearne
Ruth Ivers
Colleen Munro
Sam Gibbons

Jack Gibbons
Caoimhe Sheehan
Tadhg Sheehan
Tim Sheehan
Abergele and Rhyl Rugby Seniors
Geoff Collenso
Gary Plucker
Sam Mathews
Lloyd Smith
Dewi Jones
Darrell Cooper
Lisa Clemmett
Lloyd Collier
James Leckenby
David Johnston
Ian Davies
Heath Byron
Jason Dempsey
Adam Gilshnan
Breffni O'Reilly
Gary Speak
Adam Barclay
William Petersen
Ryan Toki
George McMahon
Neil Oliver
Mark Wakefield
Malcolm Kerr
Michael Todd
Stuart Rundell
Bob Marks
Matthew Nightingale
Ed Howard
Jamie Flood
Blair McMurray
Carol Menzies
Ivor Menzies
Isabel Halliday
David Halliday
John McGrath
Peter McGrath
Danny McGrath

Sophie Freestone
Sophie's mum and dad

AUCKLAND – 3RD TEST
Andrew Ward
Ewen Johnstone
Nick Hillyard
Roger Meadows
Robbie Regan
Steve Thompson
Stephen Thompson
Simon Richards (aka 'Tart')
Will Thompson (aka 'H')
Roy Powell
Derrick Symonds
Spike Powles
Robin Harrison
Andrew Palmer (2)
Holly Redfern
Louise Redfern
Colin Thornewill
Jordan Lovatt
Barney Tibbatts
Shaun Tibbatts
Thomas Grafton
James Grafton
Jim Evans
Alan Rose
Nick Flynn
Sam Lawrence
Andy Beller
Kelly Brennan-Kleyn
Lee Donald
Professor Andrew Walton
Ciara Walton
Colette Walton

Sir Colin Chater
Shaun Stewart
Deborah Baird-Palmer
Gillian Chater
Rachael Yost
Nadia Rokan
Rachael Bass
James Bass
Andrew Palmer (3)
Karen Armstrong
Martin Armstrong
Patricia Cray
Rosie Cray
Steve Cray
Peter Nash
Andrew Pointon
Francesca Padley
George Collins
Neil England
Daren Parsons
Steve Pitts
Chris Baker
Glove puppets Leo and Llew (with Ceri's hands you know where)
Orna Nicholl
Conor Manning
Keara Nicholl
Julian Shaw
Kim Petersen
Geoff Petersen
Tim Petersen
Holly Foreman

POST-SCRIPTS
Joseff Esposti
Jo Esposti
Tony Esposti

Simon-James Smith
Andy Toy
Sheila Toy
Caroline Mc Glone
Martin Downey
Helen Sheridan
Graeme Cook
Clare Cook
Liam Cook
Pam Tod
Emma Francis
Steven Francis
Sara Vesey-Holt
Kelly George
Maggie Lord
Yorkie Lord
Pete Jones
Phil Miles
Mick Payne
Ash Barker
Gerard Geenty (aka Gersh, aka 'Arold)
Emilie Declippeleir
Tammy Muir
David Muir
Wayne Tacon
Richmond Good Old Boys - Fat Tony, Shagger, Damo,
Tom Stokes
Fat Tony's son, Hugo
Paul Wallace
Sam Wallace
Logan Wallace
Wayne Davies (aka Nurse Doctor)
Seryna Davies
Tom Davies…

…and the latest addition to the Lions family…
Gruffydd Davies

Sam and Jack Gibbons – this picture taken at the first test was picked up by many news organisations

FOREWORD: by Rory Underwood MBE

England's all-time leading try scorer and former Lions player in the 1989 and 1993 tours to Australia and New Zealand

In 1888, the promoter of the first tour to Australia and New Zealand, Arthur Shrewsbury, demanded "something that would be good material and yet take them by storm out here". Little did he realise the part he would play in creating the phenomenon that is the Lions traveling fans.

For rugby players from Great Britain and Ireland, touring as the British and Irish Lions is the highest accolade that can be bestowed on you. To wear the red shirt of Wales, the white shorts of England and the green and blue socks of Ireland and Scotland and call yourself a Lion fills one with pride, of what the strip means and has meant for over a hundred years, in this country and round the world.

The allure of following the Lions has driven many a rugby widow to despair as all savings and holidays go towards the 'next' Lions tour. The devoted Lions support has swelled in both numbers and fervour over the years and is now one of the characteristics of a Lions tour that makes it so special.

As a Lions player, to walk around Johannesburg, Sydney or Auckland in the week leading up to a Test and see a mass of red shirts moving through the streets, is a heartening and humbling feeling that reminds you of the magnitude of the responsibility that you carry. The sight and sound that welcomes you into the stadium as you take the field is a privilege that few have experienced; only those of us who are lucky enough to emerge from the tunnel and walk onto that hallowed turf can attest to that. The sea of red and cacophony of noise that greets you as you emerge is a visual and audio feast, it further emboldens you as a team, to face the challenge of the Blacks, Boks or Wallabies.

The record books will show the wins, draws and losses of all the Lions series over the years, in all the countries that they have played, but only those that were there will know the part that the Lions fans will have played. The Lions fans are an irresistible force that are quite rightly thought of as the Lions 16th man, envied by the opposition and begrudgingly admired by home supporters.

With 'Focus on the Fans', Ken has captured the essence of the Lions supporter, the passion, belief and spirit that has become synonymous with Lions tours. If you are one of the lucky ones to have supported the Lions, then these stories and images are memories you'll cherish for years to come; if not, then be warned, that being consumed into this world may see you booking your plane ticket for four years hence, and the next Lions tour. Enjoy.

Rory

Pictures on this page courtesy of Rory Underwood MBE and Getty Images

THE TOUR ITINERARY

Ashton Keynes

London

Hong Kong

Auckland

Whangarei

Auckland

Christchurch

Dunedin

Arrowtown

Auckland

Rotorua

Hamilton

Auckland

Whanganui

Wellington

Rotorua

Auckland

Whangarei

Auckland

Singapore

London

Ashton Keynes

CONTENT

26th June	**Whanganui to Wellington**
27th June – 1st July	**Wellington – What A Week To Remember**
2nd July	**Wellington to Rotorua**
3nd July	**Rotorua to Auckland – The Roundabout Route**
3rd – 9th July	**Auckland – History In The Making**
9th - 12th July	**Full Circle**
	Post Script

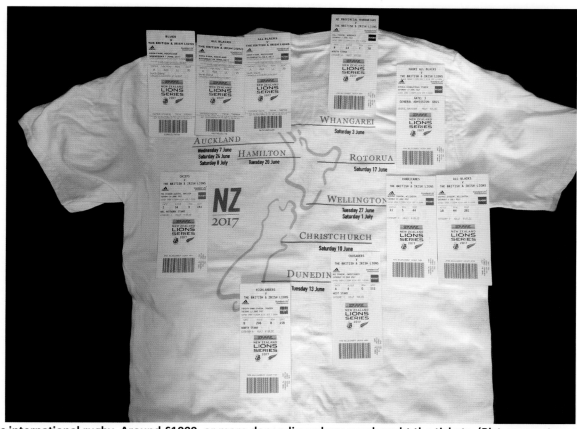

NZ$1793.53 worth of top class international rugby. Around £1000, or more depending where you bought the tickets. (Picture courtesy of and ©Gerard Geenty)

Why FOCUS ON THE FANS?

Lions Tours are never just about the rugby. They never have been.

In his introduction to 'Behind The Lions', rugby journalist and author Stephen Jones talks of wanderlust as having been one of rugby's important distinguishing characteristics since the game was initially codified.

He's right too - although many might argue that wanderlust is simply a national trait of the British & Irish, and has always been so. Whether the folklore of William Webb-Ellis supposedly first running with the ball in his hands in 1823 is true or not, the game of rugby was created at a time when The British Empire was rapidly expanding its boundaries. That pioneering gentlemen should introduce their preferred sports to their new horizons is entirely understandable.

Which could well be the reason that since the very earliest days of the sport, tours have been a feature of rugby clubs at every level the game is played. There is a very strong case for rugby to claim pre-eminence in the world of sporting tours, with the Lions tour unarguably its pinnacle.

The building of the Empire most certainly explains why, with a sprinkling of visits to other colonial cousins en-route, the primary destinations for tours of the now British & Irish Lions have always been South Africa, New Zealand and Australia, the colonies who most fervently embraced the sport of rugby.

These days the unique coming together of the cream of English, Irish, Scottish and Welsh** rugby union players, who would ordinarily be battering the hell out of each other when playing for their own nation, has become for many of them the highest professional goal to aim for. Those who achieved selection for the Lions down the years often describe the tour as their finest rugby career memory. Many of the fans who now accompany them on tour describe doing so as the trip of a lifetime. I understand exactly why.

Adolescent envy: That's not adolescents being envious, it's my envy of today's adolescents. I admit I am incredibly envious that it is now the norm for vast numbers of school or university leavers to take a year out to 'travel' at a young age. The accepted wisdom these days is that life experiences add to the intellectual roundness of young human beings - almost compensating for the physical roundness added by the amount of alcohol consumed during their sojourns. But only almost.

In 1977 I was a fairly bright 18-year-old school-leaver from a council estate starting work in National Westminster Bank's Slough 128 High Street branch on a salary of around £1150 pa. Even then I found the idea of the southern hemisphere both exciting and enticing, despite my first foreign travel being still to come (a day trip to Calais in 1978). In that very different era to today it was almost unheard of to even know of someone travelling down under for any reason whatsoever. At that time, such a journey seemed beyond imagination to me. I certainly never imagined that forty years later my wife, Val, and I would be taking our fourth Antipodean trip in 8 years, this time to follow the Lions in 2017.

Even at their tender ages, both our daughter and our son have spent many months more in Australia than we have aggregated on our four journeys south of the equator so far; and for good measure, on their respective travels to reach there they saw much more of Asia than we probably ever will.

So, when former Lions captain Bill Beaumont and then RFU Chief Executive Ian Ritchie graciously allowed me to interrupt their conversation in Auckland this summer to ask Bill for his recollections of fans supporting the Lions on his '77 and '80 tours, I wasn't greatly surprised that he chuckled before replying:

"It was forty years ago. There were no bloody fans!"

**no favouritism here, strictly alphabetical order only*

Bill Beaumont & Ian Ritchie

That rugby fans began to follow the Lions in far greater numbers from the late eighties and nineties onwards is in my opinion a combination of two key factors.

Firstly, relatively lower air fares as a percentage of income combined with the low cost of living in the southern hemisphere countries meant far more people could afford long haul travel in the late '80 and the '90s. Local prices haven't changed greatly since then by the way – it's the massive falls in the value of the GB pound since then that makes Australia and New Zealand appear expensive to Brits now.

Secondly, the advent of professionalism meant the associated rise in commercial activity related to the sport was inevitable, including 'monetising' rugby fans. Soccer recognised many years previously that its followers could be motivated to spend a significantly greater proportion of their income to watch the game they love. The danger has always been pricing 'ordinary' fans out of the game.

To which point, I honestly think the Lions commercial operation is in danger of shooting themselves in the foot. I base that on the proportion of Lions fans in New Zealand in 2017 who travelled on official tours versus the far higher number who travelled independently, and the feedback I heard from both camps. Fans we spoke to who were on official tours say that the organisation and pre-test match entertainment was definitely top notch – but also that it absolutely had to be for the eye-watering amounts they'd paid. As for match tickets, as you'll read, that caused a good deal of eyebrow raising when fans got to New Zealand.

But what was it that made me want to go on a 22-stage tour to and around New Zealand and back; with 6 flights aggregating a shade under 25000 miles (40000km); 3 cars hired, in which according to Hertz we drove a total of 3235 miles (5175km) - the vast majority of those on single carriageway roads; living out of suitcases for 7 weeks; changing our accommodation 16 times in that period; then put together nearly 600 photos and a shade under 79,000 words about it?

It was never just about the rugby.

I'm a freelance photojournalist now. I first had the idea to compile a book about fans attending a major sporting event while reading an article in bed, 6 weeks or so before the 2006 FIFA World Cup Finals in Germany. Unlike any other host country before, all of whom routinely made it clear that fans without tickets would not be welcome, Germany said to come along anyway, as they intended to make the tournament also the world's biggest party.

That night I woke up about two in the morning with the idea of **THE FANS' WORLD CUP** spinning around my mind. I envisaged a photographic essay of fans gathering to support their national teams. The intermingling of team colours from the 32 participating nations, together with shots of fans experiencing the emotional drama of matches, offered the prospect of striking visual imagery.

Knowing that England fans would make the short hop over the channel in their tens of thousands, I also wondered if their expectations would be met by the German idea of a party. I scribbled down the thoughts tumbling around my head and went back to sleep.

When I woke and read what I'd written I felt the idea had some legs, so fleshed out the night time thoughts into what seemed to me a good candidate for a book.

That's when I discovered that getting a book deal with a traditional publisher apparently involves not just capturing their imagination, but giving at least a year's notice of your intentions. Nonetheless, I did manage to find a small specialist sports publisher who hadn't been trading for very long who liked the idea, and whose directors thought - like many others - that England would do very well. My idea offered them the prospect of having 'something for the back burner' in case (for a change) England's footballers met the aspirations of the nation they represent.

The online bookmaker Sportingbet plc and a very close and very generous friend, Brian Pawley, also liked the idea. Between them they covered my expenses to carry out the assignment.

For those who don't remember – or don't follow or don't care about football – the England team's ignominious exit to Portugal on penalties in the quarter-finals was the last of a distinctly disappointing series of performances.

However, the tournament had been coined THE FANS WORLD CUP by the media, thanks to Germany delivering superbly on their party promise – especially the creation of Fan Zones to replicate a match like atmosphere for those without tickets. The publishers thought I'd hit on an idea that had the potential to be a hit, and loved what I produced, so promised they'd try to get a distribution deal despite England's mediocrity. Sadly, and no matter that the book content would be about the fans not the football, no retailers wanted another book from the world cup on their shelves. No doubt they feared it joining most of the players' books recording the event in bookshop remainder bins merely weeks after publication.

I did however get awarded a Royal Photographic Society Associate (ARPS) distinction for the selection of THE FANS WORLD CUP images I submitted on joining the society – the highest possible award on entry – so it wasn't a complete waste of Sportingbet's and Brian's money (at least from my perspective).

The panel of FIFA World Cup images submitted to the Royal Photographic Society Distinctions Jury

England's failure to qualify for the next major tournament meant the exercise couldn't be repeated soon. Other work commitments - together with the fear of walking round the next two world cup venues, South Africa and Brazil, on my own with £10,000 worth of camera kit on my back meant the idea stayed on hold.

I was fortunate enough to be busy for a few years on other work projects, so didn't give any more thought to a follow up until after the Olympics in 2012, when I had free time to mull over my next piece of work.

From 'The Fans' World Cup' to 'FOCUS ON THE FANS': That the London Olympics was such a massive success was in no small part due to the way Brits all over the country engaged in huge numbers and with exceptional fervour. The atmosphere we fans created was credited by champion after champion as one of the key factors in driving them to achieve peak performance.

Sport in general had also seen eye-boggling increases in commercial revenues from broadcasters and sponsors in the intervening years.

Yet it still seemed to me that fans don't get the recognition we deserve for what we bring to elite sport.

Those who spend millions (some even billions) to align themselves with sport do so entirely because of us. They want us to watch their programmes and buy their products - entirely reasonable of course, and one assumes successful, given the enormous sums involved. If fans didn't turn up in their tens of thousands at sporting events, and watch in their millions on TV, elite sport would be nowhere near as well funded as it is. **I wanted to tell a story that reflects the part we play.**

Additionally, times and technology have changed dramatically over the last 10 years. With the superb advances in camera phones, and the corresponding explosion in their use to not just record events, but also share them with the world, I felt the time was perfect to resurrect the concept of a fan focused book. Only this time, it should be possible to really engage fans in helping to create the end result – harnessing some of the thousands of images fans would take, and telling the stories that drive multitudes of people to travel widely to follow their chosen sport.

On 2nd October 2012 I decided that the idea of celebrating those who follow The British & Irish Lions on tour was a perfect example to illustrate the lengths sports fans will go to in order to witness elite sport at its very best. Travelling half way round the world for up to 6 weeks of touring around host cities, following a team created from the best of English, Irish, Scottish and Welsh rugby as they take on the southern hemisphere's strongest club sides and international teams requires massive commitment of time, energy and finances.

I figured that the endorsement of The British & Irish Lions themselves would be of great value to the prospective success of the book, and a recognition from the Lions that the travelling fans are indeed considered as the 16th man by the players. A Dublin based business - British Lions Designated Activity Company (BLDAC) – manages the commercial operations of the Lions brand, including Lions Rugby Travel and the relationships with corporate sponsors. I'll mostly refer to them using the phrase 'Lions Rugby' as that is how the people I spoke with referred to their own organisation.

An initial call to Charlie McEwen, then Director of Sales and Marketing for Lions Rugby, elicited a positive reaction. Unfortunately, by the time I got to talk to the agency responsible for licensing official products relating to the 2013 tour to Australia, it was considered too late in the day for the project to proceed.

I earmarked June 2016 as the right time to begin talking to Lions Rugby about the 2017 tour – a full year ahead of its commencement – and got on with my life.

When I called Charlie, by then Chief Operating Officer, in the summer of 2016 to remind him of the idea he said: "Find a way to make this happen, Ken." He introduced me to Essentially Group, another agency, contracted to undertake marketing activities for The British & Irish Lions 2017 tour. I'd never expected Lions Rugby to contribute financially to the project - the finance for the venture was always going to come from our own or a sponsor's resources. For a variety of reasons, becoming a Lions Rugby official licensee proved unworkable in the end. The late stage at which this finally became apparent (April 2017, less than two months before the tour commenced) meant preparation to make FOCUS ON THE FANS happen was just about as far from perfect as it could have been!

We - my wife, Val, and me - set out aiming to produce a book that:

- tells the story of our part in bringing FOCUS ON THE FANS to life before, during and after the tour
- presents a collective memento of why some of those fans who travelled to New Zealand did so, and their Lions tour experiences
- illustrates a little of what makes New Zealand the country it is

It meant that most of our tour involved chatting to thousands of fans during the seven weeks we were away.

Of course, there were gaps between games that required filling, and that meant the need for all of us to travel to the next venue. This afforded opportunities to visit some of the wonders that New Zealand's astonishing topography provides in the way of dramatic landscape scenery and fascinating geographic features. The book therefore also records the places we visited *en-route* between locations and on non-match days, where we invariably ran into other fans also enjoying what New Zealand has to offer beyond rugby. It's never just about the rugby.

As many of them confirmed to us, the rugby is the excuse to come here, but it's by no means the only reason. A surprisingly high number volunteered that the rugby results were not even the most important aspect of their tour. Being there was what really counted.

What became very apparent too, is what the presence of so many fans brought to New Zealand, its people and - most importantly - to the players and management of the team the fans travelled to support, The British & Irish Lions.

It would be very remiss of me not to start the whole account with a heartfelt thanks to all the Lions fans Val and I met and spoke with in New Zealand. You made that stage of our work on this project an absolute pleasure. That the idea was so well received as a concept by everybody we spoke with made our whole experience a joy to be undertaking – even while traipsing around the bars of the host cities without stopping to enjoy a drink more often than not. Believe me, we'd have loved to sit down and talk for longer with you all over a few drinks.

We know we only managed to engage directly with a fraction of the fans who went on tour and are grateful to those of you we did for allowing us into your tour.

We sincerely hope this end result meets your expectations.

You'll read about how fans enjoyed New Zealand itself, of Kiwi hospitality, travelling mishaps, kindnesses received and rendered, sacrifices made to be there, and the many other thoughts, opinions and recollections fans themselves have contributed. We certainly enjoyed hearing them. To those whose contributions never made it into the book, we thank you for taking the trouble to relate them to us. We can assure you, all were just as assiduously listened to, read and enjoyed as those that made the final cut, but space demands that editing be done. The book's already nearly a hundred pages longer than we originally anticipated!

I am deeply indebted to our mutual friend Robert Taylor for facilitating my introduction to Lions legend Rory Underwood - whose magnificent try for the Lions in the 2nd test in New Zealand in 1993 will never be forgotten. Of course, I owe a huge thank you to Rory himself for the fine words he has drafted.

As soon as he heard what FOCUS ON THE FANS aimed to do, Rory told me he wanted to express his appreciation of the role fans play from the players' perspective. I am certain every fan will be heartened by Rory's tribute to the contribution they make to the psyche of the players representing them on the pitch. You certainly proved him absolutely right in New Zealand this year.

The Lions Tour 2017 proved to be a historic series of superb rugby matches, tense drama and, ultimately, sharing of the honours between two outstanding squads of players and coaches, all taking place in the astounding country that is New Zealand. This all materialised in a very special atmosphere created by the estimated 20,000+ fans clad in their unifying red shirts in cities across the country.

To answer the question this chapter title poses, 'Why FOCUS ON THE FANS?', it's because you deserve the acclaim; you add a massive amount to the richness of Rugby's greatest test series; you bring a huge boost to the countries you visit, financially as well as in the ambiance and mood you create.

We're so glad we joined you, and that we can bring a message, sent to me by email the day after the extraordinary final test in Auckland:

"The most memorable part of the tour has been the Lions fans. They were awesome!" *Warren Gatland*

Proper Preparation… and why it doesn't always work out that way!

I've spent a good deal of my working life training people, both in business and in sport. A maxim I still swear by for every situation and circumstance is:

'Proper Preparation Prevents Particularly Poor Performance'

(or another much shorter P-word instead of Particularly).

It's a goal that in my view should always be striven for, but I recognise isn't always achievable - even if you do all you might to try and make it so. As you're about to read…

I've already told you the idea for this book had started much earlier - arguably with THE FANS WORLD CUP project in 2006 - but more specifically, with the initial approach to Lions Rugby in June 2016. So why didn't 'FOCUS ON THE FANS: Lions Tour 2017' become an official Lions licensed product?

In my first meeting with Lions Rugby in July 2016, I was told that they expected around 20,000 fans to travel on official tours via Lions Rugby Travel, a joint venture with the highly experienced and very reputable Mike Burton Group. Their figures were based on the fact that travelling on an official tour was the only way fans could guarantee securing the all-important test match tickets.

I had intended trying to find a commercial sponsor, as the risk of me underwriting the £70,000 budget to collect material in New Zealand and print the initial book run would impact too heavily on our retirement plans. That would have meant the sponsor would also need to pay a license fee to Lions Rugby. To avoid complication, I put finding a sponsor on hold and reworked a budget to be personally affordable (instead of two photographers, just me, with no payment until the book sold).

I also intended getting press accreditation to access stadiums during matches so I could capture the emotional drama fans express as they watch the game, so asked Lions Rugby who was organising that accreditation. By the time I got the answer it was already too late to get press accreditation, which meant I couldn't get into stadiums during matches, which in turn made me wonder if it would be worthwhile continuing the project at all. I managed to establish that there would be Fan Zones for all the test matches, where those without tickets could watch games. That was where I'd done most of my work in Germany, so continued to try and move things forward with Lions Rugby.

I was so pleased that Lions Rugby agreed in October 2016 that I could pre-sell the book to their Lions Travel customers. The obvious advantage being that it could make the project self-financing if advance copies were sold. I'm still not sure exactly why it took from October until 28 March 2017 for me to be introduced by Lions Rugby to the people who run Lions Rugby Travel, and it doesn't warrant an inquest to establish reasons. When I did meet them, I immediately liked the two Lions Rugby Travel marketing people I met. They had responded very quickly once the Lions introduction had been made, and both were very enthusiastic about FOCUS ON THE FANS. The information they delivered though, felt like a devastating blow to all my plans.

Far from the 20,000 fans that had been guesstimated 9 months earlier, and which I had used as a base for all my planning, only around 4,500 fans would be joining Lions Rugby Travel official tours. A further 1,500 would be on tours hosted by officially licensed tour operators sub-contracted by Lions Travel. The latter would be excluded from any communication relating to FOCUS ON THE FANS. Data Protection.

The only marketing support the Lions could offer was a paragraph of about 30 words to be included in a general email to Lions Rugby Travel customers who had not excluded receiving third party emails. More Data Protection. Now the potential value of Lions endorsement seemed to be a fraction of what I anticipated. When I saw that the operational restrictions of the licensing agreement - I fully understand the need to protect the Lions brand - involved considerable extra expense and felt very restrictive, I was less convinced about the value of an official association with Lions Rugby.

It was time to reassess the whole viability of the project - again.

After chewing it over for a week or so, I politely declined to take up the licensing offer and considered abandoning the whole venture. Yet all indications from news stories suggested that New Zealand still expected around 20,000+ visitors. These reports were based on hotel and flight booking data. Would so many fans really be travelling independently? It appeared to be the case. Which for me, made it all the more important to tell their story.

The delayed withdrawal from discussions with Lions Rugby also meant I hadn't done much to try and spread the word by social media – not that social media is a communications channel I'd used to any extent previously. I thought I should make an effort though, if only to see if the response was encouraging enough to justify a decision to go.

I quickly posted on a couple of rugby forums to try and communicate with fans who might be travelling to New Zealand, describing FOCUS ON THE FANS and that I'd appreciate hearing Lions related stories. Almost immediately a member of Planet Rugby who goes by the name of **'backrow'** posted, telling how forum members had chipped in to help a hard-up, deserving couple go to New Zealand. I bit, responding that this sounded just the sort of inspiring tale I was hoping to hear. The almost immediate flurry of posts containing emojis wetting themselves laughing led me to a very rambling and entirely mickey-taking thread that backrow had participated in, which bore no relation to the Lions tour at all. I could only raise my hands and acknowledge I'd been had. I should have read a few more threads to get the feel of the forum before registering and posting.

So much for capitalising on social media.

I am a paid-up member of The Chartered Institute of Journalists though, so set about thinking how I might use that to gain coverage.

The Daily Telegraph has for a long time - rightly - been considered the best national for coverage of rugby, so I picked the phone up to **Andy Fifield**, the paper's Sports Editor in charge of Features and Planning. Andy liked the idea of FOCUS ON THE FANS as an angle on the tour he didn't have covered, and thought my offer to blog weekly about fan experiences in New Zealand was something he'd like to do. His sticking point was budget. He hardly needed to tell a freelancer like me that budgets are a huge issue for newspapers these days. I've seen rates paid to freelancers more than halve over the last ten years. There was already a team of Telegraph reporters going out to cover the rugby of course, so he had no budget to pay me. At that stage getting the word out about FOCUS ON THE FANS was much more important than immediate income, so on the principle that fair exchange is no robbery, I offered to blog weekly if Andy would allow me to also promote what I was doing at the end of each blog, encouraging readers to engage with the project. He agreed readily.

The blog would be for Telegraph Online. It's a huge compliment that it was deemed high enough quality to go into the Premium content section, but that also meant the news was tinged with disappointment that only those with a subscription would be able to see my blogs. When all is said and done though, having a senior editor in a national newspaper offer to publish my work and publicise my project was a massive win at this late stage, so I didn't feel inclined to question that decision. Back in the 1990s, The Telegraph was the first national I ever sold an article to, so I also felt good about working with them again.

I'd invested so much time, energy and effort into bringing FOCUS ON THE FANS to the point where it could become a reality, Val and I made a decision based on:

- we really wanted the experience of a Lions tour
- we would probably never do it if we didn't now
- we had the revised focus of The Telegraph Online as an additional purpose
- whatever we spent of our savings in the 7 weeks we planned to be away wouldn't make us poor and hungry in retirement

We also decided we'd add the royalties we would have paid to BLDAC to what we'd already earmarked for rugby related charities should we make any profit on the venture.

We booked flights.

Getting there, getting about and getting places to stay

Organising logistics for a seven-week tour of anywhere is a major challenge. With ten months of uncertainty while talking to Lions Rugby, I was never going to commit to the expense of flights until a definitive outcome with them was settled upon. As you've read, that wasn't until less than a month before the tour commenced. Much earlier than that though, I'd figured from having visited New Zealand a couple of years previously on holiday that plonking 20,000 tourists in and around any of its cities would more than stretch the availability of accommodation. I also expected that hoteliers, B&Bs and Airbnb providers would all be looking to maximise their potential earnings during the Lions tour.

So, I had dealt with the logistics of our tour in reverse order of the chapter title.

Places to stay: A bit of background first.

My best friend's son lives in Beijing, so when in November 2015 an ad popped up on my screen proclaiming cheap Air France flights to the Chinese capital, it caught my eye. Closer examination revealed attractive fares to many other destinations, including San Francisco, a city I'd long wanted to visit. Travelling from Birmingham via Charles de Gaulle seemed a small price to pay for the remarkably good value £460 return fare offered on that route, departing at the end of April. Thinking this might be a flash sale I called Val out of her shower to make an instant decision. We settled on three weeks in California and booked via my usual agent Dial-a-Flight, whose extra £5 per person compulsory ATOL charge above booking direct is well worth it, as they are often able to reserve favoured seats at the time of booking and have proved invaluable dealing with problems when airlines get it wrong.

Then we formed a loose plan of what to see and where to stay: week one would be around San Francisco; then south via Yosemite National Park towards LA, so we could take in two more national parks – Joshua Tree and Death Valley; further down to San Diego, a city many friends have raved about; finally, meander up the Pacific Coast Highway to San Francisco for our return flight.

Being semi-retired but without pensions, we are a bit more careful than we used to be about discretionary spending. Thanks again to the weakness of the pound, three weeks accommodation and meals in California was clearly going to be expensive. I began investigating home exchange.

You pay a fee to join an organisation who facilitate exchanges among subscribers. Members can exchange simultaneously, non-simultaneously, or simply offer hospitality to other members if they so choose. No other money changes hands, so our £115 membership fee for the year would cover 14 nights of our 21, leaving only seven nights of hotels while on the road to be paid for in addition.

It sounded to me like a no-brainer - especially when our son told us about a friend of his in Ireland. He'd swapped his tiny two-up two-down cottage in a small village for a multi-million-dollar New York apartment overlooking Central Park. A businessman of Irish descent wanted to visit the place of his grandfather's birth.

Val wasn't so sure. We checked our home insurer's view. The customer service agent I spoke with hadn't been asked about home exchange before, so took a while to check. It seemed all was well, and that the main implication was theft from the property, which would understandably be excluded. Val's angst duly settled, we decided to take the plunge. We then got a follow up email from the insurer which excluded virtually every aspect of our cover save the house falling down around our guests. If you do consider home exchange check with your insurers their approach to how it affects your policy terms. Our Direct Line policy came up for renewal before we left, so we changed to a provider with a more amenable view in respect of home exchanges. We settled on joining Homelink.

All worked really well, as it did for us again in February and March 2017 when we visited Australia for a family wedding which turned into a six-week holiday.

So, when it came to organising seven weeks of short-term accommodation around the Lions Tour, I thought it worth seeing if Homelink members would offer us hospitality or an exchange. In early February 2017 I sent messages to all members in and around the host cities who offered hospitality stays in their Homelink profile, and to others I thought by the way they'd written their profile, may be tempted to buy into what we were doing.

Within 48 hours I had multiple offers from every location except the venue for the first match of the tour, Whangarei (pronounced Fon-grrr- eh), where there were no Homelink members.

When we confirmed we'd like to stay with **Allison Zanelli in Rotorua**, she replied asking how we'd got on in the rest of the country. I emailed back to say how brilliant I thought Kiwis were, as we'd covered everywhere except Whangarei. Within thirty minutes Allison sent another email saying that her sister lives in Whangarei and we would be staying with her. Above and beyond, Allison. Likewise, **sister Colleen**.

Our sincere thanks to everybody who made us an offer to share or have exclusive use of their homes. We chose the members we did simply based on proximity to the city centre, where we envisaged we would spend most of our time, as that was the most likely place for fans to congregate.

Our Homelink heroes as we like to think of them are:

Whangarei: **Colleen and Mike Collins**

Auckland: **Shirin Caldwell, who volunteered three separate stays to fit the match schedule**

Christchurch: **John Richardson and Jo Ewing**

Dunedin: **Glyn and Howard Smith**

Rotorua: **Allison Zanelli and Dave Matthews**

Hamilton: **Susan Black**

Wellington: **Jo Cribb and Mike Waterman**

We would meet all but Susan, as she was to be in Canada when we arrived in Hamilton. John and Jo would meet us than decamp to their holiday home. By the time you read this, Shirin and John & Jo will already have visited the UK and used our place as part of their holidays here. Susan plans to visit in 2018, as do Allison and Dave since we met. Everybody else was offering us a hospitality stay with them.

Although I was very well set up for the whole tour, before finishing with accommodation I want to pay tribute to Adam Gilshnan.

As you already know, in late March I was still trying to assess whether we'd go at all, and had tried to find out how many fans were expected to travel independently, to see if I could make a case for trying to produce FOCUS ON THE FANS as an independent project. As well as the press articles I came across that estimated around 20,000 Lions fans were expected during the peak test match period, I also stumbled upon a report that a Facebook page **'Adopt-a-Lions-Fan'** had been set up, specifically for the purpose of demonstrating how hospitable New Zealanders are.

This initiative was the brainchild of **Adam Gilshnan**. Like many other New Zealanders, Adam was annoyed by reports of hoteliers and B&B owners profiteering from the tour by hiking up prices hugely during the times the Lions would be in their cities. Inspired by the hospitality and generosity he'd been on the receiving end of when travelling in Europe, Adam took it upon himself to do something about the situation, never expecting it to touch the hearts of so many Kiwis who showed their willingness to supplement the availability of hotel rooms by offering their homes to visiting fans.

Within a couple of days, the site had registered nearly two thousand offers from people willing to host Lions fans.

As well as his full-time job in the NZ Health Service, Adam has spent an average of over 3 hours a day administering the site - to put people in touch with each other, and to ensure it wasn't being used inappropriately by scammers or people who were really trying to sell accommodation. That a huge number of Lions fans paid tribute to their 'adoption' in tweets, on Facebook, to press reporters and to other fans is reward enough according to Adam.

That so many fans have described their hosts going above and beyond just providing a bed is a tribute to the spirit in which this remarkable country's citizens embraced the invasion of Lions tourists.

Adopt-a-Lions-Fan stories have included so much more than simply providing accommodation. Amongst the further kindnesses we heard about were: many instances of plying their guests with food and wine; giving lifts all through the stay to save fans spending on taxis; donating warm clothing in the bitter South Island weather; lending one group a car for the week; helping prepare flags for fans to demonstrate their support for the Lions; and even one host who merrily handed over the keys to his property when he had to travel on business unexpectedly and said to pop them through the letterbox when his guests were ready to leave.

Then there's the tale of **Alex Edwards** that became a legend in its own tour time. On a very wet night in Auckland, Alex had travelled to Ponsonby Rugby Club, believing he could park there overnight. With the lights off and nobody around, he poked his head into the clubhouse, to find a committee meeting happening. When he explained what he was doing, Alex was offered to sleep in the house of one of the members present, rather than endure thundering rain on his camper van roof.

Little did he know the sympathetic soul making the offer was Reiko Ioane's mum, Sandra. Alex met both Reiko and brother Akira without any inkling of who they were, merely remarking to Sandra and dad Ed after the boys had left the house that they were big lads, and wondering if they played rugby... they are both, of course, Auckland Blues and New Zealand All Blacks players.

Getting About: I used to book car hire through Irish based comparison site Cartrawler, selecting the cheapest available option of the better-known suppliers - until the occasion when we had a problem after I snapped my cruciate ligament while skiing in Austria. The car was supplied by Dollar in Munich. Poor customer service from both companies was compounded by Dollar subsequently charging nearly €700 of damage repair bill that turned out - some months later - to be 'a mistake' on their part. I've always used Hertz for car rental ever since.

Like any global business, Hertz have their moments when things don't go to plan, particularly it seems with their internal IT systems occasionally. But I judge a business on how well they deal with things when they do go wrong, as it inevitably will at some point for all businesses. I had to fight tooth and nail to recover my money from Dollar, telling them I was prepared to initiate court action, with no help whatsoever from Cartrawler.

Conversely, I've found Hertz to be very responsible in their attitude to customer service, most notably with a breakdown in the remoteness of Yosemite National Park. So, although Hertz are normally pretty competitive anyway, I am very happy to pay a little bit extra up front on occasion to hire their cars.

I've done a fair bit of travel writing in the last couple of years, always paying my own way (although I'm quite open to freebie trips if anyone from an airline or holiday tour operator is reading). I always record who we paid for the travel essentials such as flight, accommodation and car hire. Sometime ago the PR Manager at Hertz UK kindly said to let her know next time I'd be travelling for work purposes and she'd see if they could arrange extra discount.

After I declined the Lions Rugby agreement, I thought Hertz might be interested in sponsoring FOCUS ON THE FANS as a marketing exercise. I asked to be introduced to the Hertz marketing team and put together a proposal for them to supply cars free of charge for our trip in return for publicising their support in the book.

My PR contact was on holiday when I tried to contact her. Her director quickly picked up the reins, couldn't speak for marketing, but in any event offered me a discount on the prices quoted by my normal Gold Club membership. Then I got a call from the Hertz corporate offices in Dublin. Somehow a senior customer service manager had heard about what I was doing, and liked the idea of FOCUS ON THE FANS. He isn't in their marketing team, so couldn't comment on the proposal I'd prepared. He just wanted to increase the discount further for me. That was a pleasant surprise.

A greater surprise came the next day, when the manager of the Hertz New Zealand marketing team made contact to say my proposal had found its way to her. She liked the idea and wanted to know more. Because I'd already made two bookings with hefty discounts for the North Island legs of our trip, she offered use of a car for free while we were in South Island, with a pick-up in Christchurch and return to Queenstown after a couple of days R&R after the Highlanders match in Dunedin.

In return, I agreed to put the Hertz logo on the flyers we were having printed for distribution to fans during the tour, and on the luminous green tabards we were having made for us to wear in New Zealand, advertising to fans what we were doing. We now had a substantial saving on our car hire expenditure, even if not completely expense free as I'd hoped, but it was all very last minute. It felt good too, that senior people in a global business like Hertz liked the idea of FOCUS ON THE FANS enough to do everything within their authority to help move the project forward in a very short timeframe.

Much appreciated everybody. Thanks.

My brilliant marketing agency in the UK - C3 Marketing - quickly adjusted the artwork for the flyers and the tabards. The flyers were to be printed in Auckland so that we didn't have to carry them as luggage. At 2am on the Friday before we flew, I'd just about managed to complete the marketing consultancy work I'd also been doing for my biggest corporate client in the run up to departure, then called the printers just before their weekend started to confirm they'd be able to print the flyers ready for pick up on arrival in Auckland the following Tuesday. Alison, our friend who with a partner owns C3, dropped the tabards round the day before we left the UK.

At last everything seemed to be coming together.

How wrong was I?

Getting There: When we had made the commitment to go to New Zealand I had checked a few airlines' direct websites and then called our usual agent for long haul travel, DialAFlight as mentioned earlier, to see the best deal they could find. We definitely wanted only one stop on the way to Auckland, and DialAFlight's quote to fly with British Airways via Hong Kong was £300 less than I'd seen on the airline's website.

Now, I must have looked at the flight **times** on the confirmation document a dozen times while trying to book internal flights in New Zealand, hotels on arrival and before departure, as well as when sorting out car hire. A few minutes before leaving for the airport on the day we were travelling, I asked Val to check I'd printed all the paperwork we would need.

In a nanosecond she spotted an error. A somewhat important one. I should have looked at the flight **dates** too.

Rather than the return flight being on July 11, a few days after the last test match, we were booked to come home on a flight one month earlier than I'd asked for, on June 11.

Not the best way to set out on a mammoth tour.

I'd like to tell you that everything went as smoothly as a Leslie Phillips "Hell-ooo" or "Ding-Dong" from then on. (I know, that's really showing my age).

I think you already know it didn't though. ☺

THE TOUR

28th May: Flight Fiasco

Some of you who were caught up in it as well won't need reminding of the weekend of the British Airways IT crash fiasco. We were due to fly late evening on the Sunday, and heard on Saturday morning that the meltdown had occurred. In the absence of any meaningful guidance from BA on its website or on social media, the advice from DialAFlight was get to the airport extra early. We did, dropped off by our lovely friend Glenys Bailey. 6 hours early.

Only to be told at the line of policemen blocking entry to the terminal that we would not be allowed inside until 90 minutes before departure of our flight – if it was still to depart at all.

On top of the return flight debacle, you can imagine why I was a bit moody sitting outside Terminal 5.

Then we thought: "Why not go and sit downstairs in the Arrivals Hall?" They couldn't be stopping people going into there to pick up passengers coming through. They weren't, but security staff were manning every stairway and lift so that nobody snuck up to departures. Not a problem, at least we could get a seat, a drink and had time to read every section of The Sunday Telegraph. (Well, I had to be loyal didn't I?)

A couple of hours later Val noticed the security was gone, even though there'd been no announcement that the restriction on access to Departures was ended.

By the time we got upstairs into Departures, still with plenty of time before our flight to get through the queues, check in our bags and pass through security, the terminal was no longer crammed with would-be passengers at the end of their tether.

It only took a leisurely couple of beers and a meal to feel considerably more chilled, even when the first leg to Hong Kong was delayed by an hour and the return trip issue wasn't resolved.

28th – 30th May: Mostly Up In the Air

We expected the plane to be chock-a-block, with any spare seats that there might have been now filled with passengers from the cancelled flight the night before.

I was amazed - and at the time hugely disappointed in BA - that there were at least 10 spare seats in our section of the aircraft alone. Surely they should have been filled with more of the 300+ passengers who hadn't been able to travel on the Saturday? Having said that, I will admit I felt less inclined to launch into a self-righteous rant about BA when the steward moved people around to even out spaces, resulting in Val and I having a row of 3 seats for the 2 of us.

Our 11.45pm departure, along with the beer and wine I'd supped and the little bit more comfort afforded by the extra seat space, meant I got a reasonable amount of sleep on the way to Hong Kong. After a short transit there we were off to Auckland for what was effectively another overnight flight. I managed a good bit more sleep. Frankly I was knackered by working long hours every day right up to the Friday before we left, whilst also trying to deal with Lions Rugby, organising our logistics and pulling together all the kit we needed: a new laptop, voice recording devices, all our camera equipment and accessories, the luminous green tabards we wore most days on tour, the flyers I'd arranged for the printers in Auckland to prepare.

The previous six weeks had been so full-on both physically and emotionally, I was grateful for the chance of 24 hours doing very little on a plane, and made the most of the opportunity to rest and relax.

30th May: Arrival in Shiny Happy Auckland

I more often listen to music for my entertainment on planes these days. I find it more restful than watching films. As our flight landed in Auckland mid-morning on the Tuesday, the track that happened to be playing on my headphones was 'Shiny Happy People' by REM.

(Quick Quiz Question: What were the Shiny Happy People doing when first mentioned in the lyrics? See the foot of the page for the answer).

Serendipitous I think, because that's how I already thought of New Zealand: full of Shiny Happy People. We holidayed there in December 2014, and felt that our trip was made as much by the people we met as by the astonishing geography of the country. Everybody we encountered always seemed dead keen to prove right all the surveys that conclude New Zealand is the happiest country to live in. Knowing that this would be as much a working trip as a holiday this time, we were looking forward to experiencing much more of the hospitality we'd found so endearing on our previous visit. Lions fans who went there for the 2005 tour, or the Rugby World Cup in 2011 would already know this too.

I was interested to see how those visiting for the first time would feel about the Kiwis, and how Kiwis would feel about the expected huge invasion of Lions fans. I was very confident there would be mutual affection – except during matches of course.

As we joined the queue for immigration checks, around 30 or so people bedecked in Lions gear appeared in the adjoining channel. Their baggage told us they must be part of the Lions squad rather than fans; the physiques of some of them told us they were in the support team rather than players. Sure enough, as we emerged from the terminal there was the Lions bus. I was told that the players would arrive the next day. I'd assumed they'd already be there, with only three days to the first match.

First fan encounter: Outside the Hertz cabin in the rental car lot, I spotted a guy sporting a Wasps T-shirt, so figured he and the lady with him may well be arriving for the tour.

Andy and Gudrun Palmer proved to be the sort of people who would definitely add to the Shiny Happy People local population. Wasps season ticket holders, they had watched their team lose the dramatic Premiership final against Exeter on the prior Saturday, had left Twickenham to go straight to Heathrow, discovering on the radio that they wouldn't be flying that night after all because of the BA problems. It took a couple of hours of queuing on the phone to rearrange a booking onto our flights 24 hours later. Perhaps that explains the empty seats. I suspect many would have given up waiting on the line long before they reached an operator. Despite all that, Andy and Gudrun were full of beans, proffered sincere congratulations to Exeter, venturing that the result was a shot in the arm for rugby union generally, and looked and sounded very happy to be in New Zealand at last. Like us, they were there for the duration of the tour.

I was intrigued that an Icelandic woman would be such an avid follower of rugby. Gudrun rationalises her complete addiction to the sport by simply saying she realised soon after Andy had introduced her to rugby that "It's the world's greatest game". She also thinks that Icelandic men should take up rugby. "They're typically very big and strong, a bit like the Pacific Island nations' players". What chance the Icelandic football fans' 'Thunderclap' being a feature of Rugby World Cup 2023 or 2027…? The enthusiastic reaction of such rugby devotees when they heard what we were planning to do was greatly encouraging. Feeling pretty chipper ourselves, we loaded our bags into the commodious boot of the Toyota Highlander that was all Hertz had left available when we had finally sorted out our reservations, and set off to pick up the flyers.

(Quick quiz answer: I bet most of you said 'Holding hands'. Wrong. The first line of the song is 'Shiny Happy People – Laughing').

We hoped Andy and Gudrun would remember to look up FOCUS ON THE FANS on Facebook, Twitter or my website.

No matter though. We bumped into them again in Christchurch ten days later. Only then did we learn **they not only watch every Wasps home game and combine all European away matches with long weekend trips, they are season ticket holders at Auckland Blues too – over 11,000 miles away from home**. Their reason? They've been travelling to New Zealand at least once a year since 1998 to visit friends – and watch rugby. In 2009, two years before the Rugby World Cup (RWC), they decided to buy season tickets as they were reasonably priced and owning them was likely to guarantee them access to RWC tickets. At that time the tickets also included international cricket matches at Eden Park, another of their sporting interests.

They were right about RWC tickets. Their season tickets secured them tickets for the opening ceremony and all group games in Auckland. In addition, they also bought tickets for two of the quarter-finals, both semi-finals, the final and the 3rd/4th place playoff. In total the couple managed to get to 11 matches. Impressive, but a long way short of the record. Yes, there is a record, as we were to discover later in Christchurch.

Friends in New Zealand use the season tickets whenever they can for regular season Blues matches.

Andy's been in touch since we returned to say what a fabulous time they had. Because they bought their Lions game tickets courtesy of their season tickets they sat with All Blacks fans. His highlights and summary are:

> *"We bumped into many of the Lions squad in various towns, restaurants and bars on our journey, but perhaps the most unexpected meeting was sitting in a takeaway in Wellington waiting for our lunch of a couple of salad wraps to be prepared, when Aaron Cruden, the All Black fly-half, came in for an order and sat down next to us. We had a good long chat with him while we all waited and he was kind enough to sign our Lions shirt (on the back of course).*
>
> *A particular highlight was away from the Lions events altogether. We had an invite via another Wasps fan back in the UK to Ponsonby Rugby Club for an evening along with other Wasps fans. Ponsonby Rugby Club is the longest standing rugby club in Auckland and has provided more All Blacks than any other club in the country. We were warmly welcomed and had the distinct privilege of meeting and talking to Bryan Williams, legendary All Black and possibly Ponsonby's most famous son. It was great to get into a "real" rugby club for an evening. Particularly one with such a rich history."*
>
> *"At the end of the third test we were treated to endless high fives and 'Congratulations' from the New Zealand fans as the crowd dispersed. Two particular comments from them stayed with me; firstly:* **'That was fantastic, but thank God it's only once every 12 years, I'm not sure my heart would take it'.** *Something I think we would all echo. But secondly, and I thought tellingly,* **'Great match - it's about time they [The All Blacks] had a real challenge'.***"*

Thanks Andy.

We found the printers on Dominion Road easily enough, spotted the spelling mistake instantly (fans were invited to 'sned' us pictures and stories), accepted the mistake was down to me, and turned our attention to finding somewhere to stay that night.

We knew of a decent aparthotel with parking on Beach Road near the city centre, as we'd stayed in it on our previous trip. The Waldorf Stadium Apartments had a room at a reasonable enough rate for us to decide not to hunt around town or on the internet – and in any event the international data roaming charges on my pay-as-you-go phone would possibly have cost more than we might save on a room elsewhere.

Task one was to sort out a local sim card for my phone. We very nearly plumped for one from the first shop we found, before realising international calls weren't included, and we'd have to renew one month later. To her credit, the young lady who served us did suggest Vodafone would better be able to meet our needs. They could. A 60-day card included international as well as New Zealand domestic calls, text and more data allowance than I was ever going to use for only NZ$ 49.

Perfect.

Weary from the journey and because our body clocks said we should already have been asleep for a long time, we resorted to a McDonald's around 5pm, followed by a stiff duty-free Tanqueray gin back in the apartment to help facilitate an early night. Unfortunately, Val's early night started a little sooner than planned, as she dozed off with half her G&T remaining, depositing it over the settee. Washing the settee cushion covers livened us both up again, necessitating a further G&T before lights out around 8.30pm

31st May: Auckland to Whangarei, via two Harvey Norman stores

Breakfast at a Turkish café on Fort Street was good.

We were never going to turn up empty handed to our hosts, but wanted to bring something a little more personal than just the wine we always planned to provide. I'd spotted a photography shop on Queen Street that offered instant printing, so downloaded one of my Natural Abstract images onto a memory stick (I also create fine art photography) – a colourful abstraction of the New Zealand Southern Alps in summer, shown right, which we'd flown over in a light aircraft during our 2014 holiday. I raced to Queen Street before we had to check out and had seven copies printed, so also needed to find frames for them. Not as easy as it sounded because I only had a square version of the image on my laptop, and couldn't find frames to match in any central Auckland store.

An internet search suggested we would be able to stop at a frame shop on a trading estate in Auckland's northern suburbs on our way to Whangarei.

Don't you just hate that anything that goes on the internet seems to just stay there – even when a business has gone out of business?

The frame shop we were hoping to find no longer existed. We discovered Bunnings Warehouse – our nearest equivalent is B&Q – don't sell frames. We returned to the motorway thinking I'd probably wasted the NZ$70 the prints had cost. Then I spotted a Harvey Norman department store somewhere in the middle of what looked like an enormous industrial and retail area. I knew from previous trips that Harvey Norman sell just about everything you could ever think of to put in a home, so

exited at the next junction and tried to backtrack through the estate. It took us ages to find the store, being well concealed below the elevated level of the motorway tucked away in a dead-end.

Success. They had exactly the size of frame I needed, complete with mount. Even better, it was very smart too. Sadly, there were only four of them, as they were a discontinued line. The very helpful photography department manager, Lee, fixed the pictures in the frames for me, discounted the already 50% off by another NZ$8 per frame, and checked stock at the next nearest store heading north – luckily for us in Whangarei. He then arranged for that store's photo department manager to put the two they had aside for me, and to give me the same deal as he had. Great service Lee.

We punctuated our otherwise uneventful journey to Whangarei with a drinks stop at the pleasant Top O' The Dome Café and the collection of the additional frames from Ivana, who proved just as helpful in fixing the prints into the frame.

Approaching Whangarei, I began to have second thoughts about whether a picture was the right sort of gift for our hosts. What if they hated it? Or it didn't match their taste in wall art? We eventually concluded it was best to light-heartedly say as an icebreaker to everybody that if it wasn't to their liking they could quietly give it away, and we'd never know.

Whangarei is a city of around 55,000 people, and the capital of the sub-tropical Northland region. It's less of a draw for holidaymakers than the small towns in the more renowned Bay of Islands a further hour north, but the city's peninsula - Whangarei Heads - is a very picturesque coastal area in its own right, with rugged volcanic peaks sheltering secluded golden beaches.

The compact central shopping district is bordered by an area called Town Basin, a leisure and marina development constructed beside the Hatea river that runs through the city. The 26-metre-high Whangarei Falls in Tikipunga, north of the centre, are reputed to be the most photographed in New Zealand.

Mike and Colleen Collins live in a rural setting in a suburb of Whangarei called Kamo. Their house is fabulous, their garden spectacular.

I swear that if you didn't know any of us, but observed our meeting for the first time, *you'd* swear that this was a group of old friends getting together after a long time apart. That's how Mike and Colleen made us feel at any rate. We shared similar views, tastes, humour, food and wine in a marvellous first evening together. By the end of it they'd offered us the use of their house again at the end of the tour, when we had a few days to kill before returning home on our rearranged flight via Singapore. The Collins would be in Australia visiting family by then. We eagerly accepted their very generous offer.

Retiring to bed we saw Mike had dug out a Lions scarf and cap from 2005 to make us feel even more welcome.

Colleen told us there's much excitement in Whangarei at the moment. The town had applied to the estate of internationally renowned (but unknown to me) Austrian artist and architect, Friedensreich Hundertwasser, for permission to undertake a project aimed at rejuvenating Whangarei's very dull Arts Centre in the style of Hundertwasser, using designs he'd incorporated into his architectural work as a basis to do so. The centre currently looks like a nondescript 1960s office block - like the ones I saw in Slough when I was growing up. Our host Colleen is a big fan of Hundertwasser, and was clearly excited about the prospect of the new Arts Centre when she described it to us.

In order to secure the precious permission, a small proof of concept building had to be constructed to demonstrate that the designers who would work on the bigger project had the ability to faithfully reproduce the eclectic style of the artist.

Hundertwasser, as many visitors do, had fallen in love with New Zealand and later in life chose to live near Kawakawa, 55km north of Whangarei. The city also had to raise the NZ$18 million funds needed to complete the building within a given period after permission was granted. The proof of concept sits alongside the current building on the edge of Town Basin and the money is raised, so work will start early in 2018.

31st May- 4th June: Wet, Wet, Wet in Whangarei

No – the venerable Scottish crooners weren't drafted in to entertain Lions fans.

Rain pounded down pretty much continuously in Whangarei

There's a very good reason Northland is classified as sub-tropical. It's very prone to frequent and torrential rain; sometimes short, sharp and extremely heavy showers but quite often persistent and ongoing extremely heavy rainfall. Being in Whangarei reminded me of something a local said to me years ago in a Londonderry pub explaining how easy it was to forecast weather there: **"If you can't see the hills from the city it's raining. If you can see the hills from the city it's going to rain."**

After the all-morning rain finally relented on the Thursday afternoon we went into town to get our bearings, then on to Toll Stadium, the venue for the opening match of the tour against a Barbarians XV. I explained to the people in the main office what I was doing with the book, told them about the mix-up over press accreditation and asked if it would be possible for me to get a shot of the crowd before the match started. All three staff looked at me like I'd just asked them to give me their first born for ritual sacrifice. Not a chance.

I decided I'd spend the rest of that rainy afternoon writing an introductory blog for Telegraph Online, explaining what I'd be writing about during the tour, telling about the book and asking fans to contribute their stories and images. I'd bought my new laptop just before we left, and had sought advice from experts who know so much more about computers than I do. I wanted something powerful to process my images quickly using Photoshop, with large enough memory to store them too. I'd been told get SSD drive as it is significantly quicker. I went for Intel's latest generation i7 processor, and a 4K screen.

I had problems though.

I'd only got the laptop back the day before we left from my regular IT guy who'd set it up for me. When I fired it up in Whangarei, with the exception of Google Chrome, I started getting error messages for any application I tried to open, as well as a good few I didn't.

Which meant each application closed down.

This would be a disaster unless I got it fixed. I wouldn't be able to send The Telegraph the blogs they were expecting.

Mike and Colleen didn't know anybody who might help, but put the word out to friends and soon got a recommendation to call a business that specialised in resolving IT problems. Unfortunately, with their outstanding workload there was no way they could even look at my laptop before the following Tuesday. We'd be in Auckland by then.

I'd also signed up with Microsoft One Drive so I could sync my work in New Zealand with my PC at home. That appeared not to be working either. Outlook wouldn't function. I could still get email communication via the web version of BT Mail thanks to the small mercy of Chrome functioning ok, but found the mousepad on the Dell appalling to use. Getting a cursor to be where I wanted it and stay in the right place for any length of time proved to be the worst aspect of this very expensive but currently useless machine.

In desperation, I tried the old maxim of turning it on and off again. No change. A few times. Then I thought I'd simply restart, rather than switching off completely. Lo and behold, the error messages stopped and I could open applications and make them work as they should. The mousepad remained a huge frustration – and still does, but at least I could do the work I had to while I was in New Zealand.

That evening Val and I donned our green tabards for the first time, loaded our raincoat pockets with flyers and drove into town to look for Lions fans. Town appeared to be shut down. Restaurant after restaurant was either empty or closed. One bar had a bit of a crowd in, but they were locals competing in a pub quiz. Amazed at how quiet it was, we went back to the house before 8.30pm. Mike commented wryly that he was surprised we'd stayed out so long. Apparently Thursday is not a night that locals go out in Whangarei. It appeared no Lions fans had either.

Friday daytime wasn't much better. The pouring rain in the morning was a very good reason not to be meandering around town. Unsurprisingly, we encountered hardly any Lions fans until in the late afternoon we discovered The Lions Den – a pop-up bar that had opened that day in Town Basin. Inside were some people in red shirts. Only one table of four mind you, but they graciously allowed us to introduce ourselves and explain about FOCUS ON THE FANS. In return they told us about...

warrengatlandsarmy.com : Michael Holland, from Thame, had set up a website before leaving home that would provide Lions fans with news. He was just about to be interviewed on local radio. While Michael spoke to the radio station on his phone we got the story from his **wife Sue,** along with **Michael's brother David and his friend Jan**. The not-quite-as-big-as-cricket's-barmy-army they had founded had a membership of precisely four at that point. There was a recruitment drive on.

David went on to explain how they had switched their allegiance from soccer to become rugby fans 15 years earlier. Michael runs a telecoms business in High Wycombe, Buckinghamshire. He had a box at Adams Park where for many years the brothers watched Wycombe Wanderers FC rise from low-level non-league to Football League status. When Wasps decamped from London to play their first match at the ground in 2002, Michael and David went along out of curiosity. Amazed by the differences in the culture, atmosphere and sheer physicality of the game, they became instant converts to rugby and haven't been to another football match since. Avid Wasps fans - obviously - they got to know Warren Gatland well while he was Head Coach between 2002 and 2005, and they remain friends.

As well as building the website, Michael had had a flag made and business cards printed. He also arranged with a pub in every host city of the tour that they would be there on match day, when he would pay for canapes to be handed round to as many fans who also happened to be in. A generous gesture indeed.

Warren Gatland's entire army?

Sue and Michael Holland

Now for **my first 'small world' moment** over here. While chatting to David we discovered I used to play football against his brother-in-law, Keith 'Chalky' White, when we were youths in Slough.

'The Last Throw of the Dice Tour': while we spoke with what is surely the world's tiniest army, another table in the Den became occupied. The self-deprecating and somewhat sardonic name that **Phil Moore, Clive Lucking, Al Pearce and Bill Dunlop** chose for their adventure tells you that none are in the first flush of youth.

The Last Throw of the Dice Tour Party

Phil's claim to rugby fame is that he was ex-Lion Mike Teague's captain once upon a time. The photo here is of The Gloucester All Blues Youth team in the 1976/77 season. Teague is second from the right on the back row. Phil, as skipper, is holding the ball. That brought back a memory for me. Teague is the only player I ever saw stand his ground and stop the great Kiwi No 8 Wayne 'Buck' Shelford in full stride. Franklin's Gardens truly was silenced for a split second as our hero bounced 5 yards backwards off Iron Mike.

Mike Teague - a big lad at a young age

Al's claim to not-so-much-rugby-fame-as-rugby-ignominy emerged when I told the guys that Rory Underwood had written a foreword for the book. That brought to mind for him the occasion when he faced Rory in a Combined Services v Civil Service match. Al is adamant that Rory smiled sarcastically at him each of the many times he zipped past Al on the wing, leaving Al to gawp aimlessly at Rory's rear end as he watched him race towards the try line.

Al told the story through increasingly gritted teeth that hinted at the embarrassment he says he felt at the time. When I told Rory this story he chuckled and said it wasn't the first time he'd been told something similar, but insists he wouldn't have treated another player so shabbily, suggesting Al may have been embellishing the tale somewhat.

Al did have more success with another rugby legend on another occasion though. At a rugby dinner where he admits he may have partaken of a little more wine than may have been good for him, his persistent requests ended up relieving Andy Ripley of his England tie – although the late, great Doctor in a deadpan put-down while handing over his tie, pointedly asked why on earth Al thought he'd want as a swap the tie Al was wearing.

School's Out: Ex-teacher **Cathy Goddard** had an amused but slightly guilty look on her face when she told me she'd taken early retirement from her job as a teacher a year ago, but had given her bosses a different reason for doing so than the real one. There's no way she could have got term-time leave to come on this tour with **hubby Steve**, and once he decided he was coming, no way she was going to miss it. The staunch Leicester Tigers fans have always wanted to watch the All Blacks play live and decided many years ago that the Lions Tour to New Zealand was the perfect way to do so.

Fibs in school are nothing new of course, but not normally from the teachers.

Girl Power: Hats off to **Pauline McDermott** from Peterborough. Touring on her own, she told me that when you've got a bucket list and the Lions in New Zealand is on it, you don't wait 12 years for the next tour to find someone to do it with. Good for you Girl.

Steve and Cathy Goddard with Pauline McDermott

How do Uni Students afford a 6-week tour of New Zealand?

Mark O'Connell and Jack Tully

It's a question Waterford students **Mark O'Connell and Jack Tully** had been asked in increasingly accusatory tones over the months leading up to the tour by people they told about their trip. The short answer they gave me is hard work and – reluctantly they admit – minimising their consumption of alcohol to levels way below those for which students have rightly become famous/infamous (your choice).

Mark worked for an investment bank in Luxembourg for the employed year of his sandwich course. Living rent free with his uncle there, and the sort of focus one doesn't often credit students with when it comes to saving their hard-earned, has seen enough squirreled away to do the entire Lions Tour on a 'bit of a budget' as they put it. The lads had a small camper van to live in for the next 6 weeks.

Jack maintained similar focus and abstemiousness for the past couple of years, and his Kiwi father proved a massive help with budgeting. As well as a small inheritance in NZ$ available to him, he reckons being able to buy match tickets through relatives in New Zealand saved them around 50% compared to match ticket prices available to those travelling to New Zealand on official Lions Tours. This was the first of many occasions I heard that sort of comparison. The issue undoubtedly raised hackles amongst a good number of Lions fans on those tours, and is one of the reasons I speculated about fans being alienated by the Lions commercial team.

Taking one for the team: Later as I went into The Lions Den for one last time before returning to Kamo, it was entirely empty.

I was just about to turn tail and go when eight Kiwis walked in.

Looking for some Lions fans to banter with, they were hugely disappointed that there was just little old me to take all the stick they wanted to unload.

I soaked it all up for a while, made my excuses (we'd arranged to take Mike and Colleen to dinner in town on the Friday night), took their picture and left.

All in good humour of course.

The would-be Lions Tamers were disappointed to find only me

We enjoyed an excellent meal with Mike and Colleen at the Grand Thai restaurant in the Grand Hotel on Bank Street that evening, but still saw very few people around as the heavy rain returned.

3rd June, Match Day 1: Lions v New Zealand Barbarians

The Party Starts: Next morning, half the stallholders at the Farmers Market Mike routinely visits on Saturdays had decided not to turn out. I don't blame them. The persistent overnight rain was now torrential. We got soaked buying our breakfast.

The good news was the rain stopped just in time for the pre-match party Whangarei's city council laid on. As we'd seen so few up to then, we couldn't help wondering how many Lions fans would gather for drinks and the show.

We needn't have worried. Hundreds of All Blacks and Lions fans mingled in and around the bars discussing in a very convivial atmosphere the prospects for both sides on the tour, while compere Luke Bird introduced traditional and modern local entertainers on the open-air stage erected for the occasion. These included a bagpipe band, highland dancers, pop bands, the spectacular Hatea Kapa Haka group and a brilliant Māori drum band.

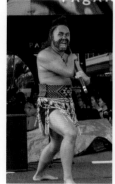

Some of the excellent entertainers who put on a show for Lions fans in Whangarei We all know how it's done but it's still fun

The first people I was drawn towards by the giant rucksack in the form of a Lion's head between them as they sat outside Rynoz Bar were **Alex and Sally Scott**. Our chat elicited that the Lion had been christened Finn – after Finn Russell, the Scottish stand-off/centre they were adamant should have been selected for the tour. As the tour progressed it was uncanny how often we bumped into Alex and Sally amongst the thousands of fans in each city.

Alex Scott with Finn…   … and wife Sally

Early doors in Whangarei

Shani and Ian Brough, Liz and Julian Evans and Peter Taylor, the fun group on the adjoining table, were joined by specially tattooed for the tour **Taz** when he saw the camera. Taz changed his name by deed poll to his army nickname. All were keen to draw my attention to the fact that Sir Elton John could be a closet Lions Fan, as their friend **Elton lookalike Howard McKenzie** (behind the wall) from Edinburgh arrived to a chorus of **'Elton, Elton, Give us a song'** ringing out from fans around.

I sent this picture of Howard to the 'Have I Got News For You' editorial office, suggesting it might be suitable content either for their **'In the news this week…'** section at the start of the show or the final **'…and I leave you with news that…'** before the closing credits. I have no idea if they used it. I doubt it as I had no reply. I imagine their scriptwriters might have come up with a tongue-in-cheek caption that would have been something like:

"As the British & Irish Lions Rugby tour gets under way in New Zealand, there's speculation that after a distressing diagnosis of a personal nature, Sir Elton John is seeking comfort in the company of thousands of men who like to play with odd shaped balls."

I should point out that I thought I ought to ask Howard for permission to send it. He's a sport.

I didn't ask Sir Elton though.

Maccams on tour: With 20 years of following a variety of sports tours already under their belts **Ron Wills, Steve Hanratty, Bill Armstrong and Bryan Hodgson** were on their first Lions Tour – for only a week. Citing the fact that times are hard in their home city of Sunderland, it was as much as they could afford to fund, but all were very keen to have experienced a taste of what they already described as the tour to beat all tours.

A couple of hours later they looked rather different in their skin-tight red onesie outfits that made them very aware of their respective manhoods and prompted a flurry of gags unsuitable to include in this book!

Perhaps they were disguising themselves from the TV cameras at the match because they should have been at work?

Maccams on Tour - albeit a short one

Should the Maccams have been at work?

Note that Bryan on the left has his on the wrong way round – the zip is over his face

Ospreys fan **Ginnene Harvey-Lovell** caught my eye next. Or rather the cast on her arm did – in Lions red of course. She broke her thumb playing hockey the day before departing for New Zealand, but wasn't going to let the discomfort spoil her trip. Brother **Ben** follows Exeter on account of them being the closest senior team to where he lives - Penzance. They both flew out courtesy of Bank-of-Dad: **Michael Lovell** now lives in Auckland after first going to New Zealand for the 2005 tour.

Ginnene   Ben   Bank of Dad, Michael

A table populated by a group of Kiwis spotted my tabard and stopped me to ask about FOCUS ON THE FANS. **Natasha and Steve Finlay with their 11-year-old lad Leon, Melissa Brake and Kerry Stevenson** set the tone for the rest of the New Zealanders we were to meet on the tour, in that they were delightfully welcoming and loved the idea of the book. Like most Kiwis at that point they were pretty certain that the All Blacks would win, conceding however that this was a very talented Lions squad, and the games should be good.

Confident Kiwis

Another pair I was to spot regularly as we all travelled round the country were old mates **Eric Sprigg and Maurice Arnold**. The reason for that could well have been Eric's distinctive deerstalker being so recognisable. Eric and Maurice are old mates in every sense – they go back a long way and would be the first to admit they aren't spring chickens any more. They're enjoying their tour in the company of 17-year-old Zelda. To be more accurate, in 17-year-old Zelda. That's what they've christened the rented camper van they are sharing throughout the entire tour. I'm not sure what camper years are equivalent to in human years, but like the guys, Zelda's definitely been round the block a few times. She's done half a million miles, so the couple of thousand Maurice and Eric add will seem like – well, just one more time round the block.

Maurice, a Leicester fan, was very happy that he'd met former head coach Aaron Mauger at Auckland airport, as he thought the manner in which the club handled Mauger's sacking last March the day after winning the Anglo-Welsh cup was disgraceful, and had emailed him the day it happened to say so.

Maurice and Eric are pictured here with former NZ Fire Service worker **Les Barclay and his mate Lloyd Matthews.** Les has seen every Lions match in his home country in the four tours to New Zealand since 1959. He was 10 when he first stood in the stands at Wellington. He's also been present at most Tri-Nations matches featuring the All Blacks during that time. Like many Kiwis he regards the Lions series as the ultimate international challenge – and the best beer-up with opposing fans in rugby.

Maurice Arnold, Les Barclay, Lloyd Matthews and Eric Sprigg   **Lauren Barclay's Mega-Scarf is seven feet long**

Les's wife Lauren has seen all the games since meeting Les too, and this year knitted a unique memento for the current tour. Her 7-foot-long woollen scarf (seen here held aloft by **Lauren, Les and friends Lloyd and Margaret Matthews**) has the colours of each team involved in the tour in match order, commencing with the lions red/white/blue and green, followed by the Baa-Baas, then each provincial team, before the All Blacks at the other end. Lauren wanted as many people as possible to know about the scarf in the hope she could auction it off at the end of the tour and donate the proceeds to charity.

Les just wanted just to witness a great series – and All Blacks wins of course.

The biggest smile I saw that day belonged to a youngster called **George Moore**. He'd just been given a rugby ball signed by the entire Lions squad. A couple of weeks later I emailed a copy of the picture I took of George to **his mum, Nicola, and dad, John**. She confirmed the smile had been pretty permanent for all the intervening time and the ball is his constant companion, even sharing his bed.

At first glance you may think young George is celebrating his prized acquisition with a beer, but rest assured, that's Dad's hand on the bottle.

George Moore with his signed ball from the Lions squad, mum Nicola and dad John

The Fan Trail from the centre of Whangarei led past the Lions Den, significantly busier on match day. Rather than have fans jostle three or four deep at the bar, from the outset owner Lloyd Rooney and his team formed them into a well organised line that snaked between the tables beyond. We Brits respect a queue of course, so the system worked very well for all the time I was in there and the bar staff worked tirelessly to keep the snake slithering forward. I'm sure the canapes being handed round courtesy of Michael Holland/warrengatlandsarmy.com helped keep best of order as well.

As many were drinking on the trail outside as were packed inside. Val had gone back to the house while I carried on talking to fans, and I thought we'd agreed when we parted that she was to pick me up at The Lions Den around 5.30pm, so we could get to the stadium in good time to hand out flyers to fans excited by the prospect of the rugby beginning.

Dave Dumelow emigrated to New Zealand a few years back, bringing with him products he used to sell in the car finishing business he worked with in the UK. His business here happens to be called Roar – appropriate for Lions support of course, and because NZRU has adopted for 2017 the slogan 'Out Roar The Lions' to encourage local fans to get behind the All Blacks. Dave's truck has a paint job in the company name, so attracted a good bit of banter at traffic lights – most of it unprintable here.

Sightseeing up the coast a little in Bay of Islands, a random Kiwi they met in a bar invited Dave and mates, Val Ager and Leigh Fitzgerald back to his for a beer, where veteran All Black legend Graham Thorne happened to be visiting. The guys reckon Graham could still have thrown the three of them around quite comfortably if he'd wanted to.

He's only 71 so they're probably right.

Leigh Fitzgerald, Val Ager and Dave Dumelow

I had just taken a picture of the shy and retiring **Lizzie Carroll-Thom** (her words, springing towards me like the Lion she'd painted her face as when she spotted my camera) when I noticed it was already twenty-to-six. Much as Lizzie and her mates seemed good fun to be around, I thought I ought to be outside for when Val arrived. There I met a young couple quietly leaning against the building watching their fellow fans getting more and more boisterous - as if to prove the direct correlation with their alcohol intake. **Michael Byrne and Paula Whelan** told me they'd just got engaged and the tour was a treat to themselves. My best wishes for as long and happy a marriage as Val and I have enjoyed – 34 years and counting.

Just about the last people I spoke to at the Lions Den were a bright and breezy (and very tall) couple of guys called **Steve Bosworth and Andrew White**, who I'd noticed earlier leading the communal singing of more traditional rugby songs that made a change from the occasional "Lions, Lions, Lions, Lions" that sprang up intermittently. They'd suffered at the hands of British Airways on their Sorry Saturday. Like thousands of others they'd spent hours at Heathrow not knowing what the hell was going on before managing to find themselves a room at a West London hotel. Eventually boarding a plane for their substitute flight to Auckland via Tokyo three days after they were supposed to, the boys had built up a substantial bill in consoling themselves for their delay. Get your wallet out BA.

Shy, retiring Lizzie Carroll-Thom

Michael Byrne and Paula Whelan

Gloucester Fan Steve Bosworth with pal Andrew White

Green laces would make these perfect Lions shoes

I think Andi Ttofa meant business

Some of Britain's finest young doctors and nurses – all working in New Zealand

I stayed with the dwindling numbers at the bar wondering where on earth Val could be, but not wanting to move elsewhere in the belief she'd arrive soon... while she hunted around the stadium wondering where on earth I was, as she thought we'd agreed when we parted that I'd said meet me there.

I was very disappointed to have missed the first opportunity to distribute flyers at the place where the largest concentration of fans would be.

You're probably wondering why we didn't call each other. Val's ancient (i.e. 2G) mobile phone became rather temperamental in New Zealand, working only sporadically. This was an occasion that it was proving at its moodiest.

A bit like me when we eventually did find each other.

The match was about what everybody seemed to expect of an opening fixture so soon after the squad getting to New Zealand. The Baa-Baas youngsters were predictably keen to impress and came out all guns blazing, playing the first half hour at a blistering pace. Many of the Lions played as if they were suffering from jetlag - later confirmed to me by Warren Gatland himself to have been exactly the case, when I had my unexpected 'private audience' with him the day before the first test.

Despite the foul weather and their apparent malaise evidenced by far too many errors, the Lions just about ground out a win that filled nobody with great confidence for the coming fixtures, which would unquestionably be more challenging.

The Lions weren't the only ones struggling that weekend - I really wasn't on my A-game either.

4th June – Whangarei to Auckland

As well as a perfect start to our trip afforded us by Mike and Colleen's welcome and hospitality, our first few days had been a marvellous introduction for Val to the world of rugby. She loved the atmosphere that had been created in Whangarei, and although she'd never watched a game of rugby in her life, had asked lots of questions during the match to begin her rugby education. She's a very bright lady, so I wasn't surprised that she was to prove a very good student.

As I said though, I really wasn't on top form that weekend. Perhaps I was more jet-lagged than I thought.

Sunday morning saw the formal Māori welcome to the Lions at The Treaty Grounds in Waitangi, about 45 minutes north of Whangarei. Mike had drawn my attention to it the day we arrived. For some inexplicable reason I didn't bother to re-check when he told me on the Saturday evening that the event started at 12.30pm. We had time for a leisurely breakfast before setting out together for Waitangi, aiming to be there by around 11.30am. We also had plenty of time for a short detour to see a couple of places on the Bay of Islands coastline before we reached The Treaty Grounds – to find thousands of people and cars streaming out of the place.

The ceremony had started at 10.30am and was all over.

Cue more disappointment to add to the previous evening's. Not with anyone else but myself I stress.

FOCUS ON THE FANS is my project so it's my responsibility to know the where and when of what's going on. I was pretty quiet though as I beat myself up internally on the journey back, so the others knew I was upset, but couldn't have known my anger was solely focused on me.

A light and fluffy croissant will always lighten your mood: Those of you who spoke to me on the tour will know that I'm pretty much deaf in one ear and nowhere near 100% in the other. I wear hearing aids, but unlike glasses do for sight, they don't restore your hearing at all for the areas of hearing where you suffer loss. Hearing aids are merely tiny speakers that make everything louder, so in environments like bars and cars where there is significant background noise I struggle to pick up what's said.

Wrapped up in my own thoughts, and with the car engine, road noise and heavy traffic creating a permanent all-around multi-toned hum, I could hear that Val and Colleen were chatting merrily and laughing as they had all weekend, but as usual with rear seat passengers, couldn't make out what they were saying. When Mike half turned to them to join in their conversation I heard:

"Do you get croissants in the UK?".

I thought I should show that I wasn't moping about the morning's outcome so much that I couldn't participate when I did have the chance, so cheerfully volunteered:

"We do, but they're usually nothing like the ones you get in France. Theirs are light and fluffy when you put them in your mouth, whereas British ones tend to be much more doughy."

When that sank in the three of them burst into hysterical, belly heaving laughter. It took 30 seconds or so for Mike to recover control enough to tell me they were talking about possums, not croissants.

One thing I'm very happy to do when I deserve it is laugh at myself. My mood was definitely lightened. This was one of those occasions when you take it on the chin, grin at your cock-up and move on.

Which after visiting the public toilets Hundertwasser had designed in Kawakawa, then dropping Mike and Colleen back at their house, is exactly what we did.

A taste of what's to come in Whangarei? Hundertwasser's public toilets in Kawakawa

Atheism rules OK! The journey back to Auckland was significantly slower than the outward drive, so it was getting dark by the time we reached the city. I'd printed off a map to find the house of our next host, **Shirin** (pronounced She-reen). We'd spoken briefly on the phone and when Val asked what she sounded like I said simply: "Very posh".

Which is what **Shirin Caldwell** unashamedly is. She's also one of the most amazing people I've met in a long while. From the moment we witnessed her big beaming smile and open-armed welcome as she greeted us at the front door we knew we'd get on famously.

Her next words confirmed it. "Come through. I bet you're ready for a glass of wine". We were.

There's nothing like the smell of a beef casserole on a cold rainy winter's evening to warm the cockles of your heart. Shirin's 100-year-old cottage kitchen had recently had a very sympathetically attached ultra-modern extension, which made the transition from cosy kitchen to bright and spacious dining and seating area work very well. It smelt great too. Supper was ready.

As we sat down to said casserole, it struck me that when we'd discussed potential arrival times on that Sunday, Shirin had mentioned her church. So, before she started serving I referred to our earlier conversation and asked if she wished to say grace before we tucked in.

Shirin and Val

"Good grief no. I'm an Atheist" was a bit of a surprise then. Even more so was the follow up: "Most of our congregation are."

During the delicious meal - the sauce had a hint of orange flavour that goes really well with beef - she explained that the Unitarian Church advocates no single faith and has no list of imposed creed or beliefs that must be slavishly followed. Open minded exploration of the world around us is considered far more important, and people who base their thinking on reason rather than dogma are the kind that they welcome. It soon became clear why Shirin enjoyed the intellectual aspect of the like-minded people she encountered at her church. She's incredibly knowledgeable and well read. Not to the slightest extent in a showy way; rather she uses her intellect and personality to engage people in the most enjoyable two-way conversations.

Once again, we felt instantly comfortable with our new friend – as we did with all our later hosts too.

She explained the reason for her speaking voice was entirely her mother's refusal to allow her to talk like the local children – Shirin was two when they emigrated to New Zealand.

"You will speak properly!" was apparently a phrase she got very used to hearing. It was no surprise at all when we learned on one of our later stays with her that as a young woman she'd modelled for Vogue magazine and had been an actress on an Australian TV series.

Small world moment number 2: The Hundertwasser print on Shirin's wall was explained by the fact that he'd been her boyfriend for a time.

A tale to make Colleen jealous.

After we'd eaten I cursed the laptop some more while starting on my second blog and the accompanying pictures, which The Telegraph wanted me to file each Monday morning. Being 11 hours ahead of the UK, this meant in effect I had all the following day to work on it too, so I soon abandoned the task in favour of more wine and getting to learn more about Shirin.

5th – 8th June: Auckland Blues – In All Senses

You're mostly Brits reading this. You'll want to hear more about the weather. Sub-tropical Auckland's winter can be like a beautiful but fickle mistress. Shaped by the city's location amid and atop 50 volcanoes, with coastline either side of the city, it's a rollercoaster of glorious sunshine and fluffy clouds one minute, turning in an instant to moody clouds and thunderous rainfall you don't see coming, only to resume normal service brightness again within half an hour. Always with the underlying potential to repeat the cycle without notice.

Starting work on a wintry, dull and rainy Monday morning in Auckland is much like it is at home – slightly depressing. Especially when things don't go to plan. My laptop decided Shirin's router – only 15ft away in her office next to the kitchen – was far too far away from the dining table to maintain a signal for more than a few minutes. I couldn't help wondering if it was the fault of Mr. Dell's components? Particularly as Shirin's tablet in the same place had maximum bars constantly.

At lunchtime there was a break in the weather. We actually saw sunshine - pretty much for the first time since we left Auckland airport. I'd finished and despatched my material to Telegraph Sport Online, so we spent the afternoon with Shirin intending to show us round some of her favourite places in Auckland.

We tried to visit an art gallery that wasn't open on Mondays.

Next stop was Auckland's second tallest volcano – One Tree Hill. Rising 182m, with 33m more of obelisk on its summit, you can see both sides of Auckland's coastline. You can also see the tallest volcano, Mt Eden, across the city to the west, and just about make out the Eden Park stadium roof to the left of the peak.

Auckland's highest point, Mount Eden, from its second highest, One Tree Hill

Auckland's west coast from One Tree Hill
Rainbows were almost ever present throughout

We'd promised to cook for Shirin that night so also visited her favourite up-market supermarket to buy ingredients, which more often than not had 'Artisan' labels on the wrapper, with corresponding 'Artisan' prices. All was very good quality though, and with the generosity Shirin had extended by accommodating us for all three Auckland matches, we were more than happy to indulge ourselves and her with fine food and wines.

On Tuesday when the rain eased at lunchtime, we drove into the city centre hoping to find as many fans as we could. The number around was still fairly minimal, but we did meet the people from New Zealand's British Consulate manning the bus that was to follow the whole tour. The vehicle had a dual purpose:

1. As a mobile consulate. If fans lost their passport or driving licence, or had other problems needing consular assistance, they wouldn't have to traipse to Wellington
2. As an advertising platform encouraging non-Brits to visit the UK

A great idea. Even at that early stage it had proved its worth to one unfortunate fan who'd mislaid vital documents in Whangarei - thankfully not match tickets.

We heard about a goal-kicking competition that was taking place at Viaduct Harbour, a former commercial dock that is now a buzzing development of bars, restaurants and apartments around the marina that became the base for the Americas Cup yachting regatta in 2003. Suppliers of pretty much all things rugby related from clothing to balls, Canterbury were a principal partner of Lions Rugby, and had a store on Princes Wharf at the harbour entrance. Their PR people had set up rugby posts at one end of the car park outside the store, and were running a competition for fans to see who could be most accurate from the furthest distance, with the prize being match tickets for the following evening's game. By the time we were within sight of the event the rain had returned with a vengeance. Water and cameras do not fellow bed mates make, so I took refuge for 10 minutes until the deluge subsided. When we crossed the road to reach the competition, the Lions fan event had finished and the All Blacks fans were taking a turn.

Despite the wet and slippery surface...   ...look carefully and you can see...   ... this one went straight down the middle

Alongside the kicking area I got my first taste of how Lions players routinely engage with fans. Five of the squad were happily signing autographs and posing for photos – and continued to do so for the 45 minutes or so that we were present.

Owen Farrell – not looking as big as I thought he must be – posing with fans

The constant rain, dull grey skies with little of interest in the background and only a sprinkling of fans braving the elements to watch the kicking contest meant there weren't great pictures to be had.

A Flash Down The Pan: During that time though, I reverted to Calamity Ken again. I managed to bash my flashgun against a railing while turning to avoid somebody running across my path after a ball had done what rugby balls invariably do and bounced in a different direction to that expected. The flash was knocked off the camera. I knew that either the locking pins on the flash or the holes they fitted into on the camera – or both – were likely to be damaged. Damn.

Intermittent showers for what little remained of the afternoon before nightfall limited the amount of flyer distribution we could undertake, with the number of Lions fans around sporadic at best.

As darkness fell we headed back before we took Shirin to the restaurant she'd picked for a meal early that evening, a Chinese place she's visited a few times.

Lost in translation: The restaurant Shirin directed us to was called Flavour House. It looked like the Chinese equivalent of a Greasy Joe's, with plain formica tables, mismatched chairs and fading photos of very reasonably priced dishes adorning the walls. We were early. Only one other table was occupied. Reassuringly, by Chinese people whose food looked tempting and was being enthusiastically devoured, even by the young kids.

Shirin told us she always liked dumplings to start, then recommended some of her favourite dishes to follow. Because each of the three varieties of dumpling we fancied trying (chicken, beef and duck) came in portions of 15, and we really only wanted to share one dumpling dish before our mains, we thought we'd be clever and ask for 5 of each flavour in a single portion. Shirin had explained the owner's English wasn't great, but he nodded enthusiastically at the suggestion and we eagerly awaited their delivery.

You're way ahead I imagine. Of course, we got three full portions – 45 rather large dumplings.

Our boggle eyed looks didn't spark any reaction from the owner, and starting to re-explain that this was much more than we really wanted very soon seemed like harder work than eating what we could and taking the rest home for next day's lunch. They were good dumplings though, as were the fish, pork and Chinese vegetable dishes that followed. They were also huge servings, so we walked out with doggy bags containing about as much as we had been able to eat. It was a good cheap meal, and the fact they aren't licensed premises means you can take your own booze in without a corkage charge.

7th June, Match day 2: Lions v Auckland Blues: we resolved over breakfast that this time we'll make sure that we get to the ground in good time to hand out as many flyers as we could to arriving fans. The morning was very sunny, so we decided on some 'We Time' before getting to work handing out flyers in the city centre bars, then moving on to Eden Park. We ventured across the harbour bridge to the North Shore, where Shirin had told us there were some great beaches.

Takapuna is certainly one of those; long, wide and fringed with stunning houses most of us will only ever dream of owning.

Looking out to sea it was clear that a fairly violent storm was taking place not that far north of where we were, while we enjoyed a lovely walk in glorious sunshine. Luckily the prevailing breeze held the black clouds to the north and out to sea the entire time we were on the beach.

Look north, look south. Ultra-contrasting weather from the same point at the same time

It felt good to be spending a little time on our own, not thinking about FOCUS ON THE FANS, or all the little niggles we'd been experiencing thus far.

A much greater niggle was to arise that evening though.

After we'd driven a little further up the coast, hit the rain that was the fringe of the storm we'd seen, decided not to look at Devonport for both time and weather reasons, we returned to the city centre and spent a little, not very successful, time searching out fans that remained there, ending up at Viaduct Harbour again as dusk fell.

Before we left for Eden Park, Val needed a comfort break first. While she found somewhere suitable I hung around the car park in case any more fans passed by on their way out of the harbour. I spotted two couples with a number of children clad in Lions shirts heading my way. I greeted them with what was to become my signature opening line when approaching people: "Hello. I'm writing a book about you."

That got the enthusiastic reaction I hoped for, and I quickly explained about FOCUS ON THE FANS. **Max Leighton** just about had time to tell me his name and that they had taken the kids out of school (with permission) for a twelve-month world tour, planning from the outset for it to coincide with the Lions in New Zealand. They were in a hurry to get to the stadium, but agreed to be photographed for the book. I took a picture. No flash.

Double damn. But not the niggle that really mattered as I had a spare flash at the house.

We were to meet the Leightons a few times more over the coming weeks, and the family were to become a rich source of news - unfortunately mostly bad with the mishaps they encountered.

Unclean! Thinking we'd allowed plenty of time to get to Eden Park before most fans, we were swallowed into the evening rush hour motorway traffic, while fans were walking the trail to the stadium or jumping on trains at Britomart station that took them there in minutes. Virtually stationary for thirty minutes or so just before the exit we needed, it was plain that cars on Dominion Road, which we were turning onto, were moving considerably slower than we could walk. We took the first parking space we found and started walking to the ground, we thought about a mile away.

Val stationed herself at the rail station end of Eden Park, while I took up position at the other end, where people who'd walked the Fan Trail were streaming in. Of course, it started raining just about as soon as we started handing out flyers, quickly becoming a considerably heavier downpour.

Because I couldn't get access into the ground to take pictures of people watching the matches due to the press accreditation mix-up, I'd thought this was the next best way to engage with as many fans as possible in as short a time as possible. We accepted nobody would stop to ask more about the book - their minds would of course be on the match about to start - but we just wanted to get the word out as widely as we could.

Within 15 minutes that idea was firmly squashed.

I felt a hand on my arm as I heard a pleasant female voice say the words: "Do you have permission to hand out these leaflets, sir?"

Turning to see the speaker I found a lady in a black polyester raincoat with silver fern and NZRU logos.

"I didn't know I'd need permission" said I apologetically. "Who would I get it from?".

She went on to show me that there is a defined 'Clean Zone' around each of the host stadiums, where it is not permitted to carry out any commercial activity without clearance from New Zealand Rugby Union. The right to establish a clean zone is enshrined in New Zealand law – the Major Events Management Act. When I explained that my purpose was merely to ask fans to send me their stories for a book I was writing about them, she politely suggested I contact the legal department at NZRU to discuss the matter. In the meantime, she would have to ask me to remove my tabard and stop handing out leaflets. I did so without argument of course.

Damn, damn, damn.

Feeling the world and his dog were against me I headed off to tell Val the bad news. We trudged dejectedly through the now pouring rain back towards Dominion Road – the limit of the clean zone on that side of the stadium.

Thanks to the earlier sunshine, Val had opted not to bring her waterproof coat, so was wet through and very cold. She took the car back to the house, while I retreated to metaphorically lick my wounds with the aid of a jug of ale while watching the game in The Dominion pub. And I mean a jug – enough to last the whole match.

Blues All Round: The bar was mostly occupied by Blues fans. Before kick-off I couldn't help that my current emotional state matched the colour of their scarves.

Although it was a curate's egg of a performance by the tourists, with some fabulous Lions play spoiled by silly mistakes which saw a narrow defeat, I rather enjoyed the game. That was mainly thanks to the excellent company of **a Blues fan called Grant**, whose easy affability and deep knowledge of rugby kept me from mithering about what had happened outside the ground. The moment of brilliance from All Blacks golden boy Sonny Bill Williams to get Blues back in the mix late in the game left plenty of Lions fans both admiring the skill of the man, while at the same time worrying about what damage he'd do to the Lions in the upcoming test matches.

With the permission of the manager I left flyers on the pub tables, hoping some would be picked up and read by fans who'd been at the match, now starting to fill the pub within a few minutes of the final whistle.

On the long walk home, I thought about dropping flyers into any bars I saw on the way. The first was an Irish pub – **The Clare Inn** – but by the time I passed, bouncers were enforcing a strict 'one out, one in' policy and the people outside were more interested in when they were likely to get in than talking to me. If I'm honest, I didn't feel much like enthusing about the book that evening, and had definitely had enough beer anyway, so, plodded on.

There were a good few people under the cover of the awning at the **Outside Obie** bar a little further down. A group of four spied the tabard and stopped me. I went into auto mode and fired up their imagination, chatting to ex-pats **Simon, John (the bar owner), Leila and Shanie** for a good half hour as they enthusiastically questioned me about the background to the idea. Sensibly, I had no more beer while there.

By now it was gone 11pm and I was decidedly peckish. I knew I'd be passing Flavour House again, and the night before had spotted a special pork dumpling deal advertised on the wall. This time I could see only one available table as I looked in, so swiftly plonked myself down at it and carefully ordered one plateful only of the special, which numbered 10 dumplings.

They were very good, as was the can of orange Tango I chose to accompany them. (Is it just me or does Tango made for Australia and New Zealand really taste that much better than it does in the UK? I don't drink it often, but every time I've had it down under I've thought the same).

With our flight to Christchurch not departing until 3pm the next day I had a bit of a lie in before packing up our kit for the journey to South Island.

Frankly, I couldn't wait to get out of Auckland. Apart from meeting Shirin and the few fans we'd encountered, it had proved to be a pretty woeful and dispiriting few days as far as the book was concerned.

I think that must have been the feeling **George Pritchard** had about the rugby if this picture he sent me is anything to go by. His email said it was taken after the Blues match.

Something had to change.

8th June: Auckland to Christchurch

After a fond farewell to Shirin we pottered down the motorway to the airport 20 minutes away. I was looking forward to seeing what progress Christchurch had made since we were previously there, and to seeing more of Dunedin. Our overnight stop in the latter city three years earlier had not shown it at its best, being shrouded in mist and rain – and that was in summer.

As we passed the airport bar in the domestic terminal after dropping our bags, I spotted two gentlemen in their Lions shirts also sporting fine looking kilts. We'd seen a good few kilts already, so it wasn't the novelty that drew me to want to talk to them. There was something about the look of these two guys that made me feel it would be okay to interrupt them as they supped their pints.

I was right. **Sandy Geddes and Norrie Flowers** proved to be the sort of people who make you so welcome and at ease, the impression they leave you with is you really want to be their pal, but feel you'd have to earn the right. I was so enjoying the 15 minutes or so that we chatted, Val moved the trolley with our in-flight bags she'd been guarding a little closer so she could join in. Sandy charmed her immediately with an age-old line:

"Ken, you didn't tell us you'd brought your daughter!"

They were soon telling me about the many rugby tours they've enjoyed hospitality on as players with Strathclyde Police RFC and as fans – one every two years on average, for more years than they care to admit to.

A recurring theme seemed to be the kindness of strangers they'd experienced all over the world. In fact, Norrie used a quote I hadn't heard but wrote down. 'Life is what it is due to the kindness of strangers'. (I can't trace those exact words as a quote, but it may reference the end of 'A Streetcar Named Desire' where Blanche says she has always depended on the kindness of strangers). Whatever the source, the words sum up the majority of the New Zealand nation for me.

While there we certainly gathered huge numbers of stories from Lions fans about kindnesses given and received by strangers without expectation of anything in return.

When I asked the guys if they planned to see the country between matches, I figured it wasn't high on their agenda because of the quizzical tone of Sandy's response: 'That would mean leaving a bar' - an accurate quote. They had one major quest for the start of their tour. They needed to find some small soft toy Kiwis to replace the Wallabies pinned beneath the Lions acting as their sporrans, there since the last Lions tour to Australia – the reason the Lions triumphed in 2013 according to them.

Norrie and Sandy in Auckland airport. Note the sporran Lions from 2013 about to eat Wallaby – soon to be replaced by Kiwis

Surprisingly we didn't see Sandy and Norrie in any of the many bars in which we handed out flyers - until the day of the final test. They walked out of The Occidental in Auckland just as we arrived. They greeted us immediately with big hugs. Like old friends. Both endorsed the absolute joy of being amongst New Zealanders for the past month. They'd had yet another ball. Good on them.

My best wishes to their friend **Paul Thomson**, who they were awaiting in Auckland airport before their connecting flight to Christchurch a little later than ours. He was taken ill a couple of weeks before the tour finale and remained in hospital when I saw Sandy and Norrie.

All change: On the flight to Christchurch Val and I discussed our experience so far. It didn't make for an inspiring conversation. The IT problems, relative scarcity of fans around the two cities we'd been in compared to our expectations, the NZRU restrictions, on top of the very unpredictable weather, had all conspired to greatly diminish the positives we had enjoyed – namely our hosts and the fans we had managed to talk to.

Add to the mix that Val was very out of her comfort zone, and my clear disappointment every time another setback arose not making her feel any better, we decided we needed to change some things to avoid this trip having an adverse effect on our enjoyment of our time in New Zealand.

Both of us don't do confrontation by the way. That's not to say we don't confront – the two things are entirely different. We work things out without shouting and screaming, and certainly not by hurling abuse at each other. We were both not happy with the way the trip had worked out so far, so took the opportunity to identify how best to make it work for us.

I thought back to the conversation with Sandy and Norrie. Whilst there had no doubt been an element of truth in Sandy's flippant comment about leaving a bar, they'd gone on to explain how much they had enjoyed seeing so much of the world through the opportunities rugby tours had provided. It struck me that we'd been so focused on the book, trying to find fans when there simply weren't that many around, we'd ended up chasing our tails with little achieved. Of the fans that were about already, it was much more likely they were taking the opportunity to see New Zealand than spending the majority of their time in city bars.

We decided we'd only 'work' at distributing flyers on match days and the day before. The rest of the time we'd simply revisit places we knew we wanted to, and explore other places that we hadn't already been to. The chances were, we'd see some other fans wherever we went anyway.

With the prospect of a minimal number of photographs of fans during matches now cemented in stone, we also knew the book would have to be much more narrative then image led, so were grateful to have been asked to blog fan stories for Telegraph Online. It had given us the focus to initiate and direct conversations with people we'd already met. We'd simply do more of that.

Arriving in Christchurch in far better humour than we'd left Auckland, we picked up the complimentary RAV4 from Hertz and stopped at a wine shop for essentials to accompany the meal we knew our next hosts were preparing before they set off for a few days at their second home. This time the car came with a GPS, so we easily found our way to **John and Jo's** house, in the hills less than 15 minutes east from the centre, offering a spectacular cityscape with a backdrop of snow-capped Southern Alps across the Canterbury Plains beyond.

After an excellent poached wild salmon with mustard sauce dish followed by delicious upside-down sponge with apple and feijoa (a new fruit to me), Jo showed us her studio. She's a professional artist specialising in indigenous New Zealand botanical subjects and insects. I was immediately impressed by her work. After John and Jo departed I wrote an email to the legal department of New Zealand Rugby Union explaining my project and asking for permission to distribute flyers at the grounds on match days.

That done, we suddenly remembered it was election day back home, so settled down to watch BBC World News on TV. Until then we'd hardly looked at telly except for the two Lions matches, so really had no clue how the campaigns had been going.

John Richardson and Jo Ewing, in Bibury near our home

I have to say, before we left the UK I'd been exceptionally impressed by the cleverness of whoever conceived and managed Labour's campaign. Not that I agreed with much of the policy content, but I recognised that focusing on issues other than Brexit at least gave them a shot at moving the debate away from the very singular reason Theresa May had called the election.

I thought the promise of scrapping tuition fees a particular masterstroke. If anything was going to mobilise youngsters to get out and vote, that was. It's a scenario I thought would be the only way for Labour to stand any chance of closing the gap. I still didn't think they would, but admired what appeared to me to be very clear strategic thinking.

Being 11 hours ahead of the UK, the polling stations were only just opening, but to discover how the opinion polls had shifted so hugely in the short time we'd been away was a major surprise. In rugby terms, the Conservatives must have played a shocker. We went to bed fearful of what we considered the worst possible result - a hung parliament. As we all now know, that's exactly what we woke up to. This was right up there with all the worst political gaffes. May's place in history secured for all the wrong reasons.

9-10 June: Christchurch – With Two 'Firsts'

EVERYTHING IS GOING TO BE ALRIGHT: No visitor to Christchurch can fail to be affected by how virtually all its city centre was reduced to rubble in the 2011 earthquake. The reaction of fans we met there depended largely on whether and when they'd previously visited the city. Those who had known Christchurch pre-earthquake and were back for the first time since, spoke of their shock at the beauty that has been cruelly stripped away. Others who first visited after the quake, like we did three years ago, felt buoyed by the belting design exhibited in the slowly emerging new city of glass and steel rising from the almost exclusively temporary structures we witnessed last time around. First timers expressed the same sort of bewilderment at the intensity of the widespread destruction as we had in 2014.

All that remains of Christchurch Cathedral

For me, the indomitable spirit of Christchurch citizens is best exemplified by three features in the city as it is now.

Firstly, Container Mall – the repurposed shipping containers that became the symbol of defiance to Mother Nature's wrath. Originally called Re:Start, the retail centre opened in October 2011 when the site had been made safe after the February earthquake. 27 units became shops, bars, banks and food outlets. Inspired, innovative and initially essential to the wider Re:Start campaign, the whole concept became a much-loved symbol of the power of collective human strength and sheer will to begin again. Many locals are now bewailing the fact that the mall is disappearing as construction of permanent buildings encroaches upon it.

Now boasting more than 50 tenants, the new owners of the land Container Mall sits on seem to have listened to public opinion reflecting the affection locals have for what became a world-renowned icon. Tenants' leases have been extended until February 2018 to allow them another peak summer period of trading, and the owners/developers say they are revisiting their plans. They now intend to retain elements of Container Mall within the multi-million-dollar development of new buildings scheduled for construction to commence in 2018.

I hope the locals get their wish for some to remain permanently.

Secondly, the message of reassurance and hope installed on the side of the city's striking art gallery. A relatively new construction that survived the earthquake, the gallery served initially as the base for the City Council to begin their rejuvenation plans.

In a variety of neon colours, these words are lit up 24 hours a day:
'EVERYTHING IS GOING TO BE ALRIGHT'

It is a variation of previous installations that are all the work of Turner Prize winning British artist Martin Creed, in this case funded and maintained by a wealthy Christchurch entrepreneur Neil Graham shortly before his death.

I don't much care about the debates I've read by various art critics about Creed's work across the world. Here it feels to me to be the right words in the right place at the right time.

Lastly, the Transition Cathedral. Known locally as Cardboard Cathedral due to its innovative construction incorporating huge cardboard tubes within its infrastructure, seen in the close up. The triangular stained glass window prominent in its façade is made entirely from fragments of the windows recovered from the fallen cathedral. I'm not a religious man but I respect the importance and symbolism of the new building, as well as the spiritual comfort it provides, to those who are.

With only a couple of days in Christchurch, we went straight to the city centre on the Friday before the Crusaders match. There already seemed to be a lot more Lions fans around. As we strolled around the still ravaged centre trying to assess the differences between our previous visit and this one, we were approached by a chap with a pull along suitcase, who asked if we knew where the Post Office was.

Little did we know at that stage that we were in the presence of a world record holder.

As we walked along together it emerged that **Justin Davies** holds an official Guinness World Record - for the number of matches watched in an individual Rugby World Cup Finals tournament. We'd been impressed by the Palmers' accomplishment of seeing eleven matches in RWC 2011. Justin saw twenty eight matches of the 2015 Rugby World Cup.

Now resident in New Zealand after marrying a girl he met when here in 2005 (no prizes for guessing what brought him here) and the 2015 RWC tournament being in England, to see so many games was an almighty logistical and financial challenge. Justin has seen 100 Rugby World Cup matches in total, watched over 400 other international matches, and is on his 4th Lions tour (though yet to complete a South African one). To mark Justin's world record, last year Sam Warburton presented him with a framed certificate during Wales tour of New Zealand. At the tender age of 45, Justin will definitely be pushing those numbers even higher for a good few years yet.

Justin Davies - Superfan

Anthony Flynn and Clodagh Toomey were enjoying a drink in the sunshine (hurray!) with friends **Damien Meere and Sarah Hayes** (wearing grey and looking distracted) in a bar at Container Mall.

They'd just arrived in New Zealand that day.

They told me with great pride that this trip was their honeymoon. The obvious question was when did they get married?

I didn't expect the answer… January 2015!!! The happy couple had been saving for this trip for the last two and a half years.

Do you remember the Gladiator TV programme? Anthony told me that in one of the squares among the newly constructed shops a local radio station had arranged for some Crusaders squad members to take on Lions fans in the programme's Duel challenge, in which the object is to knock your opponent off their platform using pugil sticks.

Small World Moment number 3: Evidently not many Lions fans knew about it, as there were only a sprinkling present. There weren't many Kiwis either. In between the light-hearted bouts, I was trying to chat to the few fans there. Approaching one guy sitting alone at a picnic table, I cheerily asked if I could hand him one of my flyers. He readily accepted and engaged me in conversation. A moment later he said something about being psychic, and asked: "Does your name begin with K?" Intrigued, I replied: "It might do".

"I reckon you come from somewhere in the west of England." he went on. He couldn't have told that from my accent - I was born in Slough, on the edge of London. Then it clicked.

"Aah! You've seen my wife haven't you."

I wasn't expecting him to then say: "Every Wednesday for the last two years!".

No, I hadn't just discovered my wife had been having a long term illicit affair. The wind-up merchant turned out to be **Tim Bird,** who runs a Keep Fit class Val goes to in our village hall every Wednesday morning. I'd never met Tim, although Val had told me some weeks before the tour started that he would be in New Zealand for the whole tour accompanied by his son **Henry**.

Mal & Isabel Morgan were watching the mock battles too. The Jersey residents left home on 7th January to join the Lions Tour. They have an excuse for such an early departure, having travelled via Scotland, Wales, Dubai, India, Cambodia, Malaysia, Singapore, Indonesia, Japan and Australia to get here - and their timing was perfect.

Although they had no match tickets nor accommodation in Whangarei, they realised when they got off the plane in Auckland they had time to catch a bus north to reach the city in time to watch the Baa-Baas match up there. 5 minutes after disembarking the bus, they snapped up tickets for the match offered at face value by a local. 30 minutes later, walking into the city centre to find somewhere to stay, they bumped into **Ian Grey**, a local resident who just stopped them to ask how they were doing. Explaining what they'd done, the Morgans asked Ian if he could recommend somewhere to try and find a room for the night. You guessed it – Ian and his **spouse Marie** put them up for the night, feeding and watering them as well as dropping them at the game.

Another intercontinental rugby friendship sure to endure.

More Wasps fans whose dedication goes above and beyond: Jackie Teeling had operations on both big toes for ingrowing toenails just before setting off with **husband Kieran** for a rugby-free visit to their daughter in Sydney. Once in that great city though, although they say they had no plans to, they couldn't resist 'popping over' for 2 matches while they had the chance. It's bloomin' cold in Christchurch this time of year. Poor Jackie is on crutches, unable to wear socks or shoes on her bandaged feet. The rest of her toes felt like long thin ice cubes as she hobbled around the coldest parts of New Zealand, rather than putting her feet up in a warm Sydney apartment. You've only yourself to blame Jackie, but we love you for doing it.

Our Irish honeymooners appeared in the square after a few minutes. Anthony even managed to shrug off the jet lag for long enough to take on a Crusader - but not long enough to register a win. There was only ever going to be one outcome.

Anthony Flynn about to take a battering

Isabel and Mal Morgan

Jackie and Kieran Teeling

After the duelling ended we were exploring the newly built shops opposite Container Mall when we bumped into **Andy and Gudrun Palmer** again. While we were extending our knowledge of their remarkable devotion to the game I spotted out of the corner of my eye a family with three children approaching from behind them. Thinking it might be the Leightons I'd encountered in the twilight in Auckland, I tried to signal them to stop while still continuing to converse with the Palmers. Remarkably, they did. I made my excuses to Andy and Gudrun, asking Val to record the details they'd shared.

I knew immediately I got a good look at them it wasn't the Leightons, and explained why I'd asked them to stop. It turned out that **the Coleman family** had done very similar to the Leightons. **Dad Paul** had planned a 6-month world tour, again ensuring they were in the vicinity of the Lions Tour at the right time, while they home schooled the children on the way.

9-year-old Luca was very excited when we met. With good reason. They'd just bumped into Sam Warburton walking round town and secured a photo and autograph. The rest of the family is **mum Jude and 4-year-old twins Izzy and Dylan**.

The opportunity for sport seemed to be a recurring theme. They'd commenced their trip skiing in Colorado, where Luca had 5 weeks slalom ski coaching and ended up racing for Team Breckenridge, winning one of the races against far more experienced skiers. They moved on to Costa Rica and Peru before he trained for beach soccer with the Flamengo club in Rio de Janeiro. That was followed by 6 weeks of soccer training with Maradona's boyhood club Argentinos Juniors Academy in Buenos Aires. The family then spent time riding horses with gauchos in Uruguay before coming to NZ.

Paul is Welsh, loves his rugby and has instilled the same passion in his children. He wanted Luca to experience rugby in New Zealand early in his life, because he believes player development is entirely different to in England (Paul coaches rugby at Luca's club). The family came to NZ six weeks before the Lions arrived so Luca could immerse himself in rugby. Paul contacted Dan Carter's old coach Stephen Dods in Christchurch, who set up Luca to play with High School Old Boys (Carter's old club) and had ex-Crusader Ross Kennedy work with him one-to-one twice a week.

When I commented on the sporting content of the tour being not just significant but very high quality, Paul explained that he used to be Chief Executive of the governing body that runs World Triathlon events. As he put it, he paid the Brownlee brothers' wages. You may have guessed that Paul was using his extensive network of contacts across the world to ensure that special memories for the family were pretty much guaranteed wherever they went.

According to Paul, there was no doubt Luca had a lot of catching up to do, but soon played himself into a team unbeaten in 25 matches in division 1 in Christchurch. He's currently keen on playing fly-half so to get specialist attention from elite coaches was fantastic for him. The whole experience has inspired Luca to dream big. He told me excitedly that he hopes to return in 12 years as a member of the Lions squad. I love kids that have such high ambition. I also wouldn't bet against it. Luca seemed very level-headed for a nine-year-old, and far from displaying precociousness, he clearly appreciated the fabulous opportunities he's had at a young age.

We ended up meeting the family a few more times before they left New Zealand for Vanuata and Fiji before the second test. On every occasion the excitement of all the children was very evident, and they were all an exceedingly impressive credit to their parents.

Luca was the lucky Lions fan that Sonny Bill Williams gave his shorts and socks to after the first test match. The gesture made his and the twins night. To top it off Ken Owens, who the family got to know through following the tour since Christchurch, also gave them his shorts and socks, so they have a set from each team. They wanted me to record their thanks to both players for such great memories.

Paul admits they stalked the Lions as a family and the kids have had their jerseys signed by almost every player. He tells me the Lions players were always very kind and patient at their hotels and training sessions and thinks they are great lads.

He has kept in contact since they left, and assured me the kids' passion for the Lions didn't diminish one iota by having to watch the subsequent matches on telly.

They completed their special tour of their own by travelling across Asia before heading home at the end of August.

The much-travelled Coleman family. Luca, Jude, Dylan Paul and Izzy

First 'First' - a great face for radio: At the consulate bus parked in Cathedral Square we heard about a fan event taking place in a suburban pub, from where a national radio show was being broadcast from 3pm to 7pm. On the way to The Fox and Ferret in Riccarton we tuned in to **The Hits Drive Time Show** and listened to a few rugby fans being interviewed between songs. The pub was pretty packed when we arrived around 5pm, mostly with Kiwis. The tabards did their job again. Before we could get anywhere near the bar we were asked by **Jason Tikao**, the show's producer, what we were doing. He then asked if I'd be willing to do a live interview with presenters **Stace and Flynny**. I'd never done a national radio spot before, but had gone there hoping for this to happen.

I've only ever done one radio interview. On a local BBC station to broadcast an event I'd arranged to raise funds for a charity trek to Everest base camp I was undertaking in 2005. Then I'd had time to prepare the points I wanted to get across, and it went so well that immediately afterwards the station asked me to record a trailer for them. Before I even got home our local Mayor rang to leave a message offering his support in any way he could. (Proper Preparation... etc).

I'd spent so many months talking to people and writing about FOCUS ON THE FANS I felt pretty well prepared with what I wanted to say. We talked in the Fox & Ferret for about 10 minutes either side of a song I don't remember. Stace, Flynny and Jason were all very complimentary afterwards.

We thought we'd earned a drink before leaving and gravitated towards the largest table in the place, where 5 Lions fans were occupying half of it. They were happy for us to join them. I sat next to **Ted Williams**, one of the fans I'd heard interviewed earlier. It's fair to say Ted's a very gregarious character. I liked him straight away. Blogging for Welsh club Betws RFC while over here, he has a wealth of rugby stories about local clubs and national heroes. Sorry Rory, but when I told him the story about you smiling as you waltzed past Al Pearce, Ted quick as a flash cited Ieuan Evans doing similar to you in a test match. I didn't want to appear to be biased so it had to go in here.

Ted's companions, from left, **Nicholas, Dick, Diana and Nicola** were just as welcoming, and all thought a book about fans and what we bring to sport was long overdue. Ted's an inveterate Twitter user and soon tweeted about meeting us.

Stace, Flynny and Jason

Nicholas Price, Dick and Diana Jones, Nicola and Ted Williams

Over dinner that evening Val and I agreed it had been a really nice day - much more enjoyable than our fan chasing in Auckland. There had been noticeably more fans around, in a more concentrated area. It felt like momentum for the tour was beginning. We'd relaxed more, chatted more – had fun!

After eating, I checked my email for any response from NZRU. There was one. Essentially it was saying I couldn't hand out flyers or wear my tabard in any 'Stadium Clean Zone', as both items contained a commercial element – the Hertz logo. I'd also explained in my email that NZRU's website had contributed to me failing to secure press accreditation, as it had directed media enquiries to be emailed to someone who had left the organisation months before – and still did so, as I'd checked again that day. I was hoping they would feel some guilt about that and allow me into the stadium to photograph fans during matches. But no, they said they would agree to me taking photos outside the ground, subject to not wearing the tabard or handing out flyers of course. It read as though they felt they were doing me a huge favour in granting that concession. It's not what I felt, as it bore no relation to why I had asked to be inside the stadiums, so was next to useless for my purposes.

It was no surprise anyway, and at least our first full day in Christchurch had seen our revised approach work well.

10th June, Match day 3: Lions v Crusaders. With Crusaders having swept aside all before them to that point in 2017, winning every match they played, facing the strongest club side in World rugby was being seen by fans as a benchmark for the Lions prospects against the All Blacks.

On a beautifully sunny but crisp, cold morning, we began our day in the city centre by splitting up. Val would work the bars and streets around Container Mall while I sussed out where the Fan Zone was. It's a small central area so we were confident of crossing paths when I'd done so.

We weren't to meet up for another 5 hours.

On my way to find the Fan Zone I happened upon a bar called Smash Palace, where I learned that the Fan Zone was literally on the other side. I thought I'd see if there was an exit on the far side of the outside seating area rather than walk round the streets to reach it. There wasn't, but retracing my steps I stopped to talk with Scots, **Jamie Little and Gavin Campbell**. Not for long though, as after their 28-hour flight landed the previous evening, they'd literally dropped bags in their hotel room and gone straight to Sullivans Irish Pub. Until 6am. They were trying to cope manfully with their giant bottles of Speight's 'Hair o' the Dog' for brekkie.

Jamie Little and Gavin Campbell

Michelle's Lions Hat**

Rory lookalike (?) Sam & Michelle Chung

At a not too distant table **Michelle and Sam Chung** sported Lions apparel. Another romance of rugby story, this couple met when Sam came over on tour. He lived in London, playing for Askeans RFC in South-east London. They now live in Christchurch, where Michelle has taken some stick from Kiwi friends for posting a picture of herself in a Lions shirt. She's used to the stick she's been getting for years for marrying a Pom.   ** Picture courtesy of Michell Chung

When I mentioned that Rory had written the foreword for the book, Sam chuckled: "Rory was my nickname at Askeans rugby club, and my mate **Steve Albuquerque** on the other wing was nicknamed Tony!" You may have surmised from Sam's surname that there's a touch of the oriental in him, although he says his teammates were definitely making more of a connection to the Underwood brothers from his background than was warranted by any physical resemblance.

I walked round to the Fan Zone and met the site manager. She readily handed me a media pass when I told her the reason for seeking her out, and assured me it would be fine for me to take photos of the fans watching the match. I was allowed to walk around the not yet open zone. It consisted of a few hundred seats in front of a screen, with no bar. Apparently, that was a restriction enforced by NZRU. It was they who dictated to the City Council the format of the Fan Zone. Which prompted me to reveal my email exchange with NZRU legal people. I didn't want my actions to upset anyone or get others into trouble unwittingly, so we agreed it best that I wore no tabard and handed out no flyers while in the Fan Zone.

Luckily there was a pub right next door - The Dux - with balconies on two levels overlooking the screen. I double checked that the bar was not part of the Fan Zone, and that there'd be no restriction on handing flyers out to its occupants, then set off past the pub back to town to find Val. I was waylaid.

Drinking outside the pub were **Les and Lauren Barclay** – you may recall them as the superfan and scarf lady from Whangarei. They introduced me to their companions, Lions fans **Jo and Rob Thomas** from Greenwich in London, telling them I was writing about fans. Rob took a flyer and told me they were writing a blog of their Lions tour too, just as they had done when they'd been in New Zealand for the 2011 Rugby World Cup. I looked up Rob & Jo's 'Tiki Tours of Aotearoa'. I imagine the 2011 trip is where they met Les and Lauren, because there seems to be a huge gap on page 2, between the pool stages of RWC 2011 and departing Heathrow in June 2017 for the Lions Tour – after which Les and Lauren get plenty of mentions as old friends.

Without being nasty, I'm slightly suspicious that their matchday reminiscences may have been affected by their alcohol intake, after reading in their blog on the day of the Crusaders game in Christchurch with Les and Lauren: **"We pass a shop with photos by Ken Skehan photographer."**

Hmmm.

I can't help but wonder what prompted this clearly inaccurate recollection. If they still had the flyer they'd know I was writing this book. Because they spelt my name correctly, which wasn't on the flyer, I can only think for some reason I gave them my photography business card as well. In which case I guess when they got back they were wondering in what context they'd collected it, and vaguely remembered it was in Christchurch.

Oh well. I suspect they are typical of most of the 7,000 or so who we actually handed flyers to. I've had a number contact me saying they'd forgotten about the book until they found the flyer in their wallet weeks after returning home.

Les expanded on his earliest Lions memory. The match was at Wellington's Athletic Park. He and his Dad stood in the wooden Millard Stand, infamous for the degree to which it swayed in Wellington's notoriously strong winds. He recalled the score being 11-8 in favour of the All Blacks. I just looked that up and he was spot on. **Quick quiz 2: Any guesses how many matches were played in total by the Lions on the 1959 tour?** I wasn't surprised to find it was more than the ten matches of the 2017 tour, but was amazed just how many more it was. (See bottom of this page for the answer).

The pub was pretty busy by this time, so I resumed my quest to find Val, as the atmosphere was excellent, but I couldn't summon her to come to me because when I tried to, I found I'd left my phone in the car.

I was wrong about the small city centre meaning we'd cross paths easily. I searched high and low without success before returning to the car. Val's phone wasn't taking calls that day, so I carried on looking for her around the centre.

*The 1959 Lions tour makes this era's tours seem like a quick break by comparison. They played 33 matches in total: 6 in Australia, 25 in New Zealand and 2 in Canada on the return home. The tour lasted from 23 May – 19 September, just a few days shy of four months.

The Rockpool Bar was jam packed. The first table of Lions fans assured me they hadn't seen anyone matching Val's description. I made sure the owner didn't mind and distributed a couple of hundred leaflets to the assembled throng. Because I was interrupting, my conversations were kept brief, except for a camper van and toilet block demolition story I promised to keep anonymous because the guy's wife was at home and 'didn't need to know'. It still took me at least half-an-hour to get around the pub, after which I continued my Val-hunt.

I spread my search a little further afield than the shopping area and spotted people sitting outside what looked like a hotel not far from Cathedral Square. While heading towards it, this group of people came running out from The Heritage Hotel foyer.

They pulled up very sharply when they saw my camera, asking me to take a picture. While taking this image I quickly explained FOCUS ON THE FANS, then handed them flyers as they resumed their race to reach wherever they were headed. They hadn't seen anyone matching Val's description in the hotel.

As the hotel was only 50 yards away I headed there anyway, where I found **Peter Beatty, David (Dai) Lloyd and Mark Davies**. They also assured me Val hadn't passed by – and they'd been sitting under the patio heater outside the hotel for a couple of hours at least. This trip was to celebrate the fortieth anniversary of when the three had met at Aston University in 1977.

On the day they left the UK, Peter's first grandchild had been born 15 minutes before they were due to leave for the airport. A swift diversion to the hospital raised a few eyebrows amongst the staff there, as the only way Peter was permitted to have the brief cuddle he desperately wanted before leaving the country, was to pretend to be the father.

They had wet the baby's head extensively during the flight – and every day since.

New Grandad Peter Beatty, David (Dai) Lloyd and Mark Davies

It was now beginning to get dusky. I was getting mildly concerned.

I thought Val would be getting worried, because, surprisingly to us, in both Whangarei and in Auckland, our hosts had said that it wasn't a good idea for women to walk round on their own after dark. They'd said that rising drug use across the country seemed to have prompted increases in violent street crime, especially against women.

My phone buzzed. A rare text from Val told me she was in the Fan Zone. Relieved that I knew she was amongst a crowd, I made my way back there.

The Dux was rocking, with a vengeance.

Blazers, Blazers Everywhere, and Military Men in Pink: On the way back to pick up my phone, I'd spotted a large group of guys in bright striped blazers walking along the street. Most of them stopped for a picture, as had a smaller group outside The Heritage sporting equally outstanding blazers.

Apologies if the names in that latter photo are incorrect. Your friend who wrote your names down in my notebook didn't have the best handwriting.

The first group of blazer boasting men I encountered...   ...and Chris Moore, Toby ?, Jeremy Stevens, Nicols Casely-Parker and Gabriel Schondent - perhaps

The two groups were of course military men in their regimental clobber, and were now mingling in The Dux.

They provided a vibrant contrast to the uniform red shirts packing the bar to full capacity in every nook and cranny. But even the brightness of these blazers was totally eclipsed when three men bounded into the bar dressed in shiny satin shocking pink suits.

Jay, Stu and Andy: making a bold impression

'Lions in Pink' as **Jay Rogers, Stu James and Andy Walton** had christened themselves, were also men with military backgrounds. The three ex-Royal Engineers who were long time mates had promised themselves a trip like this when they had got to know each other in the army nearly thirty years earlier. Jay now lives in New Zealand, and was responsible for logistics of the trip; Andy works as a deep-sea diver, and flew in from his last job in Russia; Stu was working in Africa before he arrived. A few other mates would join them later.

They'd also brought with them 10 kilos of Lions related gear to distribute to fellow fans – including the blow-up lions, soft toys, union flag bow ties and hats they are modelling here.

We were to run into Stu and Andy at almost every subsequent location on the tour. Jay had to return home after his Christchurch rendezvous. Without doubt they brightened up everybody's day wherever they appeared. Not just because of the suits either. They were genuinely an absolute joy to be with. I can't recall any occasion I saw them when they weren't either smiling broadly or belly laughing with those they were in conversation with.

Since we returned I've heard from Andy that a few of them are setting up a tour company, Lions In Pink Tours. They will offer fans wanting to travel to the next Lions tour in South Africa a value for money way to go that will offer the sort of organisation military men can bring to a project; with decent accommodation, and entertainment that he says will have a 'focus on the fun'. I wonder where they got that phrase from?

Anyone who travels with them will be supplied with their own pink suit too. It won't be compulsory to wear it though. I hope the plan pans out for them.

Small World Moment No. 4: While we were enjoying a bit of a break and a drink, Val told me about a young lady she'd met, who asked Val where she was from. Val told her the Cotswolds, near Cirencester. "I know Cirencester a bit. Where exactly?" asked the girl.

When she told her Ashton Keynes the girl asked if Val knew The Wingroves.

Kay and Dave Wingrove happen to be amongst our best friends.

"I was bridesmaid at her daughter's wedding!" said the girl.

"I was at the wedding" said Val. **Jodie Davies was with her other half Chris**. I think Val was so gobsmacked she forgot to get their photo.

The crowd thinned out a bit when the time came for those with tickets to make their way to the stadium, but I was surprised at the number of Lions fans who remained in the pub. Although then I remembered that I'd read somewhere the Crusaders game sold out within the hour they went on sale in New Zealand.

A very good time was had by all in The Dux pub adjacent to the Christchurch Fan Zone

Perusing the Fan Zone before kick-off to see how many were already in, I met **honeymooners Annie and Adam from Bude, Cornwall.** It seems that delayed honeymoons might have been a trend a few years back. They got married three years ago. Before they did, Annie had challenged Adam to surprise her with arrangements for their honeymoon.

She didn't expect to wait so long for it, so was definitely surprised with the big reveal on their wedding day. This tour.

Adam was confident his masterplan would be met with approval though. He knows Annie loves her hubby almost as much as she does her rugby.

When the match began I started taking photographs in the adjacent Fan Zone, but the lack of animation from the seated Crusaders fans and poor light meant I soon got bored with the pretty non-event images taken.

I could hear the fabulous atmosphere in The Dux – the grey building behind - still packed to the gunwales, mostly with Lions fans.

At half-time we decided we'd watch the second half with a drink in the pub.

No doubt the way the Crusaders season was going, the locals were feeling confident of beating the tourists. The 12-3 Lions victory was all the more satisfying for halting their winning streak. Not least because no other team that season had shut out Crusaders in the way the Lions prevented them scoring a try. A great game plan, well executed, saw us all feeling ecstatic with both result and performance.

We left to go back to the house soon after the final whistle. Val had driven, so hadn't had a drink during the game and felt like a glass of wine before retiring.

Second 'First' - All Shook Up: We settled down in the upstairs lounge to catch up with news from home. It was mostly predictions of post-election apocalyptic fallout for Britain.

Suddenly, we had what felt like an apocalyptic few moments of our own. A noise I described at the time like horses cantering up the stairs was followed by rumbling sensations through the floor. It only lasted a couple of seconds, but was enough to make us both jump from the sofa to investigate the cause. Unable to identify any tangible evidence in the house that would account for the experience, we came to the conclusion that we were no longer earthquake virgins.

Locals we told about it next day described it as a minor shake, as apparently happens very often. While writing this section it struck me that there must be a record of earthquake activity. There is. On the official quake records for New Zealand, which show all shakes above a magnitude of 2, of the eight entries recorded that day in the Canterbury region two were around that time, both less than twenty miles from Christchurch. We think we must have felt the 10.38pm one, which was a magnitude of 4.16, officially categorised as 'rather strong'.

I was intrigued enough to see if it was possible to identify how many quakes occurred from the time we landed in New Zealand to the time we left.

Across the country as a whole there were 1797 shakes above a magnitude of 2 between May 30th and July 11th. We didn't feel 1796 of them. The nine strongest - between 5.01 and 6.55 magnitude, officially rated as destructive - were thankfully all sufficiently far offshore to cause no damage.

It seemed a fitting end to our last full day in Christchurch.

Looking out from the house over Christchurch to The Southern Alps

11 June: Christchurch to Dunedin

I remembered from our previous trip here that the journey between these two cities wasn't the most scenic or varied drive. Occasionally you follow the sea for a little while, but otherwise it's a fairly boring succession of small towns that all look remarkably similar until you hit Timaru, a fairly soulless large town that's a bigger version of the small ones. We had an overnight there last time. We didn't bother stopping this time. After Timaru it's a similar procession of small town New Zealand until the outskirts of Dunedin, where the hills return. So, no stop-offs other than a comfort break somewhere entirely forgettable.

The best thing I remember about this journey was in Dunedin city. Our driving in Christchurch had been fairly minimal and very straightforward. There's not much left in Christchurch city centre to use as landmarks for directions. In Dunedin though, directing us to our next hosts, Miss Sat Nav said: "Turn right just after the big church". I'd never heard quite such specific directions on my Sat Nav at home. We noticed lots more examples after that.

Our next hosts, **Glyn and Howard**, were just as welcoming and friendly. Their house was at the top of a steep hill just over a mile up from the Octagon, smack in the centre of the city. The heavens opened just as we got there.

We'd arranged to eat out at a favourite restaurant of Glyn and Howard's. Plato may not be in the most salubrious part of town – it's a former seafarers' hostel on Birch St. down by the wharves – but it's well worth finding if you're ever in Dunedin. A seafood restaurant whose menu changes by the day, the food was superb.

12-13 June: Dunedin and Otago Peninsula

The next day dawned bright and breezy. While Howard continued his half-completed project to build his own wooden access tower that would reach the eaves of the house, Glyn suggested she show us her favourite beach in the city before we head off to Otago Peninsula for the day. We had a bit of a magical mystery tour as we followed her car first up to a high viewpoint above Saint Clair beach. The rollers coming in along the entire 2km bay were certainly impressive. No less so when we drove down the winding cliff road to the esplanade along the front.

Great surf at Saint Clair Beach – shame it was a work day

We got to know Glyn a little better as we chatted while walking along the front, enjoying the sea and its sounds. After coffee and cake in a smart esplanade café we bade her farewell and set off for the peninsula. We chose the Highcliff Road rather than the seafront Portobello Road and were soon climbing towards spectacular views on both sides.

Forsyth Barr Stadium and the east side of the city

Dunedin Harbour from pretty much the start of Otago Peninsula

A typical Otago Peninsula view from Highcliff Road

A seal sleeps in the penguin colony – waiting for a snack when the birds return at dusk?

There are lots of small roads leading to secluded beaches and dramatic cliff scenery. This is exactly the sort of day out we enjoy, so explored as many side roads as we thought would be worth it, all the time heading for the albatross colony at the head of the peninsular. We weren't fussed about going into the colony itself as we'd seen albatross on a boat trip from Rotorua last time we were in New Zealand, so even though this is apparently the only land-based colony of albatross in the world we thought we'd give it a miss and just park outside.

We enjoyed a walk down to Taiaroa Head where the Pacific enters Dunedin's long narrow harbour, then walked down to the nearby Penguin Colony on the other side of the spit. We spotted red jackets right at the bottom of the path, looking back across the harbour to the city. When we reached the shore and asked them to turn around for a piccy we saw it was **Taff (Kevin), Phil and Gareth**. We'd met briefly in Christchurch. Nice guys. They were on an official tour and had high praise for what they'd so far experienced.

Back in the car park we were just saying cheerio to the guys when I spotted a lady walking towards me wearing a scarf which was half the red of Wales and half the All Blacks. I couldn't resist stopping her and asking whether she was a Wales fan who had watched an all Blacks match or the other way around? The three older people with her turned out to be her parents and an aunt. It was her dad who explained to me that she was definitely a Lions fan over here, even though she's a Kiwi, as she was **Warren Gatland's wife, Trudi**. She was delightful, and happy to chat for 20 minutes or so about the tour so far, Warren's mood, and thoughts on the upcoming matches. As you will read later, that chance meeting turned out to be of massive value the day before the first test in Auckland.

Trudi Gatland with dad Terry, mum Margaret and Auntie Noelene

It's not what you know… it's what you can convince others you know! As we had to pass through The Octagon – a central area outside Dunedin Cathedral where main roads converge and there are a number of bars and restaurants – we thought we'd stop and see if we could catch some fans. We were delighted that Guinness World Record Holder Justin spotted us passing the bar he was drinking in with an old mate, **Johnny Morris**. Especially when Johnny told us a fabulous rugby story – not Lions related, but well worth repeating.

In 2010, with the New Zealand based Rugby World Cup a full year away, Johnny contacted the New Zealand tourist board. He told them he was a Welsh documentary film producer, and had the idea to make a programme about all the host cities for RWC2011, with a view to showing them on a Welsh TV channel pre-tournament. After a couple of months with no response he thought they mustn't be interested. Then he got an email asking him for more details.

At this point it's probably important to know that **Johnny had never made a documentary, had no real idea about how to do so, nor any contacts who might help.**

He blagged his way through an exchange of emails scoping out the idea, while searching for a documentary maker in Wales interested in doing the work. Eventually the NZ tourist board commissioned him to undertake the project, by which time he had found a professional TV documentary company who wanted to work with him. They spent months recording material in each of the twelve host cities, with all travel, accommodation and subsistence expenses being met by the tourism board.

The best was yet to come though. As a result of doing the documentary Johnny was given Access All Areas press accreditation for the entire tournament. He could pick and choose what games to go to at no cost whatsoever, and get behind the scenes to meet past and present rugby legends.

Brilliant blagging.

RWC Blagger extraordinaire Johnny Morris,
with RWC Guinness World Record holder Justin Davies

Before we ate we booked a motel for our next stop in Arrowtown – a couple of days R&R before returning to North Island. Glyn and Howard were also hosting a Scottish couple as Airbnb guests who arrived just after we got back. After supper together, we discovered **Karl Hendry and Elaine Hughes** had brought vodka, we had gin, so a good night was had by all as we exchanged stories of our lives and our respective trips.

Both ex-army, they'd met in Afghanistan on an entirely different type of tour to this one. They were now on an extended honeymoon – they'd got married in January in Jamaica – and had been travelling the world since leaving Glasgow in February. They visited Thailand, Cambodia, Vietnam, Malaysia, Australia and Fiji before arriving in New Zealand. They were in a temporary home in Timaru for a few months while they house sit for the owners who are away for an extended holiday. Seeing the Lions on telly made them want to join in, even if only for a short while. They hired a car for the week leading up to the Lions game and made their way from Timaru, visiting Lake Tekapo and Queenstown on their way to Dunedin.

Sadly, we didn't see them again after that night, so don't have a picture. Suffice to say Karl is very tall and lean and the very funny Elaine (funny ha-ha not funny peculiar) is less so of each. We were in the house and in bed way earlier than they came back, and we were up and away before they surfaced each morning. Karl did email me a while after the tour to say how amazing the atmosphere was and how good it was to see the Scottish connections in the city of Dunedin.

Match day 4: Lions v Highlanders

Just before lunchtime we walked the 20 minutes down the hill to The Octagon. The bars were already packed with fans from both sides, and there was certainly plenty of good natured banter flying around. To give you a flavour, here's a selection of images we took that day before the Bagpiper-led procession of fans to the stadium six hours later.

The bars were just as packed inside as well

Matt Hanly from Limerick manfully trying to wind up 4 Kiwis

Elliot White, Simon Foot, Olly Maxwell and Alex Fenton
flew in from Sydney just for this match

Jack Westenra and Chris McNamee traveled from Garston,
the furthest settlement from the sea in all New Zealand

Terri-Anne Busbridge, Sapphire De-la-haye, Ben Bacon,
Rachel Bacon and Jack Surcouf – maybe not in that order!

Val got 6 names of 7: Calum Fraser, Sen Dhayalan, Rob Gill,
Oliver Beaumont, Paul Heatley, Felix Goodone, A N Other

I'm fairly certain this is Jack...

... either Terri-Anne or Rachel...

... and Sapphire with her 'tache and cigar!

Tim O'Donnell hitches a ride...

... while Tina O'Donnell sits this one out

Hong Kong hopovers Calum Auld and Gordon Ferrier

Proud Dad Brian Leary with sons Brendan, Simon and Haydn...

...and the Lions fans who photobombed them when they saw me taking the picture

The crew of HMS Gatland

He won't thank his dad for this if he ever sees the photo – self captioned behind

D'you want a flake with that? Barry O'Neil and Michael Silke

Kiwi Neil, Lance Robinson and Mark Robinson and friend Anthony, celebrating Andrew Hearne's upcoming nuptials

Anthony McGladdery, Emily Acton and Jake Bristow

Jane Bentley, Steve Bentley, Random Intruder, James Reeves and Katie Phillips

Liam Black and James Kelly – no prizes for guessing where they're from   **Justin Roberts, Cath Hawbrook and Pete Bleddyn-Jones drowning their camper woes**

Tim and Tina O'Donnell joined the tour in Christchurch. They shared a taxi from the airport with a couple of Kiwis, who insisted they pay the O'Donnell's share of the fare when they arrived at their destination. Tim and Tina were extremely complimentary about the Crusaders fans they'd met – both before and after the match that saw the home team lose their straight win record. Their start to their tour couldn't have been better. Until on their way between Christchurch and Dunedin they'd visited Mt Tekapo, where Tina slipped on some loose scree, took a tumble and ruptured her left ankle ligaments. She's the seated lady above showing off the boot she was having to wear. Tim's the guy next to her 'riding' a lion. You'll see Tina in the saddle later.

Respect – two ways: Despite being on their second camper van after the first one supplied suffered a series of failures that resulted in no heating, no door lock and no door (it fell off while they were trying to fix the lock) and whose water storage decided to leak just before they got on the ferry at Wellington, **Justin Roberts, Cath Hawbrook and Pete Bleddyn-Jones** assured us they were still having a great time. Once again, they reported a special start to their tour. After the first Lions match in Whangarei they visited the first capital of New Zealand – Russell in the Bay of Islands - spending an evening in the local bowling club. Towards the end of a very pleasant session they were called upon by the members to sing the Welsh national anthem. Having duly obliged, they asked the members present to perform a Haka for them.

One thing we had already learned from our various hosts is that Māori customs command great respect. Much Māori land, waterways and ancestral customs are regarded as very sacred, or Tapu, and all New Zealanders are very much encouraged to respect all things decreed by Māoris to be Tapu. The Haka is one such custom, and should not be performed without permission from a Māori chieftain or his representatives. Seemingly, the son of a chieftain counts as someone able to authorise a Haka performance, as there was one present. Justin, Cath and Pete fully realise it was a great privilege to be treated to a Haka performed in their honour.

Another claim to rugby fame emerged when four Kiwi guys asked if I could take their picture. **Brian Leary and his three sons Brendan, Simon and Haydn** were all together for the first time in two years. They all played rugby, but it was Brendan who had played alongside all-time New Zealand legend Andrew Mehrtens when playing for Canterbury Boys team in the 1991-92 season – just four years before Mehrtens made his All Blacks debut. They're in the montage on the previous pages, just before they were photobombed by a group of young Lions supporters who spotted me taking the first picture. What was so nice afterwards was to see the two groups representing three generations and five countries chatting about rugby together.

HMS Gatland crew: The seven guys in fleeces and safari hats toasting their giant lion were far too busy enjoying a drink to engage in conversation, so merely said call us HMS Gatland. They could be in the navy – who knows?

Farmer Alun Owen's tour will cost him a lot more than most. On top of his 6 weeks in New Zealand he had to agree to buy his wife and daughter a horse before he could book the tour. I was able to tell him that while we had a good time in Whangarei, he hadn't missed a huge amount by staying in Tenby to finish the harvest before coming out to see the Blues game in Auckland. Sorry Alun – the photo I took was far too blurred to use.

A short hop – from Hong Kong! Financiers Calum Auld and Gordon Ferrier, pictured in kilt and Tartan troos respectively, surprised me when they told me they'd come over just for the Highlanders match, and would be flying home the next morning. Home turned out to be Hong Kong. Just the 11 hour each way short hop then? They'd spent an amusing time having lunch in the Dunedin Club. I don't recall how they found themselves to be in there, but do recall they reckoned the average age of members was over 80, and nobody there had any memory of much after 1980.

Andrew Hearne – wearing the sheep's hat he insisted should be described as horny – told us he was on his stag do with his ex-brother-in-law **Mark Robinson, Mark's brother Lance, from Porthcawl in South Wales, and Kiwi friends Neil and Anthony**. Andrew and Mark had met after marrying two sisters, and by extension, is also how Andrew met Lance. Mark came to New Zealand with his wife many years ago, while Andrew's missus divorced him. Evidently, Andrew declared for many years after the divorce that he'd never get serious about a woman again. Two months earlier than we met, he'd met girlfriend Emma Hancock, who he will have married by the time you read this; the date is set for September 2017. The stag-do will last for 5 weeks of the Lions tour. Possibility of a few headaches? I think so.

My favourite story from Dunedin also involves a wedding. **Paul Roser and Christina Jackson** were married at sea on May 17th by the captain of Cunard's flagship ocean liner Queen Mary 2, while cruising between New York and Southampton. Let's hope this isn't an omen for the happy couple, but the captain told them afterwards that at the time of the ceremony they were very close to where the Titanic sank…

Christina's a Brit, Paul's a Kiwi. Cue double celebration. The first was in a private box at Glorious Goodwood's summer race meeting for the UK crowd. They then flew to New Zealand, joining the Lions Tour to coincide with the match against Paul's other beloved – Crusaders. The wedding party for Kiwi friends was in a private box in the AMI stadium in Christchurch during the Crusaders game against the Lions.

The couple met in 2007 while working on a yacht together. They discovered a shared love of rugby during the Rugby World Cup of 2007, while they were based in the US and trying to find places to watch matches. They started dating during that tournament, have attended both RWCs since and plan to be in Japan for the next one.

Their rather extended honeymoon lasted the rest of the Lions tour.

At Glorious Goodwood for the
UK friends' celebration

Christina's brother presented her with a Lions shirt
to put on over her wedding dress

The very special wedding venue

Christina excited to find the Lions bus

In Christchurch for the Kiwi friends' celebration

Raining on the parade: It had been bitterly cold but bright all day. As darkness set in the rain came, so a lot of fans opted to ride to the ground on shuttle buses running from outside the bars in The Octagon rather than joining the bagpiper led parade on the 30-minute walk there. These are all people who just wanted a picture when they saw me taking others and didn't give us names.

We followed the piper as far as the Jury Room on the corner of Stuart and Cumbernauld Streets, which a fan we encountered recommended as quieter and cheaper than the bars in The Octagon, with a good range of beer, and like a good old fashioned London pub.

He was right (apart from not having hand pumped beer). So we dumped our sopping gear, ordered a bottle of the red for which Otago is most famous – Pinot Noir – and a couple of what turned out to be huge and very tasty steaks.

The match: Thirst and hunger sated, we settled down with about 10 Kiwis to watch the game and continue Val's rugby education.

A similar story to the first couple of games. Some excellent Lions attacking play and dogged resistance established a strong lead against a lively but understrength Highlanders team, who capitalised on Lions errors and indiscipline to work their way back into the match, and sneak a deserved one point win in the last 10 minutes.

Most enjoyable though, and once again, a joy to watch the game with such knowledgeable rugby fans. A bus up the hill – it's incredibly steep and the rain persisting down still was incredibly cold - and we hit the hay with all well in our world.

14 June: Dunedin to Arrowtown, with a detour to Wanaka

The miserable weather continued for the first couple of hours after we set off for Arrowtown, with heavy rain and mist masking the not unpleasant, but compared to most of New Zealand, definitely run-of-the-mill scenery we passed through for the first couple of hours of the journey. Alexandra was a surprise. Some 190km from Dunedin we didn't expect to find a town with a population of 5000 after seeing only tiny settlements along most of the way. Known as the hottest, driest and coldest town in the country, it also claims the southernmost vineyard in the world.

The road between Alexandra and the next major town, Cromwell, winds alongside the river Clutha through a spectacular gorge.

A small part of Cromwell Gorge

Just before Cromwell there's an oddity on the opposite bank. It looks like a series of stepped layers have been cut into the rock, disrupting the contours of the mountain so it stands out a long way before you reach it. I was trying to work out whether it was some kind of big statement modern sculpture or a quarry. It seemed too big for the former and too small and neat for the latter.

As we got closer I could see the area below the step layers had been laid with what looks like neat flagstones, upon which there was lettering that had either weathered or been scrubbed partially away. It wasn't until I was looking over pictures at home that I remembered it. I thought the letters might be the quarry name. I still haven't found out exactly what the layering is, but did manage to blow the photos up enough to establish the letters were protest graffiti - HANDS OFF BEAUMONT. Apparently at various times throughout the years energy companies have proposed giant hydro-electric dams further downstream which would mean flooding the small town of Beaumont. Mystery part solved.

We decided on the spur of the moment to visit Wanaka, which sits at the southern end of its eponymous lake. A fan in Dunedin who lives there had recommended it, saying the place was even better than Queenstown – a favourite of ours from our last visit. Wanaka is indeed a very pleasant place, much smaller and quieter than iconic Queenstown, but I'd definitely argue Lake Wakatipu from the Queenstown shorefront is far more scenic. Whilst it's a nice drive through snow-covered mountains from Cromwell, there must have been a large element of home town bias in the Queenstown comparison.

We were planning to take a pass across the mountains from Wanaka to head straight to Arrowtown but our car had no snow chains, so we obeyed the sign banning us from even trying the route. Which meant a return to Cromwell to reach Arrowtown along a main road. A good decision as a local we later met in Arrowtown had crossed that pass that day and said chains were essential.

We had booked at the **Shades of Arrowtown motel**. Set in nice gardens at a quiet end of the main street, we were given a two bedroom unit with a kitchenette. The rooms were spotless, with excellent quality fixtures, fittings and furniture – especially the modern shower room. **Owners Brenda and Frank** bought the place in January 2017 to provide an income after retiring from their professions of Swimming and Skiing Instructors respectively. Both occupations are not renowned for their pension rights. I think they're really well suited to their new roles, have set up the motel superbly, and wish them every success.

So many people had told us how brilliant Arrowtown is, which is why we opted to stay there rather than Queenstown. I can't help wondering why the huge fan base?

We arrived mid-afternoon, and set out to explore. It's quaint, I agree. However, there's not a great deal to see in town itself beyond the main shopping street, and in winter it's bitterly cold as it sits in a sort of steep sided bowl, so even on a sunny day, in Arrowtown the sun disappears behind mountains very early. We decided we'd explore the old Chinese settlement the following day.

We took Brenda and Frank's recommendation to eat at the Fork and Tap pub early doors. Literally a stone's throw from the motel, it's a very decent place – in no small part due to the fantastic range of local craft beer and cider brewers' products they stock, including hand pumped ales – rarely seen in Kiwi pubs.

I think we were in there by about 5.30pm. By six it was packed with a good spread of families, couples and groups of blokes, creating a really great atmosphere for a Wednesday night. Well fed and watered by 8.30pm we went back to the motel for an early night.

June 15th: Queenstown and Arrowtown

We were last in Queenstown in summer, December 2014 and loved the place. Nestled into the shoreline of Lake Wakatipu, surrounded by mountains on all sides, it's truly a majestic setting. I was keen to see it in winter, so after our superb breakfast in Settlers Restaurant opposite the riverside public car park in Arrowtown, we drove the 20km to Queenstown along the mountain roads through Arthur's Point. It was only a week before the ski-lifts were due to open, but there wasn't much sign of the snow needed to make skiers happy.

Last time we came to Queenstown we'd treated ourselves to a flight in a small plane over to Milford Sound. That meant crossing The Southern Alps in a spectacular 35 minute journey that saved around 10 hours driving there and back. The combination of craggy peaks and mountain lakes before flying down the sound itself is simply stunning. Although it's an indulgence, I'd very much recommend it if the weather's good and your budget can stretch to it. This time we settled for being only 450 metres above the town, taking a ride in the Skyline Gondola up to Bob's Peak, from where there are superb views of the mountains and lake.

Queenstown on Lake Wakatipu

We met a few Lions fans up there, among them **Stephen Jack and Thomas Buckley**

Jonny Murray had celebrated his 16th birthday on June 13th by watching the Lions play Highlanders in Dunedin. His dad, **Gavin** had emailed Highlanders' sponsors Pulse Energy ahead of their trip to tell them about the Jonny's birthday. As a result, the family was invited to a meal at Emerson's Brewery in Dunedin courtesy of Pulse Energy, where Jonny was presented with a shirt signed by Highlanders and All Blacks half-back Aaron Smith.

Julie and Gavin Murray with sons Jonny and Charlie

Fair play to Julie. She hates heights and had to be persuaded to appear in this family photo, only doing so by backing into position so that she didn't have to see over the edge of the viewing platform. Val doesn't like heights either, so took measures to avoid looking out of the gondola window on the way up and the way down.

We met **Phil, Gareth and Taff** again, who told us there was a magnificent lookout along the lakeside road to Glenorchy, a small town at the head of the lake, some 50km from Queenstown. We were about 10km along the road when I noticed for the first time the fuel warning light had come on. The on board computer info told me we could expect to drive a maximum 60km on the remaining fuel, so I figured we had plenty enough to get us to Glenorchy, and continued to enjoy the fabulous views across the lake to the mountains beyond.

We'd gone another 15km or so when we realised we didn't know anything about Glenorchy, including if there was a gas station there. While I virtually crept along the road to preserve the little fuel we still had, Val tried to find the nearest petrol stations on the satnav.

There didn't appear to be one at Glenorchy. I pulled over while we debated whether to risk continuing our journey.

A car passed us while we were parked – a notable event on New Zealand's quiet roads – and as we now crept forward to preserve fuel while looking for a spot to turn round safely on the single carriageway, we spotted the occupants on the side of the road ahead ahead, taking photos across the lake. We thought we'd ask if they know Glenorchy at all. They didn't, but one of them had an app on his phone that showed all petrol stations in New Zealand. He confirmed nothing was showing at Glenorchy.

While chatting to them about why we were there it emerged they were over from Melbourne, and that **Sinead Ryan** had been selected as the Melbourne Rose, to represent the city in the upcoming Rose of Tralee festival back in Ireland. There are apparently 65 'Roses' selected around the world, chosen from women in their twenties of Irish descent, who are charged with promoting Irish culture and womanhood in the year they hold their position. Sinead took a little persuasion to don her sash and pose for us.

Melbourne Rose, Sinead Ryan, with fiancé Charles Kelly, and friends Emma Walsh and Alan Cremin

&!!/* Sat Nav! Back in the car, although I didn't mention it, Val soon noticed that the computer was now telling us that during our stop the projected distance we could travel before the fuel ran out had dropped from 40km to 25km, so according to it, we now didn't have enough fuel left to get back to Queenstown. I know these readings are never 100% accurate, and assume manufacturers err on the side of caution, so wasn't unduly worried. Val was less than convinced by my assurances, even though I nursed the car back towards Queenstown at the most economic pace I could, and freewheeled as far as possible on uphill stretches.

I knew the longest and steepest of these would be just outside the city, so cursed our luck when we rounded a bend to see a massive lorry and trailer carrying huge tree trunks, each about 40 feet long and six feet wide, was just finishing its turn onto the road in front of us to make the climb up the hill. There was no opportunity to pass on the winding ascent so we were stuck in the least fuel efficient gear for a very slow 10 minutes as we followed the lumbering lumber truck.

When we finally reached the edge of Queenstown we followed the satnav instructions to the nearest petrol station. Having previously praised it, over the next twenty minutes I cursed the blessed machine. At the first site there was no petrol station. It was a small supermarket. The next nearest fuel was showing as about 2km away – up the steepest roads in Queenstown through a housing estate to a dead-end at just about the town's highest point. No petrol up there of course, and almost certainly never had been. Unwilling to risk wasting more precious fuel on she-who-should-no-longer-be-obeyed, I freewheeled down the hills to the main road heading for the airport. I was sure I remembered a fuel station along that route from our previous visit. Thankfully I was right and we put in more than enough petrol to complete the journeys back to Arrowtown and to Queenstown airport the following morning.

We spent a pleasant afternoon wandering around bits of Arrowtown we hadn't explored the day before, in particular the old Chinese settlement. It's largely a collection of shacks fashioned from flatstones or hacked into the mountainside. On a chilly winter's day it wasn't difficult to imagine just how challenging life must have been for the immigrant community scratching a living exploring largely spent gold fields in the second half of the 19th century.

Nice to run into **Ted Williams & co** again after meeting them in Christchurch. Also nice to hear from them that they'd enjoyed very much the Indigo restaurant I'd recommended in Napier. I wrote about it after my last trip as the best Indian meal of my life.

Talking of which, evenings end early in small town New Zealand. After we'd both fallen alseep on our late afternoon return to the motel, finding a restaurant still willing to serve us at 8pm was a challenge. All but one were either closed or about to close. We were quite happy that the one place open and serving was the only Indian restaurant in Arrowtown. We're quite the fans of a good curry, and the Mantra's food was excellent - nicely spicy with great and varied flavours. Not quite the historic standards of Indigo but pretty damn good.

June 16th: Arrowtown to Rotorua via Auckland

An early departure for the 15 minute drive to Queenstown airport left plenty of time for brekkie in the terminal before our 9.35 flight to Auckland. Ours was on time, the next one was cancelled.

After a very quick call in to Shirin's to pick up clothes we'd left there rather than carry to South Island, we were on our way to Rotorua. The first part is not as dramatic a drive as most in New Zealand. The seemingly omnipresent rain we had in North Island kept us company yet again for most of the way down the State Highway 27 and then Highway 5. Satnav redeemed herself by unexpectedly directing us to bypass the town of Tirau, and then to avoid most of the very long queue on the long hill down to Lake Rotorua. The traffic lights at the bottom would easily have added twenty-five minutes to a journey that had otherwise seen next to no vehicles.

Allison and Dave's house is tucked away down a steep drive decending between houses on the street. The drive opens out to an impressive looking bungalow with a wide frontage and sprawling gardens beyond. Very nice. We'd already stayed with Allison's sister of course, so they no doubt had the lowdown on us. Both retired teachers, they work almost as often as when they were employed, regularly being called on as supply teachers covering for sickness in their respective old schools.

Because both of Allison's daughters live in London, she and Dave are very active Homelinkers. They are set to become even more active exchangers, as one daughter is now relocating to New York.

Small world moment number 5 – our very first exchange in San Francisco was with people Allison and Dave had exchanged with the year before.

We shared food, wine, stories and much laughter in a very pleasant evening of getting to know each other a bit better, and picking their brains about what Rotorua had planned for the tour in their city. This largely centred around a world record attempt to have the most people performing a Haka at the same time.

Officials from the Guinness Book of World Records would be there to ensure all conditions were complied with, and it was hoped that over 7000 people would turn up to take part.

17th June: Rotorua – Rotten Eggs Rule

17th June, Match day 5: Lions v Māori All Blacks

Some of the estimated 7800 who smashed the record   Picture credit Dave Rogers Getty Images

The Giant Haka was a big idea, initiated by the **International Rugby Club**, an online club affiliated to Northland Rugby Union, whose aim is to bring the global rugby community closer together. The idea itself sounded simple – have enough people turn up to wrest back from the French holders the record for the number of people participating in a Haka. The city council stepped up to support the proposal, as did most of the schools in Rotorua. The whole event was superbly organised and executed and much fun was had by the 7800+ of all ages who performed to resecure the record for its rightful homeland.

In the warm up, Rotorua born All Blacks legend **Wayne 'Buck' Shelford** addressed the crowd.

Buck was playing for Northampton when Val and I moved to the nearby village of Gayton. The new mates I made in Gayton were all rugby fans, so introduced me to the game. I was amazed that after the match the players joined us fans in the club bar, and I was treated to 20 minutes conversation over a beer with Buck on my very first visit to Franklin's Gardens.

Buck was kind enough to pose for me in Rotorua so that I could send a pic to my Saints friends along with his best wishes.

Two Scotsmen were picked from the crowd at the finish for the enthusiasm with which they performed in rehearsals and the record attempt itself. **Andrew Pollock and Jhuan Roux** (born in South Africa but lived in Scotland most of his life) are from Aberdeen.

They were rewarded with free tickets for the match against Moari All Blacks that evening.

They were soon surrounded by other Lions fans still seeking tickets, and quickly offloaded their prizes as they already had their own tickets.

More beer tokens for them.

I'd spotted Andrew in the warm up too.

Could have been the resemblance to another Scottish Andy.

And the 'Murray' emblazoned across his chest.

Have a look at some of the moves that caught the eye.

Spot the family resemblance – Ian and Peter Lindsley

Plenty of Lions swelling the numbers in the Giant Haka

Some were confident in their abilities...

... and some were not so confident

The many Lions fans who took part in the Haka decamped to Eat Streat, a smart development of restaurants either side of a covered walkway that has underfloor heating provided by Rotorua's most famous geological feature – the geothermal ground and springs that account for the permanent background smell of sulfur around the city, and provide the rotten eggs reference for this chapter.

And Dad Came Too: Eat Streat was absolutely jammed with Lions fans. The first we encountered were a fun group. After booking to come on the Lions tour with girlfriend **Geri Thomas, her Dad Brian, and friends Nick Smith and Mairead McGinley, Mike Hollister** found that his work is soon taking him to the States. He and Geri decided they'd marry so that she could get a visa to go with him. But where and when, given they'd already spent a bundle on the Lions Tour?

Realising Las Vegas was half way to New Zealand... two weeks earlier they'd snuck off there without telling anybody in advance, got themselves very drunk and very married – and assure me it was that way round.

Viva Las Vegas - Mike and Geri Hollister with her Dad, Brian

So Dad was effectively joining them on their honeymoon (and was very pleased – what he saved on a wedding has more than funded his Lions trip).

The Lightbulb Moment: Around the corner we met **Sophie and Nigel Starr**, who shared another Romance of Rugby story. Before they got married in December 2015 they started planning the sort of special honeymoon they wanted. Sadly they didn't have the spare cash to do it then. They resolved to save towards one while they planned the detail, settling on New Zealand in late 2016 as their preferred option. Accepting they'd been enjoying life perhaps too much to save what they needed, the planned 2016 trip was postponed until 2017, when ... DING!!!... they realised that's when the Lions would be there. The summer break they had in mind was very quickly replaced by a winter Lions tour, and they had greater incentive to make sure they put enough aside to enjoy it to the full. Which they definitely appeared to be doing. I know I took a picture of them but can't find it anywhere on my cards. Sorry.

I had a brief chat with a delightful Irish couple, **Simon Chadwick and Aifric O'Malley**. Poor Aifric was managing very well with the crutches she was hobbling through Eat Streat on. She was expecting to be using them for some time yet as she'd badly sprained her ankle only a couple of days earlier. She preferred for them and her poorly joint not to in the photograph.

Lesley and Reg Warne were another couple who had saved hard to mark a special moment in their life together – their 30th wedding anniversary was the reason behind their trip to New Zealand. I don't remember what I said that made her laugh!

Lesley and Reg - very happy to be in Rotorua

Opposites Attract: For ex-pat **Glyn Jenkins**, his betrothal after meeting **Kiwi wife Wendy** during the 2011 RWC came with strict conditions. Their marriage vows included commitment from Glyn to support the All Blacks against any teams other than England and Wales. I bet love, honour and especially obey was also in there.

Wendy's wedding vows ensured no rugby fallouts with hubby Glyn

Back on her feet: We just finished talking to Glyn and Wendy when we spotted **the O'Donnells** again. **Tina** had recovered enough from her ankle injury to don her own costume and join husband **Tim** hitching a ride on a lion, albeit one still wearing a heavy support boot and strapping.

Tina and Tim

All roads lead to Rotorua: Three guys drinking together told widely differing stories of their journeys here. **James Broomer and Brett Crowton** work for Lions Rugby principal partner Land Rover in China, had got tickets through the company, so had 'popped down' from Shanghai for 10 days.

By contrast, their mate **Will Caspari** had worked 12 hour days on a potato farm for 3 weeks to afford the trip from Christchurch. All were very happy to be here though.

James Broomer, Brett Crowton and Will Caspari

Nigel Bellamy became well known during his first trip down under, when the press spotted him and his stuffed red dragon, Dewi, following Wales in RWC 2011. Cardiff postman Nigel got the travel bug on that trip, saving hard for the 2013 Lions tour to Australia and again to be here in New Zealand.

Dewi and Nigel attract fans of their own

My first encounter with **Paul Roles** was simply a grab shot as he walked through Eat Streat sporting his brilliant painted red beard.

We were to meet a few more times in subsequent match locations, when it became clear he's just the sort of larger than life fun filled character you assume he will be when seeing him for the first time.

Yvonne Morgan and husband G (he wouldn't tell me his real name, simply saying that G is what everyone knows him by) were the first people I met who had hosted guests under the Adopt A Lions Fan scheme.

Well done you, and for entering into the spirit of the tour by dressing up so ridiculously for the occasion.

More Opposites Attract: A moment after the Morgans literally scampered away, I met another couple whose affiliations were potentially conflicting. Lions fan **Peter Wren-Hilton met Kiwi wife Jacquie** in London, before they moved to New Zealand in 2003. They asked me if I would help them replicate a picture of them looking back over their shoulders taken by a friend during the 2005 Lions tour. Wearing the same flags they sported 12 years earlier, they have a picture. Happy to help.

The combination of Lions fan/All Blacks fan couple continued on our walk over to to have a look at the Rotorua Fan Zone in the Events Centre in Government Gardens. **Paul Percival**, proudly sporting his Lions shirt, asked if we knew whether he had to pay for parking at that hour, before **Kyla Bourne** stepped from the car in her All Blacks kit. They met while teaching in Auckland.

One for the Boys: After all this romance a bit of Bromance. A day amongst rugby fans should after all contain a blokey element. So here's to **The Thirsty Fencers,** who had earlier worked up a matchday thirst by skinnydipping in Lake Taupo on what was a very cold morning. They were glad nobody like me was there to embarrass them by snapping the effects of the cold water on parts of their bodies as they emerged from it! They then hotfooted an hour north to Rotorua, further building a thirst by joining in the world record breaking Haka, closely followed by slaking said thirst with a significant number of beers before the match against the Māori All Blacks. I suspect their celebration of a superb performance and result by the Lions resulted in a repeat of the beer intake.

Hopefully they didn't close their day as they opened it by skinnydipping in Lake Rotorua while under the influence.

The message I got from them later struck a chord with me. I've travelled the same road they describe very accurately and amusingly below, although my journey along it was not in the depths of winter as theirs was:

When the three thirsty fencers Lions touring party set off to see the sights of Coromandel Peninsula, they didn't expect to experience three films in one trip.

They set off up the West coast through the winding route 25 . As light was lowering, the decision to head east across the Coromandel was made. Heading east out on route 309 turned out to be a little more eventful than planned. The bitumen road soon turned into mud. The track, as it was now, wound slowly up hill with severe drops down one side - the side they were driving - the road now barely wide enough for one car let alone a camper van.

*When they met the occasional speeding native it was pot luck as to how much road could be used. Not only sheer drops, but the road had simply eroded away leaving giant holes. White crosses of past travellers who never made it littered the roadside. All this was reminiscent of the **Top Gear** programme's account of Bolivia's death road.*

*As they preceded along the very slippery track for over 26k there was little sign of civilisation let alone a main road. The dramatic palmed landscape, dimming light and lowering mist were just missing the dinosaurs of **Jurassic Park**.*

*Slowly progressing along the narrowing track thinking things could not get any worse, a bright yellow sign appeared from the dusk, "PIGS ". Thinking this was a joke of some kind, that they didn't get anyway, they continued on, only to be then confronted by not one but over forty pigs roaming wild - or so they thought. Once the initial surprise of witnessing pigs far from civilisation was over, they then noticed many rusting vehicles in the scrub and clearings,and a few old buildings and caravans appeared. All this reminded them of the film **Deliverance**. A quick hasty pedal to the metal and they finally made it back to tarmac.   A movie night was planned!!!*

Moments to remember

1. *Swimming in Lake Taupo in winter at 7.30am is apparently a mad thing to do according to the locals.*

2. *Swimming in the pacific sea in Waihi beach got similar looks.*

3. *Obviously the rugby wins in Rotorua and Hamilton and the hospitality*

The city council had created a superb Fan Zone. The lady responsible for it admitted while showing us round that she was exasperated by NZRU's decree that it must be an alcohol-free event. I hope her efforts were rewarded with a big crowd, but wasn't around to find out. I can't imagine any other Lions fans were either.

By the time we made our way back to the town centre it was dark and raining heavily. We hitched a ride on the free shuttle bus to the stadium, which we knew was about a 2km walk from Allison and Dave's. What we didn't know was the bus dropped fans off about 1km away from the other side of the stadium, which had to be circumnavigated as well to reach the road we needed. After all day on our feet in Rotorua we were pretty knackered and very wet by the time we reached the house only just in time for a quick towel-down before kick-off.

The match: A very strong performance saw the Lions dominate all areas of the game, running out 32-10 winners and bringing real hope amongst Lions fans for the prospect of a win in the first test against the New Zealand All Blacks a week later.

We celebrated with red wine and post-match pizza from Allison's freezer before bed.

June 18th: Rotorua to Hamilton

On Sunday I started my blog for The Telegraph before Colleen and Mike joined us mid-morning.

They were down from Whangarei visiting Mike's relatives so I'd suggested Val and I take both couples to lunch. We went to The Landing Café on Lake Tarawera. It was a shame that the rain was so heavy, our hosts told us there was no point stopping to admire Blue Lake and Green Lake on the way. Neither could we see the hills at the opposite end of the Lake Tarawera from the café because of white cloud and the driving rain. Good job the food was up to muster.

The rain had eased by the time we finished our very enjoyable lunch accompanied by much mirth and merriment. We were able to get a photo by the lake before the rain returned and Val and I set off for Hamilton.

Our new friends, Dave and Allison, Mike and Colleen

Our first time here, I thought Hamilton looked a very smart town as we drove around the ring road to find **Susan Black's house**, collect the key and locate a Countdown store where we bought groceries for the next few days.

Susan, as I said, was in Canada on a Homelink exchange trip.

I'd planned to contact as many rugby clubs at home during this week, it being the run-up to the first test, and had found a website that listed every club affiliated to every County RFU, complete with contacts. I figured a lot of rugby clubs would be opening their clubhouses up for breakfast on test match Saturdays, and I wanted the fans who were watching at home to be a part of this book if possibe. So I thought I'd create a poster which I would send to the clubs listed to put on their clubhouse noticeboard, suggesting that someone capture a photo of their members watching the first test and send a copy for possible inclusion.

While Val cooked I worked on the poster and sent it to 17 Avon region clubs before dinner was ready. Afterwards I reread the blog and selected the accompanying photos to be processed and sent with it next morning. Tired after a long and active weekend, we settled in for a quiet night plonked in front of the telly - something we'd hardly done since leaving home three weeks before, and then only to see the election result. It was a very welcome relaxing evening.

Unlike Monday 19th, which was pretty much a write-off.

June 19th – 20th: Hamilton – Hiccups and (quiet) Hurrahs

I'd woken early, thought I'd crack on with the mailing, and by 9am I'd emailed my blog, processed the pictures I'd selected and sent them across to The Telegraph using the WeTransfer web app I routinely send large files by. I'd then merrily plugged away adding the contact email addresses in the RFU databases to the template message I'd used the night before, intending to send it to hundreds more clubs.

Or so I thought.

After a couple of hours plodding methodically through, and very pleased with my morning's work so far, I thought I'd check incoming emails for a break.

A few of the previous night's had been bounced back. That's when I noticed my laptop had decided not to send messages in Outlook, but to store them in my Outbox, where over 150 - including my blog - were sitting doing nothing, and could not be sent, moved or deleted.

As I could access BT Mail's web application, The Telegraph was at least easy to fix. A quick email to apologise for its later than usual arrival would have reached the London office long before anybody would be at work anyway. Using the web app to repeat sending the rugby club emails was a far longer process than within Outlook, but I thought worth persisting with. Many hours later I was ready to try and sort out Outlook on the laptop.

It took hours of searching online to find and try out solutions suggested in response to people who had posted similar problems in the past. There weren't many relevant to Windows 10 and Office365 though, so a lot of the hoped-for remedies I tried didn't work. I honestly don't remember how I finally managed to clear my outbox in late afternoon. By which time, it was apparent from the deluge of bounced back emails that the County RFU databases are very, very out of date. What I thought had been a good idea to publicise the book to a segment of its target market had resulted in next to no effect.

After all the previous mishaps we decided not to dwell on what was really no more than a wasted day, cooked, played cards and drank wine. Perhaps slightly more than we would have (or should have in the case of the latter) but what the hell?

20th June, Match day 6: Lions v Chiefs

On a bright, beautiful Match day morning we decided we'd visit one of the city's best known attractions – Hamilton Gardens. Our expectations weren't especially high given the wintry time of year, and we were neither blown away nor disappointed. It was evident that a serious amount of hard work goes into creating the showpiece gardens, and although there was a sense of the whole place being in maintenance mode, I imagine a late spring or summer visit would be glorious.

We were very glad we went though, as much for the people we met as for the gardens. There are a lot of individually created gardens dedicated to single countries. Unsurprisingly, there isn't a Belgian garden. But there was someone who surely must be the only Belgian national who is a Lions fan. **Marc van de Peer** was so very proud of being a Belgian rugby fan. To cap it all, he was wearing a Munster shirt and told us he travels over to Limerick to watch them as often as he is able to.

If I knew any Flemish (or if it was featured as a language on Google Translate) I'd salute you in your native tongue Marc.

Marc van de Peer - the only Belgian Lions fan?

Further on, in the still very verdant tropical garden, we met **Jo and Ian (the latter universally known as Ducky) Mallard. They are** Tigers fans who live in Melbourne. That's the Melbourne in South Derbyshire, which gave its name to the city Easy Midlanders regard as the young Aussie pretender (as well as to the Prime Minister serving when Queen Victoria came to the throne, Viscount Melbourne).

David Coates and Jim Hughes appeared and joined in our conversation. David was in his Scarlets shirt. They were all speaking mostly about the marvellous hospitality they had experienced so far when a couple of natives wandering by became the focus of their collective admiration for all things and people Kiwi. I liked the pic Jo sent me of them in Queenstown, where they skied for three days.

Jo and Ducky In Hamilton's botanical gardens…

…on the slopes in Queenstown and caught in the crowd on TV

David Coates and Jim Hughes with random Kiwi couple...   ... and with Hamilton Adopt-A-Lions-Fan host Dee...   ...and with Auckland hosts Margaret-Ann and Robert

David and Jim were just telling us they had twelve nights of Adopt-A-Lions-Fan-Accommodation within their trip when around the corner came **Huw Jenkins**, another Scarlet, who spotted his fellow fan's shirt and stopped to chat too.

On our way out later we crossed paths with Huw again. He asked if we knew where the footpath was from the Gardens to the city centre. We didn't, and in any case offered him a lift as it was where we planned to go. Huw declined, chuckling as he explained he was under doctor's orders to walk as often as he could. While we all wandered across the car park and attempted to find the footpath, he told us he was staying in Hamilton with an old friend who he'd been best man for in 1981. His friend had invited people round who were at the wedding, and Huw took great pride that many remembered his speech. He left it to our imagination as to what he said that was so memorable 36 years on.

He'd also had a completely chance meeting with a member of The Hamilton Male Voice Choir. A chorister himself at home, Huw was immediately invited to join in one of their rehearsals, where he was warmly welcomed and grateful for the chance to fully air his lungs with gusto. I asked if I could get a picture of him.

Having already surmised Huw is an outgoing and jolly character, I wasn't greatly surprised when he spotted the open air stage adjacent to the kiddies' playground, leapt up and struck this pose.

The inimitable Huw Jenkins

Scouting round the city centre for the first time, we were seeking somewhere to park when we happened to pass what was clearly the team hotel. The Lions bus paintjob is very distinctive and the twenty or so fans milling around outside the foyer entrance was also a bit of a giveaway. We happened to find a multi-storey in the next street, so parked up and went to meet a few fans.

Our first encounter was a Swedish lady carrying a giant soft toy lion.

Maria Nordstrom had lived in England for 22 years and played rugby for Richmond and then for Cheltenham Ladies. Now living in Auckland with her new partner **Mark** (more rugby romance - they met during the 2015 Rugby World Cup), they'd been both hosts and guests under Adopt-A-Lions-Fan. Five Scottish fans stayed with them for the Blues match. Since then Maria and Mark had themselves been hosted in Christchurch, Dunedin, Rotorua, Taupo and here in Hamilton.

Small world moment number 6: in Whangarei Maria bumped into her old coach from Richmond who she hadn't seen for 25 years.

Simon Elliot, Caroline Theobald, Sue Woolford and Bob Woolford between them represented England, Scotland and Wales.

They were looking to adopt a Paddy to make it a full Lions den.

Brothers **David and Rhys Williams** were in New Zealand with their good friends **Elle and Andrew Long**. Rhys told us how his journey here very nearly ended in Australia, thanks to the Brexit vote. He'd been travelling for over a year, and flew into Cairns from Vietnam. Planning to spend time there before hopping across to New Zealand, he needed to prove he had the equivalent of AUS$5000 in his bank account to support himself during his stay. His paperwork included a recent statement showing his British bank account had... dropped in value since the Brexit vote and was now worth only AUS$4600. He was surprised and grateful that they let him in anyway. Val and I already knew the UK has a similar requirement for youngsters visiting on holiday visas. The first time we flew to Australia we were seated alongside a kid who had flown into Heathrow from Melbourne without his bank statement, and was being shipped straight back to Sydney on our flight. He'd arranged for his dad to fly from Melbourne to Sydney to meet him with the necessary, so he could fly back to London next day. I bet his jetlag was the worst ever.

Paul and Julia Oaten travelled to New Zealand with **John and Caryn Snell**.

All from Taunton, Julia told me that watching the last Lions tour in Australia on TV had captured their imagination. They'd looked at official tour packages including tickets bought from Lions Rugby, but heard from a cousin in New Zealand that the tickets were massively cheaper if bought in the host country. Their words.

They worked out that booking everything for themselves, the whole tour could be done by two people for the price of one Lions package. Not wanting to wait until their late sixties by the time the next New Zealand tour would come around, they decided Julia would pack up her job, Paul negotiated extended leave from his, and they would blow a bit of the kids' inheritance. John and Caryn liked the idea too. They managed to get tickets for nine of the ten matches.

The skirts were made by the ladies especially for the occasion.

This scary young man, right, is **Ethan Bates. Dad, Simon,** is originally from Newcastle but he and **mum, Sarah,** now live in Auckland.

The first bar we encountered was The Quadrant. We heard the noise coming from its outside seats long before we saw the pub. At which point Val decided this was not a day when she felt she'd enjoy walking into the very busy bars around central Hamilton to gatecrash fan conversations. As it was bright and sunny - though very cold - she'd work the streets handing out flyers.

I then spent what must have been the longest time I ever have in a pub without having a drink.

The first guys I talked to were **Colm Murphy, Conor Murphy and Ronan Boylan**. Again, no prizes for guessing their nationality. Colm and Connor aren't related. While Ronan had flown straight to New Zealand to join his mates, the Murphy non-brothers had left home considerably earlier - in January. Conor told me with the great zest that always accompanies engaging Irishmen telling a story well, how they'd taken 6 months to get to New Zealand, which included:

- 3 months touring Vietnam

- trekking to Everest Base Camp at 17500ft altitude** (where they danced their socks off at the highest rave in the world - another official world record attempt apparently. The boys just thought it nice that a party had been arranged for their arrival)

- exploring Indonesia

- partying hard again in Bali

- relaxing on Australia's stunning Gold Coast

- celebrating three further New Years since the one just before they left Ireland – in Vietnam, in Nepal and the Māori New Year in New Zealand.

I'm betting they made and broke resolutions for every New Year.

Conor kindly emailed me when he got back to Ireland in August with a more detailed account of their adventures:

Hello.

Me and my two friends, Colm Murphy and Ronan Boylan (all 3 of us are Munster men) met you outside an Irish bar in either Rotorua or Hamilton (can't remember which) and also did a very quick interview about our travels to get to NZ.

I remember you asked if we could send in more information after if we had any. I (Conor) just landed back in Ireland and can give a brief summary.

*Myself and Colm left Ireland on the 25th of January, travelling to Saigon where we celebrated Tet (Vietnamese New year) before buying two Honda Win bikes and biking more than 4000km all over Vietnam for two months. This also included Colm and our friend **Damien O 'Sullivan** (who joined us from Ireland for 2 months) going for a day trip into China.*

All 3 of us celebrated St Patrick's day in Hanoi - on stage doing Irish dancing with lots of Vietnamese people and an American Irish Dancing instructor.

In late March the 3 of us headed for 3 busy nights along Ko Shan road in Bangkok before heading for Kathmandu in Nepal.

*For the next month we climbed up to Everest Base Camp, via a plane journey to Lukla airport (the most dangerous airport in the World). ** We were involved in a World Record for highest party on Earth at Base Camp and also celebrated another New Year, Nepalese New year where the year is 2074!*

Me and Damien eventually got our first helicopter trip ever, down from the Himalayas while Colm completed the far famed 3 passes.

After this our friend Damien returned to Ireland while me and Colm went to Indonesia via 3 days in Singapore.

Two more people joined us in Bali, Austin Lyne and Sean Daly. However unfortunately I had to spend 8 days in hospital in Bali recovering from my trip to Everest Base Camp.

In total a month was spent in Indonesia mainly at beaches and relaxing. Myself and Colm had both a very unlucky and then lucky hike searching for a good view of a sunset over Bali when we got split up and got lost before eventually finding separates routes down Mt. Batur at night-time.

Next stop was Gold Coast, Oz. We were extremely lucky and grateful to catch the flight from Indonesia as we hadn't applied for visas for Australia, so the application and acceptance of the visa was done at the airport in a massive hurry!

For Oz it was back to just me and Colm and we managed to see our first Aussie rules Game when The Gold Coast Suns beat the West Coast Eagles for the first time in their short history.

It was now the end of May and we had our final week of summer before heading to winter in New Zealand.

On the 5th of June me and Colm reached our final destination of NZ along with our final New Year, Māori New Year (that was our fourth New Year for us in 2017!). Our first Lions game was the Blues vs the Lions.

Then on the 16th of June Ronan arrived after 30+ hours travelling to NZ. We went straight to the double header in Eden Park for Wales vs Tonga before seeing the All Blacks for the first time in the flesh in an amazing display of pure rugby against Samoa. Ronan struggled to stay awake during the poor opening game but was wide awake for the brilliant All Blacks display.

The next day we hired our Jucy camper and headed for Rotorua and then Hamilton for the next two warm up games, as well as sightseeing both Hobbiton and going to Mordor.

Our final journey in our Jucy camper was a very long trip from Taurangi to Auckland where we owe a massive thanks to a French man working in a very expensive and full camper site, who gave us excellent directions to a quiet and free camping spot in Devonport!

This camping spot was right next to the beach and more importantly the ferry that led straight to Auckland Queen's Street and also the Lions Den.

A perfect location for Test 1!

By the end of the series all 3 of us had seen as least 5 games involving the AB's or Lions, with me catching Test 1 and 3, Ronan getting Test 1 and 2 and Colm getting Test 3.

Side note: both me and Ronan celebrated our Birthdays during these manic two weeks in NZ.

After Test 2 Ronan had to head home for work.

By mid-July I was heading for Ireland too, via a week in both Toronto and New York.

Colm stayed in Auckland and is now working as manager in a hostel out by Mt Eden.

Thanks Conor.

**Trekking to Everest Base Camp immediately earned my respect, as it's something I tried in 2005 and failed spectacularly to achieve. Only many years later I understood that a previously undiagnosed (and now permanent) medical condition meant I was always going to be the first in our group to suffer altitude sickness. My descent from 15000ft with fellow sufferer Andy was a little adventure on its own, because he didn't get better as we came down – the only recognised cure for altitude sickness. Andy became unable to walk more than a few steps without experiencing severe asthmatic type symptoms. At lunchtime the following day, Andy's at-rest heart rate was around 220 beats per minute. The Sherpa accompanying us and I agreed we needed to leave him in the care of the monks at Tengboche monastery overnight at about 12900ft, get to Namche Bazaar (the settlement with telecommunications at a little over 11000ft), where we'd sort out a rescue helicopter for Andy. We'd spent one and a half days trekking from Namche to reach the monastery on the way in. I'm immensely proud to this day that by running all the downhill stretches we managed to reach Namche in under 3 hours, where I then had to pay $3500 to arrange for the chopper to come first thing next morning. Hopefully Andy would be alive and be able to repay me. He was, and did after we returned to the UK.

Bizarrely, just as we finished swapping Everest stories, four guys came by wearing these shirts. The quote is a reference to a legendary speech by Lions forwards coach Jim Telfer before the first test of the 1997 South Africa tour. In a squad rich with world class players amongst the backs, the forwards were perceived as the potential weak point for the tourists. If you read the players' comments in 'Behind the Lions' it's quite clear Telfer made the difference throughout the whole tour, to elevate the performance of a group of players expected to get beaten up by the powerful South African pack.

His 'Everest' speech were the right words delivered in the right moment to inspire the whole group to become more than the sum of the parts.

Rolo James, James Lambert, Frank Skinner and Gareth Price were the fine young men showing they knew their Lions history.

Next stop was the man photobombing the picture above of the Irish lads I'd spoken with. **Andrew Bell - Bello** - is a lovely guy. We met, briefly, a few times after our first encounter in Hamilton. Bello's 2nd from right above. His wife **Ann-Marie,** furthest right, had organised the trip for Bello's 40th birthday. **Doug Price** is her brother, 2nd from left. The others were part of the tour group they joined up with.

When visiting Ninety Mile Beach in the far north, Doug was driving their camper when he heard the beach is sometimes used as a substitute for Highway 1 when the road has landslips or floods, and that in 2013 Jeremy Clarkson drove the entire length (strangely, only 64 miles) for a Top Gear challenge against a racing yacht.

It had to be done of course.

I'm sure Doug wasn't the first and won't be the last to get his camper van stuck on the beach. I suspect though, that those who got stuck before him would have helped any locals who might have rushed to their aid to dig out their vehicles. Luckily, on this occasion, there were locals around with the right tools to help them get mobile again. However...

... Bello tells me Doug did not dig.

Each subsequent occasion we crossed paths was a pleasure to see how much he and his companions were enjoying their tour. Bello's 'team', as he described them to me, complete with nicknames he'd assigned, comprised:

Andrew 'Bello' Bell (aka Erasure)

Katie Dooley (aka Next Husband Please, aka Pretty Much Welsh)

Ann-Marie Bell (aka Dot Cotton aka Kung Fu Panda)

Rhys Beddow (aka Captain Safety)

Doug Price (aka Warren Gatland's Lovechild)

Robert Samuel (The other one)

Daniel Trick (aka Lieutenant Obvious)

Desert Island Dave (The not-so-flying Scotsman)

Rachel Trick (aka Dory, aka Dancing Queen)

Stuart Knox (aka Knoxy aka Bossy Boots)

Since he returned Bello has supplied some of the thousands of pictures he took, starting with the welcome event I missed at The Treaty Grounds. Your taste of that event is courtesy of him.

Pictures on this page and the following page courtesy of Andrew Bell

Here are some more general ones he sent me, including various members of not just his team.

Behind Bello and his gang were two of the Lions In Pink. Jay had had to return home, but as you can see, **Andy and Stu** were still in the pink in every sense. They were comparing notes with another former military engineer, **Andy Morley**, who I later found out when we had a beer together in Wellington, had come out to New Zealand on his own and was just enjoying mingling with fellow tourists.

Military Engineers Andy Walton and Stu James - aka Lions in Pink - meet former Royal Engineer Andy Morley - and a few photobombers

I'm sure it was **Richie Jermyn's** indubitably Irish suit that first brought him to my attention, and it was from the second glance his way that I noticed the hair extensions he'd had done. I think Richie was already wondering himself if the Lion cub sized ears and (fairly short it must be said) orange mane he'd had woven into his rather darker own hair had been a step too far. When I met him in Auckland before the third test they were gone. He said he knew not where, but I suspect their undoing may have been by his own hand. Richie was with pals **Iain McGann and Rob Anderson**.

Still not yet having reached the doorway to the pub, I thought I'd check to see if Val was OK. She said she'd station herself in the shopping square 100 yards or so further down from The Quadrant, but I couldn't see her there, or outside the bar opposite so returned to The Quadrant.

A gap-toothed guy from Runcorn who'd clearly already had a few stopped me in my tracks as I reached the outside area again. When he realised I was a southerner he began to roundly abuse me just for being so, and would not be interrupted, even by his mates.

When he heard what I was doing though, he softened, and even deigned to shake my hand. It was still only about 2pm. The match didn't kick off until 7.35pm. I can't help wondering if **Neil Wilkinson** managed to stay the course that day. Not, I think, Jonny's twin separated at birth.

I managed to squeeze through the throng outside to find that the inside of the bar was just as packed and even noisier. Inside, The Quadrant seemed a very appropriate place for **Bertie Burleigh** to tell me that in 2005, Lions fans had drunk over 250 kegs of beer in The Peggy Gordon - the very famous pub (his words) he owned in New Plymouth. I imagine he was very sorry there was no match scheduled for Yarrow Stadium on this tour.

Bertie Burleigh

Former Wales and Lions winger **Shane Williams** was holding court amongst an admiring group of Welsh fans and I thought at one point I'd caused a scrap as people jostled each other to try and be in the photo I took of him. All calmed down soon enough though.

Shane Williams was out and about with fans a lot

Spookily, the very next person I spoke to told me about a near-to-blows encounter he'd had with a Kiwi in a bar – the first negative experience I'd heard.

Lloyd Williams was already a tiny bit peeved that the B&B in Rotorua he'd booked before leaving the UK turned out to be a scam, and didn't exist. With some ninety minutes before the Māori All Blacks match kicked off, he and **Max Bray** had nowhere to stay after the game. You may recall it was a very wet night. They'd all but resigned themselves to a cold and miserable night in the hire car, when with twenty minutes to spare before kick-off they'd found a hotel who'd just had a cancelled reservation due to a flight cancellation caused by the weather. What goes around comes around.

The next day the boys were playing pool in a bar in town. A group of ten Kiwis were exchanging banter with them when one who appeared to have had a skinful changed the tone of the situation, becoming aggressively abusive, despite most of his mates telling him not to be such a knob.

Lloyd says he was contemplating using the cue he was playing with as part of his defensive tactics before one of the Kiwis recognised the degree of escalation his mate had provoked and dragged him away. Drinks for Lloyd and Max duly appeared and all was calm again.

Hardly the worst bar conflict you'll have heard of, but all the more surprising to hear when everybody else has raved about Kiwi hospitality.

I tried to chat to a few other people but found it very difficult to make out what they were saying. Why is it that in a crowded room everybody seems to talk more loudly than they would normally in a vain effort to be heard, which, of course, increases the likelihood of not being heard? I concluded it It was almost impossible to hold a conversation with anyone and set off to find Val again. It was starting to get dark and she was still nowhere to be seen. I crossed to another pub – The Local Taphouse - to see if anybody on the outside seats had noticed her. Tables there were more spread out, so at least I could have conversations with people.

I don't recall exactly why **Ian Harris** proffered this advice, but it's the sort you remember. His pearl of wisdom was: **"When in Thailand, you have to be firm with the Lady Boys."** Companions **Elwyn Owens, his son Dylan and James Dare** seemed to enjoy my questions in reply: "Firm with the Lady Boys' what?" and "How exactly did you find this out?" None of them recalled seeing Val.

While pondering Ian's wise (?) words, a chorus of 'Jingle Bells' came from the next table. It was soon apparent why, and was soon taken up by everybody present. **Kevin McIntosh** duly acknowledged his greeting by first conducting the singing then taking a bow.

The quick thinking Mickey-takers are pictured below.

Evidently nobody could think of an appropriate mickey-taking song quickly enough to accompany Val's arrival 30 seconds later in her luminous green FOCUS ON THE FANS tabard over a bright red rainmac.

Or they simply took pity on her as she looked very cold.

Dylan Owens, Ian Harris, James Dare and Elwyn Owens

Val had been round the shopping centre and stopped in The Quadrant thinking I was probably well ensconced with some fans and enjoying a few beers. Which reminded me that I'd eaten and drunk nothing but a small bottle of water all day. While we discussed what to eat and where to watch the match, we explored the food options in the mall we were in, which happened to be where we'd parked. I was just trying to find a menu in a smart bar full of Lions fans, when a young guy looked at my tabard and asked about blogging for The Telegraph.

Jordan Howes is an impressive young man. He was in New Zealand with **his Grandad, Tony, from Leeds**, who had wanted to go on the tour but was reluctant to because of his age. Jordan successfully persuaded him that was exactly why he should go, and offered to go with him. Currently working for the Keith Prowse travel agency serving corporate travel needs, it was Jordan's out of work activities that impressed me. When I mentioned my lifelong soccer affinity before discovering rugby, Jordan told me about his work with **Football Beyond Borders (FBB).** It's a charity that works with children who love football, but who underachieve academically. Typically they work in economically disadvantaged areas, mostly around South and East London, using football themed educational and media related activities to inspire disengaged students to develop the behaviour for learning, literacy skills and self-motivation.

However, as part of their international activity, Jordan led the first tour of children to play football in Palestine, and tells a brilliant story of crossing religious and cultural boundaries with kids in Mostar, Bosnia - a community completely torn apart by racial and religious conflict, particularly during and after the break-up of Yugoslavia.

Mixing Muslim and non-Muslim local children to join with the kids he'd taken there to play football, they were all tasked with finding out and understanding what life was like for the people they were about to be teammates with.

After that, the mixed teams happily played football together, a universal language and culture of course.

Despite not stopping for a single beer all afternoon I'd really enjoyed my day. The atmosphere and mood I'd encountered in the bars had been fantastic and a real pleasure to be part of.

By contrast, Val had hated her day on the streets, even though it had been her suggestion to do so. She had started off feeling fine in the sunshine, happily distributing flyers to passers-by. The first person to decline taking a flyer had a major impact on her confidence. By the time a second person said 'No thanks' she had almost decided to give up. She had wandered around fairly aimlessly for a couple of hours since then, half-heartedly offering the flyer to diminishing numbers by the minute. I completely understood. This whole project was a massive step outside her comfort zone, and I was hugely appreciative that she'd even agreed to do it with me. There aren't many women I know who would spend the best part of seven weeks traipsing round New Zealand to accost large groups of men in bars. The fact remained though, that when she gets talking to people she's brilliant at building rapport very quickly, so I resolved that she'd only have to do no more than that for the rest of the trip.

Val was much heartened by the inspiring tales we heard from Jordan, and by my assurance that I'd make sure she wouldn't end any other day during the rest of the trip feeling like she had that day. We decided we'd head back to the house and walk to the nearby pub to eat and watch the game, so that both of us could have a beer or wine, or as it turned out, both beer and wine.

On the way back to the car we encountered a few more people who wanted photos taken:

Dominique Forrest, Dan Westerby and Chris Ward sat outside at The Local Taphouse, as did Andrew Richards, Fiona Williams, Jessica Talbot and Alex Gammon.

We were honoured to meet **Her Majesty Queen Elizabeth II out for a beer with her granddaughter-in-law Kate,** heavily disguised as **Mark and Charlie Leddy** from Manchester (or maybe the not so heavy really disguise was the other way around); while **Barry Smith, Mark Thorrington, James Whelan and Michael Bryon** were keen to show off their very big Welsh flag. Barry was also keen to tell me New Zealand beer is addictive. Many times.

I have no idea who these guys are – but they insisted on Val joining their photo. She seemed to be enjoying the grope don't you think? ☺

The match: We got to the pub, The Cock & Bull, with five minutes to spare before kick-off, to find we were the only Lions fans in a crowd of Chiefs supporters in front of the big screen.

Exeter Chief, Jack Nowell, seemed inspired by the opportunity to star against his club namesakes in a thoroughly professional Lions performance that restricted the Chiefs to only two penalties in their 6-34 defeat. Val and I restrained our joy though – it doesn't do to risk antagonising an already rather miserable group of fans, however friendly the nation had been to us so far.

Their team was, of course, depleted by the absence of their All Blacks stars. I was getting very hopeful that Gatland's game plans to squeeze opponents to the point of frustration and mistakes was so well executed against The Crusaders, Māori All Blacks and Chiefs, even the blip against the Highlanders wasn't dampening our rising spirits leading into the first test.

21st June: Hamilton to Auckland via Waitomo Caves

I know. It's a seriously roundabout route, but this was the only day we could feasibly fit in time at Waitomo Caves. We'd not managed to fit it into our intinerary on our 2014 visit, so were keen to this time.

Before we left I was packing the kit we'd need if we encountered fans. I set on the coffee table one of the voice recorders we'd deemed not worth bothering with using because of the dreadful sound quality on playback. The brilliant sunlight that morning glinted on something I - and plenty others who'd also examined them - hadn't previously noticed. When I'd unpacked the things originally I'd removed the thick and very obvious plastic film covering the microphones at the top of the machine. The sunlight now highlighted the very much thinner and very less than obvious film that covered the speaker at the bottom.

I left it in place to verify with Val that I hadn't been as relatively thick as the mic film, then peeled it off and found that, whilst a little tinny, you could now at least understand what was being said. We laughed. Honestly!

It's worth going to Waitomo. The boat ride trip is a good introduction and where you'll see the most glow worms at one time from the gentle cruise through the grotto at the end (2017 cost NZ$50). It's a further NZ$45 for all three caves, only NZ$6 more than combining two caves, but we were all caved out a good bit before we finished the third. I'd recommend adding to the boat trip one of the two cave combos – the Aranui (extra NZ$24) if your attention span is short; the much longer, more varied and we thought much better Ruakuri if you have the time and patience (extra NZ$39). You have to fix the times you will visit each when you buy your tickets, so it's well worth checking all availability options so you don't sit around for longer than you need to. You can't use a camera on the boat trip and their PR department hasn't responded to my request for one. So here are pictures of what you can expect to see other than in the boat ride cave.

PR as it should be done: As well as seeing the caves we met a few Lions fans – including what we thought must surely be the youngest Lions fan on tour. More about her shortly, but first we had run into **Sonia Clark and Colin Davidson** in the car park. Not literally thank goodness.

They'd arrived at Auckland airport only one hour before the team were due. They decided they'd wait to greet the players.

With plenty of media around looking to fill their waiting time, Colin was interviewed a number of times - and appeared on New Zealand national TV's 6pm news.

They also got chatting with Matt, Jo and Mark from Standard Life Investments (SLI), the Lions principal commercial sponsor, who were waiting to greet the playing and coaching squad. Colin happened to mention it was Sonia's birthday next day, whereupon they were promptly presented with 'Golden Tickets' to attend a closed Lions training session at the QBE stadium a couple of days later.

A car was sent to pick them up, deliver them to the training ground and take them back to their hotel. They met and chatted with all the players and management team. A wonderful unexpected added bonus to the start of their tour, which gave them memories you literally can't buy.

This picture and following 16 pictures courtesy of Sonia Clark

Memories of a special, unexpected birthday treat for Sonia

More was to come their way though, and just as unexpectedly. A couple of weeks later when Sonia and Colin bumped into the same SLI people in Dunedin, they naturally took the opportunity to thank them again. Sonia had foregone her ticket to the Highlanders match to allow **Colin's daughter Kathy**, who lives in Christchurch, to see the game with her Dad on her own birthday. When the SLI people bade Sonia to enjoy the game, she mentioned what she'd done, and was provided with another ticket courtesy of SLI so that all three could watch it live in the ground. Good to hear. Well done Matt, from Standard Life Investments.

Kathy, Sonia and Colin get to watch the Lions together…

… courtesy of Matt from Standard Life Investments

Extra Baggage! Waiting at the cave ticket office for the shuttle bus to Ruakuri we noticed **Jeremy Ankers and Rachel Parkes**. When they booked their tour with Lions Travel fairly early in 2016, little did they know they'd have extra baggage by the time it came to depart. **Baby Josie** was unplanned, but by then four months old, she was gurgling in her Mum's arms. Jeremy told me she wore a teeny weeny Lions kit to matches. Which prompted me to ask whether they were asked to pay anything extra for adding Josie to their booking. Although it's standard practice for airlines not to charge for one so young, as infants don't take up an extra seat, Jeremy was amazed that the same argument wasn't true as far as Lions Rugby were concerned. They wanted to charge them extra, saying that Josie needed tickets for matches. Understandably annoyed and disbelieving, Jeremy contacted NZRU to explain the circumstances and

counsel their view. He was told categorically that Josie was welcome to every match he and Rachel were attending without the need for an additional ticket. Lions Rugby relented when NZRU confirmed that to them too.

This picture courtesy of Jeremy Ankers

It was a long old trek back to Shirin's home in Auckland, where another stonking meal of wild salmon greeted us as warmly as its cook. We spent a restful and enjoyable evening bringing Shirin up to speed on the rugby we'd watched and the people we'd encountered on our travels south and back; all of us concluding that the prospects looked very good for a fabulous first test in three days time.

I was to be even more hopeful after getting the inside track from the Lions coach himself.

22nd – 25th June: Auckland Comes Alive and 'A Private Audience'

A day off – of sorts. We were both tired after nearly four weeks of what seemed like constant travel, long days and working to gather material. The morning was showery and dull, so we thought we'd have a lazy day. Val's involved grocery shopping for the meal she would prepare for us all later. Mine was a bit of catching up with other things going on in my world beyond the Lions trip, responding to emails from home that hadn't required urgent attention, thinking about the plan for the two days leading up to the match on Saturday evening, and starting to sort through potential content for my next blog.

I also emailed the guy who hired me to work for Nationwide back in 1991, to arrange to meet. I hadn't seen Mike Cutt in years, although we had kept loosely in touch through a mutual friend I'd originally introduced him to, and who I also ended up working with a few years later. Mike had been in contact to say he was coming out on **his sixth Lions tour**, this time with his two sons. They'd be arriving in Auckland just before the first test.

Brief Encounter: On the Friday morning I got a text from **Jo Cribb**. Jo is the lady whose house we would be moving on to stay at in Wellington after the first test. Before stepping down to spend more time with her two children, she was the CEO of New Zealand's Ministry for Women, so an ideal person to address a Women in Leadership Summit being held in Auckland that day. Its venue was The Hotel Pullman in the CBD, where the Lions squad was staying. Jo suggested I drop in at lunchtime to say hello – we hadn't previously met – and see who was around. Val and Shirin decided to stay at home out of the rain, while I left for the city centre to suss out the Fan Zone location and then meet with Jo.

From our time in Rotorua and Hamilton I already knew the fan population was increasing considerably. I fully expected their numbers to be swelled with new arrivals in time for the first test. Walking from where I parked to the Fan Zone on Queen's Wharf it was immediately apparent that was the case. Rory's sea of red was beginning to wash over the streets of Auckland.

The Fan Zone was already buzzing. Set alongside a building called The Cloud, where the 4500 official Lions Travel fans would enjoy their pre-match hospitality and entertainment, a huge warehouse had been converted into a giant sports bar. At least someone had come to their senses and installed a 50 metre long bar inside to satisfy the thirst of the thousands expected to cram in to watch the game on eight giant screens. All Blacks players were busy signing autographs and there looked to be plenty of temporary stands where I could perch myself above the throng to photograph people in the crowd reacting to on-field events during the match. It's what I'd done in Germany, and I knew watching the crowd would mean me only seeing glimpses of the game, but I was first and foremost here to do just that.

There were more bars, booths serving street food and seating areas outside, where I sought out the site manager to explain what I was trying to achieve, make sure I wouldn't be compromising any NZRU diktats and ask for permission to take pictures within the Fan Zone. The delightful Michelle provided me with a media pass and assured me she was perfectly comfortable with me taking pictures during the match - and any time up to or after it. This Fan Zone had been set up by the city council rather than NZRU, so the Lions fans' predeliction for supping lots of booze both pre-match and while watching rugby had been the driving force. They'd done a great job.

Very happy with the morning's outcome, it started belting down on the short hop to The Pullman. I paid for an hour on a meter 100 yards or so away, and waited inside for the fifteen minutes until the summit broke for lunch. I'd looked up Jo's picture, and my text to her saying to look for a short, fat, grey-bearded, balding late-50's bloke who was in a sopping wet luminous green tabard, unsurprisingly meant she clocked me straight away. We passed about fifteen minutes introducing ourselves and chatting before I thought it right to let her get some lunch. I liked Jo straight away. We'd meet again the following Tuesday.

You make your own luck – Chance Encounter: In great spirits I headed for the bar to see if anybody might be around for me to talk to. I quickly sussed that most of the many red shirts around were being worn by fans, sometimes evident by physique, but mostly because they wore ordinary trousers rather than Lions tracksuit bottoms as players and coaches did. We'd said we wouldn't interrupt people who were eating to talk about FOCUS ON THE FANS and – not unexpectedly at lunchtime – virtually every table occupied by Lions fans was also occupied by plates of food. No matter, I felt I'd achieved anyway, so was slowly making my way towards the exit when I spied a couple who had finished their food.

Graham Newling and his partner Judith Williams from Newport, South Wales were most welcoming when I asked if I might leave a flyer with them. I soon found out this was Graham's sixth Lions tour too. They had made all the travel, accommodation and match ticket arrangements for it independently and were having an absolute whale of a time. I'm very pleased I made the decision to accost them and very grateful they allowed me to, as if we hadn't had the exchange we did, my next encounter in all likelihood would not have occurred.

After moving on from Graham and Judith, I saw a group of guys in red shirts and tracksuits standing around a table next to a bench seat. Players possibly? No – I didn't recognise them, but by their age realised they were more likely coaching staff. As I passed the last one I caught a glimpse of Trudi Gatland sitting on the bench. Not expecting at all that she would remember me from the time we'd spoken on Otago Peninsula a couple of weeks earlier, I thought it worth a brief: "Trudi" and a nod as I passed. When she looked up to see who had addressed her, I genuinely was very surprised when her face lit up as she responded: "Ken. How are you? How's the book coming along?"

I took that as an invite to stop and chat. Within the fifteen seconds she remonstrated playfully with me for not greeting her a few days earlier in Hamilton (when I apparently didn't notice her walking past me) the men standing had dispersed. Warren Gatland, who had been sitting down and therefore screened behind them, was now right next to Trudi and right in front of me.

Trudi introduced me, explaining about the book. Warren gave a friendly smile, so I took the opportunity to say I was also blogging for The Telegraph and that my editor would naturally expect a journalist to ask if we might have a conversation when presented with an unexpected opportunity like this. I quickly followed that by acknowledging that he and Trudi may have not had much 'We time' while on tour, so offered to bugger off if they would rather be alone. At least I could honestly say to the editor I'd asked. Warren laughed and invited me to sit down while they finished their cokes.

I hadn't for a moment imagined I would be in this situation at any time on the tour, let alone in a chance encounter in a hotel bar. As I took a seat across the table from them, I quickly grappled to find an opening that would elicit a positive response to start us off.

The last two performances from his team had been superb, so my instinct was to comment that he must have enjoyed the last week – meaning the rugby side. I was all ready to talk about how it was going so well, with building momentum, and mostly great execution of the tactics he was employing, but his reply threw me, I'll admit.

"Actually, I've not enjoyed it much at all. It's been a horrible week."

I didn't have a chance to ask why before Trudi was quick to point out with her wry smile as she pointed to my newly acquired badge;

"People like you, Ken. The media."

Warren went on to explain it was the New Zealand media. The very personal insults and assaults on his professional credibility were less than he believed he deserved from his home nation. Some of them had come from people he regarded as friends – although I got the sense they may be off his Christmas card list now. Just because he was returning with a strong rugby team to take on the All Blacks. He was sure it was happening because the Lions performances had hugely diminished the belief in Kiwis that this series was to be a pushover.

Although he doesn't read what they print or watch much of what is broadcast about him, the Lions series in New Zealand is such a massive event for the host nation it's virtually impossible for him to avoid. The preceding week had seen unprecedented levels of abuse hurled his way, much of it from people he felt had no right to comment on his tactics and team selections. It was always going to be raised by UK & Irish media at the start of press conferences too - and we were talking before the country's biggest newspaper depicted him in a cartoon with a clown's red nose that dominated its front page.

Even the most professional people are only human, and thus aren't immune to personal attacks. Clearly, Warren was upset and hurt. It's also clear he is exceedingly professional. Whilst he doesn't let the vitriol affect his professional performance, his relationship with his players, coaches and with his wife, he admitted it still smarts.

And there's more: He wasn't thrilled with Premiership Rugby either. A schedule that left him with only three full days for the players to acclimatise before the first game in Whangarei meant many of the team were suffering the jet lag that watching fans correctly concluded was the reason for such a scratchy victory in the Barbarians match. Gatland thinks a minimum of ten days acclimatisation before playing competitively is essential. Neither would he ideally want a tough match against an outstanding rugby club side like The Chiefs so soon before the first test. But the coach doesn't set any of the match, commercial, local community PR and the media schedules of course. He was definitely proud of his players, not just for their on-field performances, but also for their enthusiasm in carrying out all the off-field commitments in the engaging manner they did.

At this point I asked if I could publish anything he'd told me, acknowledging he'd been very open. He told me I could use anything he said to me, provided I reported it accurately, which with a sideswipe to the press generally, he said hadn't always happened. Words had apparently been twisted in the past. I offered to show him what I prepared for The Telegraph in advance of sending in my copy. He was pleased.

Voice of the people: We moved on to the future of Lions tours, which has long been a topic for debate. There are many past tours held up as having been defining moments for the future of The British & Irish Lions. There are many in the top echelons of rugby whose views are faithfully reported in some quarters that Lions tours matter much less than they used to. Warren's comment was whilst this may be true for some Premiership chairmen, he truly believes that's not the case for the players, not for the coaches, and especially not for the fans. His concluding argument on the matter though was that ultimately market forces, not politics, will determine the Lions future to be in safe hands. **"You only have to look at the streets outside to see how much the best international rugby test series means to rugby fans. The voice of the people will win through."** Politics did make a brief appearance when he cited Brexit as a similar example of people power.

His appreciation of, and faith in, rugby fans' voices being heard is evident when he describes how much the fans contribute to making the Lions Tour the uplifting experience it is for players and management. That was particularly pleasing for me to hear, as that's exactly what was behind the idea for this book.

I explained I'd meant with my first comment the rugby was what I thought he'd be enjoying. The increasing momentum had so many of the thousands of Lions fans there truly believing the Lions can beat the All Blacks; and All Blacks fans significantly more concerned about the prospect of losing than they were prior to the tour. His demeanour switched instantly to professional rugby coach mode.

It's difficult to convey the focus and absolute certainty in his voice when he told me: "We're going to win tomorrow night. We know. We're going to win. I know how we can win, and the players who can best deliver the result." It certainly wasn't arrogance, or the bluster you might expect from some coaches. It came across simply as the convincing tone of a man who knows exactly what he is doing and is genuinely convinced his players will execute the game plan.

I believed him.

I decided I'd find a quiet corner to write up an additional piece for The Telegraph and - subject to the Gatland's approval as promised - send it for the Sport Online team to wake up to. I'd finished the first draft when I remembered I'd only put an hour on the meter, and it was already over. I returned to the bar to see if Warren and Trudi were still there. They weren't, but my slow wander towards the conference rooms - and possibly my media badge - caught the attention of one of the hotel concierge team. When he asked if he could help me, I asked how efficient traffic wardens were in Auckland. That prompted a response of "Very efficient, sir," and a question as to why I might need to know. I explained I was hoping to catch Warren before I left but was already over time on my meter. Not a problem. The concierge would collect the car and park it in the drop-off area at the front of the hotel. Fabulous, I thought as I handed over the car key.

I established from a Lions PR person I found that Warren was in a conference room doing a radio broadcast, so shared her table while I fine-tuned my article, and waited until he came out. He was all set to quickly read through it until the PR lady apologetically dragged him away, saying he really didn't have time before his next scheduled meeting. I thanked Warren for his willingness, said not to worry, I'd email it to Trudi instead. A couple of hours later I got a reply saying:

"That's absolutely fine Ken. Go ahead. Kind regards. Trudi."

Andy Fifield (of The Telegraph) emailed as soon as he read the article to congratulate me and say it would be online within the hour.

It was on my way out of the hotel that I spotted Bill Beaumont and Ian Ritchie and got the 'No bloody fans' quote.

Soon after posting the news of my audience on Facebook, Dermot Ross added a really nice post of his own:

It's a family affair: After a bit of a late lunch back at the house, Val and I came into town again in early evening. Strolling into the Fan Zone I was delighted to spot the two families who were on extended world trips with their kids - **the Leightons and the Colemans** - had crossed each other's paths. Both sets of kids and parents seem to have hit it off.

They had been swapping stories inside the Fan Zone and were now off to have their evening meals together before bedtime for the youngsters. There weren't a huge number in the Fan Zone itself, but as we walked along the waterfront area of the CBD every bar and restaurant was jammed with Lions fans.

We met a fella with a pretty thick Aussie accent who called himself **Brisbane Rob**. The night of England's final test in Australia in 2016 he swears he had a serious number of beers with Graham Rowntree, whose advice he subsequently sought about a personalised number plate he was considering buying for his car. It's **LION**. Graham apparently said to buy it. Rob showed me a picture of a pick-up with the Lion plate, but has forgotten to email it across. It turns out Rob is English, has only lived in Brisbane for 10 years, but found selling to customers was much easier when he accentuated his Aussie accent. He'd had his future son-in-law driving him around wineries all day. You could tell. Particularly when he collared a couple of passers-by and coerced them into dancing in the street with him, below right, while he took The Killers band name literally and murdered their hit: "I got soul, but I'm not a soldier". Good fun.

Barry Smith, Mark Thorrington, James Whelan and Michael Byron were wandering around the marina bars, this time without their giant Welsh flag we'd seen them with in Hamilton.

They hadn't visited lots of wineries, but a number of bars must have profited greatly from them continuing to prove Barry's previously expressed belief that New Zealand beer is addictive.

In excellent humour though, they told Val how much they loved her, that I was alright, and insisted on another photo outside a restaurant Brisbane Rob might have claimed ownership of.

It was getting late, we knew we had a long day coming up, and there was a strong likelihood of whoever we spoke to now being pretty sozzled, so headed home.

July 1st, Match day 7: Lions v New Zealand All Blacks, First test

A hearty breakfast set us up for the day ahead. I read an email from **Gary O'Brien**, a Lions fan in exile in New York, who had read on Telegraph Online what I was doing and sent a great photo of himself, his son **Jonny**, their dog wearing a lion's mane and their Lion mascot, then we were off to the city centre. Gary had started out watching the midweek matches live but found his workday was somewhat impacted by the 2.35am kick-off, so resorted to recording them for viewing after work.

Pictures on this page courtesy of Gary O'Brien

Mike Cutt had replied to say he and his boys had all come from different countries to meet here, so he was having a beer with them and some of their mates at lunchtime, but would be in the Fan Zone at around 2pm. I was looking forward to seeing Mike very much. He's a really good man.

While Val went to the marina to leave piles of flyers in the many bars there, I went straight to the Fan Zone, which was already packed – almost completely with Lions fans. It didn't take long to dawn on me that the whole place had been shifted around since the day before. All the raised terracing I'd seen and thought I'd use as vantage points had been removed. I could no longer get above the fans watching the game to spot people amongst the crowd and capture their reactions to what was happening on the screens. Oh well, I was long past getting frustrated by anything that detracted from my pre-tour plans, so began looking around the place.

Of the thousands in the building, it was remarkable that the first two groups I happened upon were people we'd met before.

The Leighton family; Max and Maria, with their children Xander and Scarlett. They'd had some bad news from home. Maria had bought Max a special edition Land Rover for his 40th birthday. It was a prized possession, but they'd had word that it had been stolen some time during the night before. There were people in the house, and it was parked at the rear, so it seems it was a professional job, as the car must have been rolled silently down the drive and loaded onto a trailer.

PR opportunity missed: Thinking about what Standard Life Investments had done for Sonia Clarke, it struck me that Land Rover might want to do something as nice for the Leightons. I thought as a Lions principal partner it was an opportunity for some positive publicity for Land Rover, so emailed the story to their Head of PR. We never heard back though.

Standing nearby the Leightons was **Mike Hollister.** After a quick word with him to get his correct email address (the photo of his group in Rotorua he'd asked me to email had bounced back – he'd written down his own address I should add), I began to walk around to see if I could catch the attention of people I didn't know who might want to learn more about what my bright green tabard said on it.

The first were a fun bunch. **Amanda and Simon Clarke, with Paul Matthews,** had all invested in Lion head hoodies. Not a bad idea for the winter weather that was proving most likely on match days. Actually, any day would probably feel cold to Amanda and Simon. They live in Dubai. We were to meet in Wellington too.

In the Auckland fanzone the day of the first test

Outside the 2nd test venue - Wellington

Not sure if this was originally intended as a line-out lift or celebration

Plenty of Lion fuel to go round

Get your tickets here!

John Tidy was looking quizzically at my tabard in the rather strange red lighting they'd chosen to use in the Fan Zone. I caught his eye before he looked away.

He and wife **Lizzie** had watched all the warm up matches at their home in South Africa. They'd been impressed with the quality of the rugby so decided to come to New Zealand to soak up the atmosphere as well.

Despite Lizzie's protestations that it was a waste of time, John had insisted on stopping by Eden Park's ticket office the day before, to see if test match tickets were still available. Amazed to learn there were, they snapped up a couple. John thought "While I'm here..." and asked about tickets for the third test, also to be at Eden Park. "How many would you like?" was the totally unexpected response.

They'd be staying a couple of weeks instead of a couple of days.

And I have an invite to stay with them when I eventually persuade Val that a holiday in South Africa is a good idea. We'll see you sometime.

Irish eyes were smiling: A couple of tables along, three very attractive young Irishwomen understandably caught my eye well before I managed to catch their very smiley eyes. I just had to stop and talk to them (mine's a tough gig but somebody had to do it). They turned out not only to be lovely, but very smart and very funny too. They had me in stitches with their banter. They introduced themselves as Auckland's most wanted on the lookout for New Zealand's most eligibles, keeping the pace up pretty much non-stop from there.

It was about fifteen minutes into laughing with them that I described what I'm doing out here, whereupon **Sarah Melvin** raised (as high as she could) her right foot to show me she was wearing a very similar brace to that of Tina O'Donnell, mentioned a couple of times earlier.

Injured a couple of weeks before travelling here from Sydney where the girls all live and work, Sarah was not going to let a little thing like a broken ankle spoil her weekend away with her mates, **Sinead Healy and Emer O'Leary**. Emer's first words to me were that she was out here to meet her fiancé, only he - and she - don't know who that is yet. They were as interested in hearing about me as I was about them, and drew from me a few stories they seemed to greatly enjoy:

- **how Val and I first met:** on a boat between Paxos and Antipaxos – after she had ricked her neck jumping out of bed late for the trip and could only look to her right side- she ended up swimming round in circles when I eventually persuaded her to try going in the water
- **our four day holiday romance:** which included me directing her through an emergency exit from a club and her dropping unexpectedly to the beach four feet below instead of being in the ladies; the bouncers wouldn't let her back in because she didn't have a hand stamp
- **our son Rob being regularly mistaken for Ed Sheeran;** particularly the time a girl in a Bristol nightclub made him sign her breasts despite his protestations that he really was Rob Skehan

From left: Emer, Sarah and Sinead

Thanks girls for 30 minutes of great fun.

Maybe I'll put Rob in touch with you. I've already told him I'd love any or all of you as daughters-in-law.

PS: My answer to the very suggestive question you ask everyone Sinead.

My kind of Uber is the ride of your life – short or long!

During the 6 weeks they were on tour, sisters **Birlyn Greenough and Bechan Jones** sported Lions hats knitted by Bechan. It's what she does for a living. Knitting – but not always Lions hats.

More Adoptions: Alison Butler and Deirdre Reilly were having a drink in the Fan Zone with their Auckland Adopt-A-Lions-Fan hosts, Kiwis **Mal and Iain Douglas.** The girls enjoyed similar hospitality all over New Zealand.

Ali and Dee also sported a home-made creation, courtesy of materials supplied by earlier hosts, as you'll read on the next page.

While the girls showed us the banner they had made, it attracted some random people who just wanted to be photographed with it.

I have no idea who they are! Nor where to send a photo.

The next day Deirdre was kind enough to email me a summary of their tour to date and plans for the rest of the trip:

Alison Butler (Ali) and I are friends from London who play tag rugby together and are both huge Ireland fans.

I'm originally from Donegal in the North West of Ireland. Ali grew up in Liverpool and has an extended Irish family. We had talked for months about the Lions tour and finally took the plunge last August, agreeing to quit our jobs and go on a massive holiday. We're both lucky enough to work in healthcare and be able to pick up work pretty quickly when we get back in August (we hope).

The Lions package we booked, as it was the only way to guarantee match tickets, was a campervan for 2.5 weeks on the North Island plus tickets for the three tests. Not satisfied with that, we were determined to see the South Island, as well as hotter climes along the way and left London mid-May to spend a few weeks exploring Indonesia. We arrived in Queenstown on June 1st. Ali flew via Auckland (I came via Christchurch) and bumped into the Lions squad at the airport after she had gone 24 hours without sleep. Excitement levels were high.

We hired a car for our 3.5 week stay in the South Island and stayed with friends where possible, but that left a lot of the island uncovered and us with dwindling funds. We had made plans via the Adopt a Lions Facebook page to park up with people in Auckland and Wellington for the tests, so decided to look at other offers and it worked out brilliantly. Although there were no tests played on the South Island, a huge number of people were offering beds and driveways all over the South Island.

After a trip to the Franz Josef glacier on the West Coast we drove north up to Golden Bay and stayed 3 nights with **Ann and Brian Jones**. They described themselves in their Facebook messenger reply to me as 'no spring chickens but rugby mad'. Indeed they were. We arrived at their beautiful farmhouse to gin and tonics, a cooked dinner and then sat down to watch New Zealand demolish Samoa. They gave us advice on where to visit while we were there, what route to take and we shared a meal each evening. They even tried to explain the complexities of the unfolding America's Cup to a pair of sailing novices. They encouraged us to make a banner and gave us some old curtain lining and a box of acrylics to do the job.

From there we travelled through the middle of the country, overnighting in a motel until we arrived in Christchurch where **Nicci Hyman and Leanne Collins** gave us a front door key and a set of massive sofas in their front room for 3 nights. We went out for dinner on our last night and on the way home Nicci took us for a drive through the earthquake affected North Island suburbs.

Having already seen the rebuilding work in the city centre and heard how unhappy people are about the slow speed of rebuilding and compensation following the devastating 2011 earthquake, it was humbling and really sad to see the miles of now parkland which was once home to thousands. Unable to rebuild as the ground is unstable people have been forced to move elsewhere in New Zealand or south of the city to start again. Nicci told us about her experience on the day of the quake and in the following weeks. It was terrifying. An insight and experience so far away from the usual tourist route, it was, I suppose, an honour to see real everyday life for the people of Christchurch.

Christchurch was our last stop on the South Island. We flew North to Auckland on the morning of June 23rd to pick up our campervan and join the waves of red fans, some of whom had been lucky enough to follow the tour through all the games.

An official campervan park was available in Auckland at a price, however the details still hadn't been finalised in April 6 weeks before we were due to leave the UK. The Adopt a Lions fan Facebook group allowed me to contact **Iain and Marilyn Douglas** who offered a parking space on their driveway for both Auckland tests. Iain was super excited about the games, having moved to New Zealand from England 25 years ago. He didn't have tickets for the games but that didn't stop him enthusiastically messaging us about the Fan Zones, the weather and the squad updates for weeks before our arrival.

Greeted by presents of our very own cuddly kiwis on our arrival, on the morning of the test we went to see Iain and Marilyn's 9-year-old grandson Sam play rugby in North Auckland. It was fabulous and our lions rain jackets got a great reception on the soggy side-line. Everywhere we have gone in fact, the locals, while convinced of their sporting superiority, are delighted we have made the trip and have been friendly and welcoming, with the very, very odd exception.

Pre-game on Saturday Iain and Marilyn came with us to the fan area in the harbour in Auckland and Iain even picked us up from the train station on the way back.

*We left them to travel north today but will be back for the final test. We have many more adoption hosts in the diary. A farm in Raglan promising a roast lamb and red wine dinner, a bed and parking space pre-test in **Wellington with Deanna,** before we head to Napier to stay with her daughter for a night. Another pit stop with **Tom and Alex near Lake Taupo**, interspersed with a few nights in campsites so we can charge the campervan battery!!*

It's a truly phenomenal country but the way people have opened their doors to us is making for a unique and amazing holiday. We've honestly run out of hyperbole to describe this place.

I hope this email and the attached photos jog your memory and help with the blog and book!

Deirdre

In the Takaka garden of Ann and Brian Jones

Watching Iain and Mal's grandson play

Pictures on this page courtesy of Deirdre Reilly

Ollie Stuchbury, Josh Skinner, Joff Jennings and Tim Harrison also made great use of Adopt-A-Lions-Fan, Joff even picking up **Lion, Jason,** as a gift from one of his hosts. Josh and Ollie were pleased to bump into Neil Jenkins and Rob Howley, taking a break from their up-market hotel by dining in Maccy D in Auckland the night before the Blues match a few weeks earlier.

Don't tell Lions Rugby! This not so subtle adaptation of the Lions badge was sported on the blazers of a group of guys I spotted in the Fan Zone. **The Knutsford Boys** created it to reflect the relative contributions to the squad by each of the countries represented. It would no doubt be frowned upon by Lions Rugby Brand Police.

On the way out to meet Mike Cutt, this guy's Lions costume was attracting admiring comments from many, but **Ross Preston's lad Finlay** looked a little unsure about being patted on the head by a roaring lion. Or maybe it was just being photographed he was unsure about.

Mike Cutt has definitely aged much better than I have, despite only just about surviving a serious motorcycle accident some years back that's left him with permanent physical challenges. He thought we were bound to win as he was wearing his lucky Lions shirt – the one he wore when the Lions won the first of the six tours he's been on, in South Africa 1997.

Mike's boys, **Toby and Frasier**, had both arrived a week earlier, one from South Africa and one from Australia. They had been camping as they travelled around North Island. Mike said they stank when he met them the day before. They hadn't been able to afford campsites, so had pitched their tent on roadsides or in fields, and there aren't many public facilities to shower in the New Zealand countryside.

They were directed to use the shower in the Airbnb place Mike was staying at before he'd taken them for a beer the previous evening. He'd had a few more with them already that lunchtime, and was soon off to the hospitality event that was part of his NZRU ticket purchase for a further few before the game.

Mike explained that he'd intended booking official Lions packages for them all, but when he asked if he could leave off flights for the boys as they were already in the southern hemisphere, he was told no – the flight was a compulsory part of the package and they'd have to fly back to London and depart on the tour flight from there. Mike worked out it would be significantly less expensive all round to make his own flight, accommodation and ticket arrangements. Like many others you've already read about, he used a contact in New Zealand to buy tickets far cheaper – even with the hospitality added the cost was less than the official Lions Travel option, and much less inconvenient for the boys. It was lovely to see Mike, even if only briefly that day. We promised to catch up for a bit longer at the third test.

I headed off to meet up with Val, encountering these guys, below left, singing along to the anthems with the 4500 fans in the official Lions Travel hospitality event in The Cloud next door; three more lovely ladies from Tipperary; then **Eric and Maurice** who I'd met in Whangarei. They wanted me to take a picture in front of the massive blow up figure in the Fan Zone, and attracted a couple of ladies to join them in it. I know not who, but hope it was the start of a beautiful friendship.

Val had actually enjoyed going round the bars in the marina. Lots of people had stopped her to ask about what she was doing, which boosted her confidence no end. She'd loved the atmosphere too. All the bars were rocking ahead of the big game, both with Lions and All Blacks fans. The mood everywhere was thrilling, she reported.

I hadn't seen this mock-up in O'Hagans myself, but I did like **Tony Campbell's picture of his mates Kevin Bowers, Antony Bowers and Jon Jenner.**

Tony's other pics he sent are below: on the way to the Auckland Fan Trail, and in the Westpac Stadium, Wellington at the second test.

Unclean - again! Fans were starting to go to the stadium, so Val and I went to Britomart Station to hand out flyers to those taking the train to Eden Park. I'd managed to get rid of most of the flyers I had on me before I was told by an Auckland Transport official that unless I had permission to do so, I should cease handing out any more. Unsurprised, I beat a hasty retreat. Outside the station entrance a couple of girls were distributing pizza offer vouchers, and told me nobody had accosted them to move on, so with waves of Lions fans still arriving, I recommended distributing flyers, while Val went to get more of them from the car.

By the time the flow of fans dwindled to stragglers who were likely to miss the kick-off, we were very cold and very hungry. We had time for a fuel boost at Nando's before returning to the Fan Zone, where I hoped to get more of the emotional images I've talked about, capturing fan reactions as they watch the match – if only from those standing in the front row!

With the eight big screens, the red lighting and limited view of the crowd, it was hardly perfect conditions to shoot fast, sharp exposures. I could tell that some fans were distracted from the game by my flashgun too – and those of the few other media photographers also snapping away. When the Lions fell far behind in the second half, one fellow gave me the finger and mouthed something you didn't need to be an expert to lip read. I thought "What the hell. Let's just enjoy the rest of the match."

Here are a selection of shots I'm reasonably happy with, from before the game started until I stopped shooting. I think they tell the story of the evening.

The match: Warren had been wrong of course. We didn't win. In fact, the second half proved all too easy for the All Blacks to put points on the board that meant the contest was effectively over with 20 minutes still to go. However, I was very impressed by Val's absorption of rugby knowledge as she gave me her view of the game while we drove home.

She thought the Lions played well at the start *(they did)*; they defended very well in the first half against an All Blacks team who looked faster, stronger and the more likely to win *(the Lions did, the ABs were)*: the game may have panned out very differently had the Lions taken the chances they created in the first 20 minutes *(it would have)*.

My thoughts? Warren had said to me the day before we had to get off to a fast start. The players did exactly that, and I agreed with Val; had the early chances the Lions created been converted to points the whole match could have taken a very different course. Warren had also acknowledged the defensive gameplan relied on perfect tackling and timing, which means the risk of conceding penalties is increased. It proved the Lions undoing, with penalties leading to all the points conceded except the final try when the game was beyond saving. I thought the All Blacks performance was as good as I've ever witnessed on a rugby pitch, and the Lions did outstandingly well to stay in the game for as long as they did. Fine margins proved the difference. The All Blacks made fewer mistakes and capitalised with clinical efficiency on the ones the Lions made. But what about the O'Brien try for the Lions? Even better than Rory's, and some fans saying it's the best Lions try ever.

25th - 26th June: Auckland to Whanganui to Wellington

We'd told Jo Cribb that we would be arriving a day later and leaving a day earlier than planned, so that we could break up the journeys between Auckland and Wellington both ways. We also thought it would be less of an imposition on, and therefore less disruptive to, their family. We considered visiting Bertie Burleigh at the famous Peggy Gordon in New Plymouth on the way down from Auckland, but decided it was too long a way round. Instead we would take in Tongariro National Park south-west of Lake Taupo and Whanganui National Park along Highway 4, rather than bash all the way down to Wellington on Highway 1.

It was a good decision. The road was virtually empty all the way. We had a great day out around Tongariro in 2014, so were happy to be driving back through the landscape there, even though it rained very heavily for a lot of the journey. The drive through Whanganui National Park is spectacular, if a little hairy at times to navigate past the numerous landslips that had caused half the road to disappear in several locations.

Val had a look at Trip Advisor on my phone as we neared the town. **Siena Motor Lodge** was showing as #1 for lodging, so we headed there first. There was no need to look anywhere else. **Ronnie Wheeler's** welcome, ready supply of information and rate offered was more than enough to stop us even thinking about looking for alternatives. Here's my Trip Advisor review.

"If this isn't the best value for money versus quality motel in the world, I want to stay anywhere better"

Reviewed 14 July 2017

Proper full-size rooms in the one bed apartment we had, with outstanding bathroom including massive spa bath.

Good quality furnishings and finish, but best of all is the attention to detail and thoughtfulness that owner Ronnie clearly puts in to the running of the motel; from the arrival 'goodie bowl' to the comprehensive information pack and services such as laundry, high speed wi-fi and restaurant meals available for delivery to your room. Ronnie's recommendation for dinner outside resulted in a superb meal, only a few minutes' walk away. I had a deadline to meet to file an article for a UK newspaper so needed a late departure which was willingly permitted with no additional charges for the room or renewed wi-fi. This motel thoroughly deserves the support of anyone visiting Whanganui.

Stayed June 2017

Whanganui itself isn't the most attractive town in New Zealand, but it's also far from the worst we've seen (Riverton on the South Island's south coast deservedly takes that unwelcome mantle in our view). The next morning, after filing my copy to Telegraph Online, we headed a little way back up Highway 4 to the Whanganui River Road, a circular route that rejoined the highway eighty miles or so north.

The first climb opens on to a stunning view of the river valley. I can see why Ronnie said it's a spot he visits regularly just to sit and enjoy.

However, pleasant as the drive after that mostly is, there are a number of sections untarmacked, including a few where it wouldn't have taken much more rain to make them impassable. Although the road more or less hugs the river side until it turns back towards the highway, it's a long, long time before any more scenes worthy of note appear.

The view from 'Ronnie's Spot' is good even on a dull day

We did stop on our way back down Highway 4 to take a couple of pictures that I really liked.

These sheep coralled together caught my eye …

… as did the light on these trees against the background. Moments later they were dull as ditchwater

Hello, Hello, Hello!

After that it was all the way down to Wellington. Traffic slowed to a crawl as we rejoined Highway 1 at Ohakea. Wondering what the problem was, we soon saw signs for a very large police weighbridge compound; the sort that when they have a blitz on checking lorries, it's compulsory to pull in for anyone ordered to stop by an officer. It appeared that today the focus was on camper vans. I imagined how peeved Lions fans on their way to Wellington would be having to wait, I assumed, for the rather large number of vans in the compound to be checked over.

I later found out from **Annelise Kerr,** who was cursing when called to pull in, that the venue wasn't being used for its primary purpose that day. Instead of weighing vehicles, the local police had set up an operation of an entirely different kind. Drivers ordered to stop in the weighstation were actually leaving a little heavier than they arrived - after being served bacon sandwiches and tea by the officers.

Brilliant idea, perfectly executed, wonderful PR.

Picture courtesy of Annelise Kerr

Heat of a different kind: Hitting Wellington commuter traffic, we arrived a little later than scheduled at **Jo (Cribb) and husband Mike Waterman's** very lovely home.

Jo had wine open and was quite relaxed about out tardiness

Have I mentioned central heating up to now? No? I didn't think so.

Picture courtesy of Jo Cribb

That's because we hadn't seen any. Not a single house we'd stayed in had that home comfort we routinely take for granted. So far we'd either remembered to put one or both of a portable heater or electric blanket on in advance of going to bed... or forgotten to and shivered our way to sleep. The first thing we noticed when Jo showed us the beautiful room we were to occupy that week was that Jo and Mike's house has central heating. No matter it is an old system of air being blown through grates in the middle of the carpets (that I hadn't seen since a girlfriend's house in the 70s in the UK). It was warm eveywhere in the house. Not that I'm complaining about the homes of anybody else who put us up – they were all lovely in so many other respects, and all provided some means to heat our bedrooms.

Mike was with their son, Isaac, at scouts, so we had time for a glass of wine and to help 11-year-old daughter, Celeste, with her maths homework test. I say help, but in reality I think she was really showing us she knew how bright she undoubtedly is by getting us to ask her how she should approach each question. She knew exactly what to do with every one. Impressive work and tactics at that age.

Before the guys returned, the four of us sat down to enjoy a very tasty stew Jo had prepared. I'd checked with Jo that she didn't mind us bringing copious slabs of the delicious Whittaker's chocolate that Shirin had introduced us to. By virtue of her being there when we arrived, Celeste bagsied first choice of the various flavours we'd bought. When Mike and Isaac returned the rest were distributed. We may have been a tad disappointed not to see a single square of it afterwards, but it was a present after all. Jo had told us she loved the picture; Mike seemed less enthused when she showed it to him. No problem – any appreciation, or otherwise, of art is in the eye of the beholder of course.

Mike's a software engineer, currently working on contract with Wellington's bus company to install more smart information at bus stops. Jo serves as a director on a number of public boards, as well as consulting to companies - mostly working from home on a variety of of projects. As you might imagine, a household with kids the age they were has a routine to continue, even when guests from a foreign land arrive, so we quite understood Jo's encouragement to look after ourselves as much as possible.

Jo mentioned she knew Bernadette Courtney, the group editor of Fairfax Media who publish The Dominion Post, the local newspaper. She thought Bernadette might be interested in running a piece about FOCUS ON THE FANS, so before going to bed I drafted an article I thought they could use and an email to send to her.

27th June – 2nd July: Wellington – What A Week To Remember

27th June, Match day 8: Lions v Hurricanes

Next day was a match day against the last of the Super Rugby franchises they would play – the Hurricanes. Another tough gig.

But the big news waking up this morning came from Bermuda. New Zealand had won the Americas Cup for the first time since 2004. The lift to the collective Kiwi psyche was unmistakeable throughout the day. It was definitely the talk of the town all over. At least, it was for Kiwis.

After sending the article and email I'd drafted to Bernadette Courtney, we decided the short bus ride from the end of the road into town seemed our most sensible transport option, so we might have some alcohol while watching the game later on. We started by finding The Tasting Room restaurant, where I'd promised to stand Rory a Beef Wellington. We'd eaten there on our previous trip and had a stupendous meal that I wrote about as part of an article for a national Sunday newspaper. I wanted to check whether we could reserve a table.

Arriving just before midday in Courtenay Place, there were already a twelve-strong group of guys seated at a table in the restaurant. Clearly Lions fans, while I waited for the manager to appear, they introduced themselves as **'The Ginvalids'** from Llanelli. They also told me they had been there since 8am! When I asked why so long, the answer seemed obvious – the Welsh Dragon bar around the corner they wanted to go to wasn't open at 8am. It would be at 12.30pm. They thought they'd wait. As close as possible. Somewhere they served beer. And gin.

When I mentioned that Rory Underwood had written the foreword for my book, **Geraint Evans** told me a story supposedly told to him by Richard Webster, one of Rory's fellow Lions in 1993. Apparently seated next to each other on the flight home, Rory settled in to read two books – each of around a thousand pages. When Rory needed a comfort break, Richard says he ripped the last five pages out of each book, then feigned sleep before Rory returned. I made a mental note to ask Rory to verify that one when I met up with him. He didn't remember.

I was told by the manager that the chef had changed since we were there, but he also promised the Beef Wellington would be just as good. I like such positivity. It suggests to me that people will make the effort to deliver on a promise. I assured him I'd book a table as soon as I heard from Rory.

Super savers: We wandered from Courtenay Place towards the waterfront, as that was where the Fan Zone was to be, outside Mac's Brewbar on Taranaki St Wharf. The seats outside the pub were already nearly full with Lions fans. Apparently we'd just missed some kind of stunt involving a guy dressed as a Buckingham Palace guard, his bearskin and lots of water. Pressed to take a photo of the 'guards' who had remained dry, a few drinkers lined up alongside them.

Two of these turned out to have set what must be a record for the longest period of saving to go on a lions tour.

Neil MacGregor and Tim Manning were both teachers until they retired in 2015 and 2016 respectively. Twenty five years ago, soon after they met and discovered their mutual love for the game, they both expressed the wish to see the Lions play live. Of course, they knew they could never go on a Lions tour while at work because, frustratingly for them, the tour always happens in term time, just before their summer break.

Knowing it would be a long time coming unless a dramatic change in fortune came their way, they resolved to put away whatever they could spare each month for all those 25 years, with a view to being on the first Lions tour after retirement finally came along. Long time friend **Tony Wilson-Spratt** was always part of the plan too.

Tim Manning, Neil MacGregor and Tony Wilson-Spratt finally achieve the dream

Neil, Tim and Tony played rugby for the Isle of Man, coach rugby and watch it as often as they can.

Rugby has always been such an important part of their lives that they have a wealth of contacts and stories to tell, so it's no surprise their account of their tour contains significant elements of both. For example, on their very first morning in New Zealand they met the 2017 Lions Tour Manager, John Spencer, walking around Hamilton on the morning of the Chiefs match. Many years ago Neil, Tim and Tony had all played alongside Mike Burton and John in a guest Isle of Man team put together to mark the opening of Vagabonds RFC new pitch in Douglas. Northampton Saints legend and 1966 Lions tourist David 'Piggy' Powell played for Vagabonds that day. John, they reported, recalled the day very well, and the hangover that followed it.

The guys had bumped into the Lions forwards' coach Steve Borthwick that morning. Tim and Neil reminded Steve of the time his Preston school teams had toured the Isle of Man and he had played against their school as a 12-year-old. Steve apparently recalled them and the trip very clearly and very fondly.

Tim and Neil even discovered a mutual friend in New Zealand they didn't know they both knew. Trevor Barker was leading Queen Elizabeth Grammar School Wakefield's team on tour and the guys happened quite by chance upon his group before the final test. Tim knew Trevor from school cricket tours and Neil knew him from university. Tim hadn't seen Trevor for 25 years; Neil for 40 years. A TV news reporter nearby pounced on them when he heard their exclamations, so the fortuitous reunion was filmed and broadcast on New Zealand's national news – complete with 'Oohs' and 'Aahs' from the Lions fans surrounding them.

They were all staying in Wellington with a former IoM rugby team mate, **Jon Everest;** they met up with **Tony's nephew Simon** - also a former pupil of Tim; went skiing at Whakapapa on Tim's birthday, and took a dip in Kerosene Creek on their way to Rotorua.

Before you start thinking what hardy souls these Manxmen must be to bathe in a New Zealand river in the depths of winter, you should know that the creek's water is naturally heated by the Rotorua area's geothermal energy to around 35°C.

Pictures on this page courtesy of Tim Manning.

Tim very kindly sent me through these pictures at the same time he pre-ordered three copies of the book for each himself, Neil and Tony:

Teachers in hot water   **... with Jon Everest and Simon**

... with Trevor Barker

Happy Birthday Tim   **... with John Spencer**

Val had a mission to buy some Merino wool as a gift for our knitting mad neighbour Louise (she likes knitting, she isn't mad), who was meeting and greeting the three groups of Homelink guests using our house while we were away, so disappeared off to the shops to track the wool down, while I carried on seeking fans to talk to.

There were plenty around. The pubs were awash with fans from early on Tuesday – inside and out, despite the chill.

Passing presents possibilities: Sadly the passing here is not the sporting kind. After Val left, I joined **Jane Shaw**, a self-employed leadership and development consultant, originally from Basildon in Essex. She was sitting on her own outside Mac's Brewbar, enjoying a pint of cider. She told me she had decided to book her official Lions Travel tour only a few weeks earlier, after her aunt passed away. Since a young child, rugby has always been the special link between Jane and her dad, **Derek Lockett**. It's what they did together that no-one else in the family took part in. They still attend Twickenham matches a few times a year. At her aunt's funeral, Derek urged Jane to follow her heart and follow the Lions to New Zealand – and helped her with the cost. Jane's loved every moment, like many others citing the special feeling and ambiance Lions fans create wherever they go as the highlight for her. She rated the atmosphere at the first test as a step up from her beloved Twickers. She also shared a little insight about the game coming up that evening – she'd sat next to Romain Poite, the French refereee and his match officials at breakfast in her hotel that morning. It concerned her a little that they were extremely fussy about their food and coffee, and were short with the waiting staff. She was fervently hoping they wouldn't being that attitude onto the field that evening. Nice lady.

Keith Duffy and Pauline Baxter from Reading owed their presence in New Zealand to Keith's late brother Martin.

His passing earlier in 2017 after a battle with cancer came before he had a chance to fulfil his much talked of plans to see more of the world. It persuaded Keith and Pauline that life is too short not to take the chance to fulfil a dream when the opportunity presents itself.

With some help from what Martin left to Keith, they embarked on their Lions tour carrying a framed photograph of Martin at all times.

Home from home: I wandered over to three blokes sat in the corner laughing loudly. They turned out to be Swindonians – the nearest big town to the village I live in. They were just reliving what they'd witnessed a little earlier that morning while walking along the waterfront. A jogger – presumably short-sighted – was running towards them, but completely missed a turn in the path and tumbled straight into the dock. **Darren Vicat, Gary Marriner and Harry Hoard** were too busy wetting themselves laughing to join in with those fishing the hapless and very wet soul out and were just reliving the moment.

Val returned from her shopping expedition and we went to lunch. While there she began developing symptoms of cystitis, the very, very painful condition that makes urinating feel like peeing razors, but as if to rub salt into an open wound, also makes you want to wee more often. She had to go back to the house, but was happy for me to carry on. While she was suffering in the loo, I chatted to a couple who had just come in for lunch. Their travelling woes made the BA fiasco seem like a trifle, as well as making me realise how little attention I'd paid to what was going on in the wider world while we'd been away.

Crisis? What crisis? Simon and Margaret-Anne Tuke were living in Qatar before coming to New Zealand. They were booked on a flight to Auckland from Doha, but the severing of diplomatic ties with Qatar on 5 June by numerous Gulf states – which had completely passed me by – meant their flight wasn't going to happen. They made fifty-six calls to Qatar Airways before finally managing to speak to someone. All they were told was: "Make other arrangements to get to your destination and wait and see about your return flight." They'd had to buy new tickets to Auckland with BA for £1000 each. When I met them they still didn't know how they were going to leave New Zealand. Credit to them, they were having such a good time they didn't really care, and would cross that bridge when they came to it.

I couldn't believe I don't have pictures of Jane, the Swindon boys and the Tukes. I must have accidentally deleted them somehow. Very sorry folks.

As I left the bar the boys from **Dunvant RFC near Swansea** were demonstrating their lineout techniques for the benefit of fans seated outside. A team photo followed, naturally, until a guitarist/singer on the stage in the adjacent Fan Zone started playing to an audience of zero people. Whereupon the Dunvant boys swiftly decamped to strut/mince/leap/silly walk and generally make fools of themselves to entertain the lonely entertainer.

The entertaining Dunvant RFC

The owners of Mac's Brewbar had set up another fanzone outside one of their other pubs, München, further along the waterfront. I set off to find it.

Matt Lambourne and John Gilfillan were the first fans I'd met who hail from the Isle of Wight.

We were joined by their friend Kevin Manning – 'Manno' – for whom this was his third lions tour to New Zealand. He'd also come over for the 2005 Rugby World Cup.

Matt, Manno and John

You mean there's more than one?

The bar was just heaving too much for me to hold any hope of getting a drink, and the noise meant there probably wouldn't be any point in trying to find people to talk to.

In the square outside five Santas magically appeared.

They explained that Santas have a bit of time on their hands at this time of year, so were taking in a bit of the tour to relieve the boredom in Lapland.

Graham Hill, Gary Evans, Warren Blakestock, Julien Daniels and Mike King were the men in red who temporarily abandoned their elves.

As dusk started to fall and I was leaving, these young ladies were dancing with the lack of inhibition reserved for children who haven't yet developed a sense of reserve, and drunken uncles at weddings who've temporarily lost theirs. With their parents' permission I took a couple of pictures. I handed the parents a flyer so they could send me their email address to enable me to send the pix to them. They haven't sent one.

A FOCUS ON THE FANS fan: By the time I'd found Churchills, another bar in the city centre packed with Lions and Hurricanes fans sharing stories and beers before the game, it was properly dark. I went to the upper floor to take a picture of the busy bar. As I descended, a Hurricanes fan pointed to me and said: "I've been reading your blogs."

Not exactly fame, but the first New Zealand subscriber to Telegraph Online I had come across. I had a good chat with **Charlie Ives** and his pal **Keith Leadbetter** before heading back out to the street, where plenty of fans were also gathered round the outside tables.

Keith and Charlie

This group's laughter hinted at some good banter between the opposing supporters, so I was pleased when one stopped me to read my tabard.

I have a dream! It would have been reasonable on a cold and drizzly Wellington evening to assume **James Della-Porta** sported his woolly hat merely for weather reasons. But that wouldn't strictly be true. He told me one of my very favourite stories of the whole tour.

James had a dream just the night before that he was visiting Waitomo Caves, where a Māori priestess had told him that if he shaved his head the Lions would win their next match. He woke early with that embedded in his mind, and knowing the Lions needed to win the second test, immediately set about carrying out the prophecy by shaving his head.

When he told his **mate Trev** of his sacrifice for the greater good, he got rather short shrift: "You bloody idiot. You should have shaved it tomorrow." In his early morning stupor James had totally forgotten about the Hurricanes match.

That he seriously thought it might make a difference... come on James! A* for Follow Through though.

After the familiar chorus of "Lions, Lions" had sprung up from an adjacent table, spreading quickly to the fans inside, James came out with the view that there really should be a Lions anthem with a little more to it than merely repeating Lions. Hmmm. I said I'd work on some lyrics but haven't managed to yet. Watch this space.

Is there a doctor in the house? Chuckling all the way back to the waterfront thinking about James' so-called sacrifice, I spent the next ninety minutes before kick-off handing out flyers to as many of the thousands of fans who were walking to the stadium as I could – outside the designated clean zone. Rather than delay fans with getting to the match on their mind, I walked alongside quickly explaining FOCUS ON THE FANS, then retraced my steps to pick up another likely group. An hour and a half of tripping backwards and forwards was very good exercise for me.

A couple of groups in fancy dress demanded pictures. I was more than happy to oblige recording their efforts.

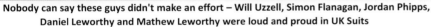
Nobody can say these guys didn't make an effort – Will Uzzell, Simon Flanagan, Jordan Phipps, Daniel Leworthy and Mathew Leworthy were loud and proud in UK Suits

These Irish lads wore red themed fancy dress - they were very late for kick-off but saw the camera and couldn't stop themselves...

Just as I was about to give up and settle down with a beer to watch the game, I saw two guys headed towards me at a very quick pace holding bottles of beer which they swigged at without slowing down – or spilling any. A well practised manaoevre judging by the look of it. With ten minutes to kick off, they asked if I knew how far to the stadium. They were destined to be late for the game as it would be at least fifteen minutes walk, even at their pace. Instead of going off to the Fan Zone I fell into step with them and explained my aim. Perhaps the most incredible story of the whole trip was what I heard next.

Without breaking his stride **Andy Spencer** related how the Saturday before he'd left Eden Park in an ambulance after experiencing chest pains during the first test. A different sort of test had established he needed heart bypass surgery, and would be barred from flying for the next month. Which of course meant missing his flight home, scheduled for twelve days later. He assured me the doctors had discharged him with no more than a "Don't overdo things in the meantime."

After getting his email address I did question where almost running a couple of miles while drinking a bottle of beer sat on the 'not overdoing things' scale. With a cheeky smile and cheery wave he told me he'd be fine. I emailed him after I got back but haven't heard from Andy. I appreciate he has more important things on his mind, so just hope he's as fine as he predicted he would be.

The match: I watched the first half at the Fan Zone outside Mac's Brewbar. Fortunately, you could see the screen from the pub's temporary outside bar, so I was able to also enjoy a beer. There was next to no atmosphere though. Similar to the Christchurch Fan Zone, the couple of hundred Kiwis scattered around the benches were almost silent. That could have been down to the performance of their team – a lack of discipline had been punished by the Lions, who held a 23-7 lead. The game looked dead and buried by half time. I decided to head for Courtenay Place in the break so I could jump on the first bus home after the final whistle.

I enjoyed the second half in The Residence, with a jug of ale and a large serving of very good fried chicken fillets, all for NZ$10. Who says this country is expensive? Despite the disappointment of a tired looking Lions team being pegged back to a draw, it made for a thrilling finale to the game, and cracking atmosphere in the largely Kiwi bar crowd. I headed off tired but content, leaving the two very pleasant Kiwi ladies whose table I'd muscled in on to finish the chicken and beer I couldn't.

Wednesday 28th saw Val wake in much greater discomfort. It was clear she would need to see a doctor. Jo and Mike's usual GP couldn't see her. We found a walk-in private medical centre the other side of the city that opened at ten.

Checking my email, I saw I'd had two messages the day before from a reporter at The Dom Post, asking if I could be available for an interview. I called their office to explain that I'd been out working all day Tuesday, so hadn't seen the messages until this morning. We arranged for me to go in to their offices at noon, thinking Val would be done by then, or if there was a long wait I could leave her at the clinic. Luckily there was nobody else waiting so Val was seen with plenty of time for me to get her back to her bed and get into town in good time for my meeting. After I was interviewed they also wanted to take photos of me, so a staff photographer walked me the few minutes to Civic Square, where I posed in my tabard at the top of the steps taking pretend photographs as nobody was about.

We'd offered to cook a roast dinner that night so I then headed off to Countdown to buy beef and accompanying veg. In the absence of a sirloin the best looking joint they had was silverside. I noticed it also said 'Corned' on the label, so asked an assistant if it was suitable for roasting. She said yes, so I bought it. Back at the house we put it in the oven. Checking progress after about an hour it was evident that this particular joint would be tough as old boots. Jo returned from a meeting a few minutes later and when we told her what we'd done, would have laughed her socks off had she been wearing them. Apparently corned silverside is not a roasting joint. It should only be boiled. A hasty rescue plan was formed, as the veg was all nearly ready. I'd race back to the supermarket, resist the temptation to seek out and re-educate the assistant who'd misled me, and buy two hot rotisserie chickens I'd noticed they also sold. Meantime, Val put the beef into a slow cooker with some stock and hoped it would tenderise overnight.

Dinner was saved; the chicken was very good and we enjoyed chatting to the kids, Jo and Mike at the table before they all disappeared to their evening tasks of homework, work work and housework respectively, while Val and I watched Australian Masterchef five months ahead of the UK broadcast.

Thursday 29th: The medicines Val had bought had eased her symptoms by the next morning. The silverside joint had recovered too and was now the tender, moist succulent and tasty corned beef it was originally intended to be. It's nothing like the horribly processed fatty corned beef in a tin sold in the UK.

The weather was bright and sunny, so we headed out in the car for a little sight seeing. A slowish amble around Oriental Bay to the tip of the headland offers pleasant if unspectacular sea and city views. A steep climb – whether by car or on foot – took us up to Mount Victoria lookout on the most perfect day we could possibly have chosen. Bright sun, no haze and little breeze meant the 360° views were as good as they could be. If only I'd brought my pro camera instead of the very good but more limiting Panasonic compact I'd bought for Val to use.

As Old as the Hills: I was chatting to a couple of Lions fans, one of whom - **Roy Powell** - was clearly a good bit older than his companion. They were part of a fifteen strong group from **Berry Hill Rugby Club.** There should have been sixteen, but **Derrick Symonds** hadn't made it out that day – a victim of man-flu. Remember that.

They had all started walking up the hill to the lookout – as I said, a very steep climb. Roy, I learned when he told me this story, is 79. He was soon struggling, and it quickly became clear he couldn't make it all the way up under his own steam. Passing a house where some major refurbishment was being carried out, one of the team went in the open front door to ask the builder if he would take a break from what he was doing and drive Roy up to the lookout in his truck. The builder happily downed tools and did exactly that.

The Berry Hill boys were a fun and clearly close knit bunch. **John Evans,** the club's treasurer, had organised the trip. He filled me in on Berry Hill's past in the John Player Cup when the club was a National League team in the 1980s. For a few years they regularly reached the stages of playing against the top teams of the day. Their history includes honourable showings against London Irish, London Welsh, Quins and Bath, with their zenith being a victory over a London Scottish team that contained four Lions players.

Roy wasn't looking forward to the effect on his knees the walk down would have, so I suggested we take him and a couple of his mates down in our car and come back to ferry others. I dropped Val off with them and set off back up the hill, thinking I'd catch the group not too far from where I left them. Not so. Figuring they must have taken one of the other roads, I drove around searching for a little while before getting a text message saying they were all back in a city centre pub, having taken a much quicker footpath down than the considerably less direct road route.

We had a quick beer together before they continued their training for the twenty stages of the Wellington Pub Crawl they planned to complete the next day.

Val was struggling again, so we returned to the house. We cooked dinner– well, the veg to accompany the huge corned beef joint, and had a quiet night in.

Friday 30th: Val sensibly thought she should take it easier during the day in case she relapsed on match day, when we knew we'd be very busy. I thought I'd drop flyers into the main bars in the City, leaving piles that we hoped fans would pick up from over the next couple of days. Val would come into the city that evening and we'd try to eat at The Tasting Room. I'd not been able to reach Rory Underwood so hadn't made a reservation.

Every bar I went into was very happy for me to leave flyers. In **Churchill,** the manager **Hayley Pynsent** liked the FOCUS ON THE FANS story and volunteered that she and Lancastrian husband, **Jonny Peel**, were welcoming Lions fans from as far afield as Copenhagen, San Francisco and London.

The last bar I would drop into was München, scene of the second Fan Zone. It wasn't busy at around 11.30am, but there were a few fans around to talk with. Outside I met **Alex and Sally Scott** again. Resplendent as usual in his kilt, Alex had caught the attention of a Kiwi who wanted to photograph him holding Sally's Lion. **Paul Whitham** is a very keen semi-pro photographer who is on the council of the New Zealand Photographic Society. After I'd taken his picture alongside Alex, Paul told me he's been taking a photo a day for seven years. He started it as a personal challenge to improve his photography skills and has just carried on the task alongside the professional work he does, as well as the shots he takes to enter camera club and other competitions.

As I looked in the tent I just caught **David Haller, Kevin Morgan, Geoff Aspinall (from Bolton) and Ronnie Hunter (from Hartlepool)** posing with **Phil Vickery**. The guys were chuffed that Phil allowed them to interrupt him to have his picture taken with all four fans. David and Kevin both live in New Zealand now.

Charlotte-Rose, a waitress in München, arrived with four pints for **David Murphy (Irish), Andy Frewin (English), Rob Edwards (Wales/living in Jersey) John Greatrex** (didn't say where from but I do recall he wasn't Scottish – they couldn't find a Scot to come with them on tour).

Ex- England and Lions star, Celebrity Masterchef Champion and all-round nice guy, **Phil Vickery,** was still in the bar (having a coffee). He explained to me his thoughts on how rugby is a sport that prides itself on its inclusive nature, the culture it fosters, the cameraderie it encourages and the strong bonds created across the world. As for the Lions, he expressed the view that besides bringing four countries together on and off the rugby field, it's the best example of how, even on a highly professional tour, the players get close to some of the 99.9% of rugby people who play and support the sport at grass roots level, and vice versa.

On the question of future Lions tours, all the reasons he mentioned make it in his opinion a unique, very special event for players and fans alike. He personally would like the tradition to continue, and hopes the game's administrators can find time for Lions tours in their scheduling.

Ray Mills, wife, Kim, and son, Euan, were just about to have an early lunch, but had time to tell me they arranged their tour independently after Kim, who works for Standard Life Investments, had won the right to buy tickets for all three test matches in a raffle at work. They had made good use of Adopt-A-Lions-Fan, arranging accommodation in Auckland and Wellington. The following Thursday Euan was scheduled to play in a Lions Fans versus Onewhero RFC match that had been arranged over Facebook. The promise of camp-beds for all Lions fans in the clubhouse - players and supporters - would mean they could celebrate/commiserate as much as they liked after the match without having to drive. Euan had messaged to register his interest but remarked that his parents would probably pass rather than rough it on camp beds. Almost immediately they had an offer to stay in a comfy bed in the home of an Onewhero club member. I never made it to the game but heard a very good night was had by all. For the record, the Lions fans in borrowed kit and boots won 17-12.

More long term savers: Twelve Welsh fans sitting in their local pub in Aberdare got so enthralled by watching the Lions in Australia four years ago, they all decided after the match that they would save for the next four years so that they could be here in New Zealand. Immediately they left the pub, each went to open a savings account at the bank. I met two of them in München.

Like many ideas conceived in the pub it proved a little too fanciful for many when their heads cleared. One by one they fell by the wayside.

All except for **Maria and Nigel Elias**, right, who saw it through and are the only two who made it here from that group. Mind you, they were so staggered by the cost of the official tours when they felt they'd probably saved enough after a couple of years, they sat with a travel agent for four hours and made all their arrangements independently.

They found it easy enough to get hold of tickets in New Zealand, so have been buying them on a game by game basis. They know their friends will regret not coming when they get home and tell the story of the magnificent time they've had on their tour.

Three young men that made a longer term commitment, which all of them have seen through, are **Will Vander Gucht, Jack Cooper and Simon Gateley, left.** They met eight years earlier at Nottingham University. As their mutual passion for rugby came to light, they resolved at the age of 18 to save as much as they could afford each month to fund being on the 2017 Lions tour, whatever paths their careers and love lives followed.

Each spoke eloquently about the camaraderie, atmosphere and unity they've observed and enjoyed amongst fans of both sides as they've travelled around this amazing country. That they saw through a commitment made at such a young age and are embracing the experience fully is no great surprise should you meet them.

By the way, Jack landed at Heathrow at 7am the Monday after the last test and was due to begin a new job with the BBC at 9am. I'm not sure what happened, but his Linkedin page shows him still working at Accenture, albeit in a more senior role.

DIY Ts: As soon as I saw **Adrian and Colleen Rowlands** walking through the Fan Zone with their friends **Paul and Sian Thomas,** I had to stop them. They wore official Lions outer gear, but I'd spotted underneath some T-shirts I'd not seen before. A very ornate gold motif depicted a Lion and a Kiwi squaring up to do battle. They'd had the tees specially made for their trip, and very impressive they were too. The soft toy dragon and lion they carried were known as Delilah and Samson respectively.

Motor mouth! I honestly don't mean any disrespect to the next fellow I talked to by the motor mouth reference. He is a 100% endearing character.

Scott Gregory had his five mates and me in stitches as he told me about some of the great time they'd been having – all related at great pace and seemingly without pausing for breath. One story concerned the white water rafting Scott had arranged on the Whanganui River, a place I talked about earlier.

It was seriously difficult to identify all Scott's words on the voice recorder, they were delivered at such a rate of knots. Hence the odd couple with (?) after them, but here goes my best effort. Gesturing at two of his mates, he set off:

"**These two didn't want to go**, they wanted to go to a spa and play in the mud; we talked them into it; it was hilarious, because back home in Snowdonia where we do it you get an hour's safety briefing before you even get your wet suit on; so we're heading down to the water and he's going to me "Scott, Scott, are they going to give us our safety brief?"; we're in the boat and he's going "When're we gonna get our safety brief?"; they said "This is how you hold the handle" and that was it; next thing you know we're down the first waterfall and before you knew it we're about to slide down a 23 foot drop, so we stopped, he had a chance to get out; he had a panic attack and God bless, we did feel sorry for him, then we took the proverbial, he being **Gary Miller, Neyland (?) RFC**; and he had a shocker and said "I'm gonna do it boys, I'm gonna do it" so myself and Lee Miller, we get to the end of the waterfall, Lee's already in the brace position; **me and Hawaii-5-0 here** are still going for it, we go over the edge, we hit the water and the boat disappears into the water; we got a picture showing it; the boat has disappeared; I'm still in the boat thinking "I'm still in it" and as it starts going up up it launches me out, launches him out, launches him out, this three are drowning, these three are still in the boat; I pop up, I saw him, I pop up, he looks at me like a meerkat(?), "Get me out, get me out"; so I go over, get him back in the boat, it was amazing, one of the best things I've ever done in my life; we peed ourselves laughing – in my case literally, 'cos I couldn't get any wetter but got a whole lot warmer; it's been like that from day 1, we've had great laughs, great laughs."

Scott wasn't kidding about the 23 foot drop either. Here's the evidence, **pictures courtesy of Colin Picton**

One of the other lads mentioned an incident on their way south from Auckland. Just as Scott had said "We haven't seen any police for miles" they heard whooping of Blues and Twos (lights and siren tones) and were pulled over for speeding, for which they were fined instantly NZ$170. One of the Miller brothers shouted "I hope you lose the test!" as the officers walked away. For a moment he wished he hadn't when they stopped... then carried on walking.

Talking of money, Scott explained - once again in his inimitable style - how they fund their drinking. "We start a kitty; we don't put any more in, it all comes from fines; so we have a president which we play spoof for; the president gets nominated, he has an hour, and he has a right damn laugh; we grass on each other; there's no swearing, no pointing, it's buffalo drinking, left hand only, and if you get these wrong you get fined, and the money just keeps coming through, and it's brilliant cos then everyone ends up arguing, you have people going beep, beep beep and they get fined for pointing, swearing and it just goes on until it gets to a certain time when **he** loses the dolly out the pram and starts blubbing, and then the game starts over." Sounds like proper rugby club fun to me.

Lee Miller, Colin Picton, Mark Kenny, Scott Gregory, Sean Grundy, Gary Miller

I headed over to Mac's Brewbar to check out the action there. It was now chock-a-block inside and out. Walking through the Fan Zone, Kim Scott told me a self-deprecating story of how she was in a bar with partner, Peter Longmore, the day before the first test match, next to a group of Welsh fans who seemed excited to be talking to someone she couldn't quite see. As they dispersed, she turned to find herself face to face with the subject of the fans' attention and asked: "Who are you then?" After introducing himself, Scott Quinnell was amused enough to ask if Kim knew the fellow with him. Not a clue. It was Will Greenwood.

Kim was even more embarrassed when Scott told the story against himself when addressing the 4500 Lions fans at the fans' pre-match function the next day.

Phil Birch and Walter Todd are best mates of many years standing, as are their respective sons, **Tom Birch and Alex Todd**. Bank of Dad was funding the tour again, as it had done four years previously when the Lions toured Australia. Tom and Alex rated their day on Bondi beach after the last Aussie test match the best Lions day ever. In the beach bar they met some of the Wallabies team. The boys were very complimentary about the grace with which the Aussies acknowledged the Lions were simply too good for them. They were then jumped on by a young Radio 1 DJ looking for some young fans to be interviewed; after which they remarked it would round off the perfect day if they saw some Lions players too. The radio show's producer said: "There's a few in that bar over there." Sure enough, Ben Youngs, Johnny Sexton, Stuart Hogg, Mike Phillips and Alex Corbisiero were all in there, very happy to chat and – now the rugby was done – drink with fans.

Like every other Lions fan I spoke with, dads and sons were loving New Zealand too.

Some New Zealanders weren't proud of some of their countrymen though.

The voice of the people: Talking to **Sean Ahearne and Ruth Ivers,** I learned that Wellington City Council had fuelled the wrath of many of the citizens they serve by raising the price of a camper van pitch while the Lions were in the city, from NZ$30 per night to NZ$130 per night, and they introduced a minimum three night fee. Sean and Ruth were using Adopt-A-Lions-Fan accommodation. When they were arranging a place to stay in the South Island, a woman responded to their request message saying they were welcome to stay at her B&B for just a thank you as a fee, purely to protest at Wellington Councillors, albeit from a distance.

I heard similar from Wellingtonians while there. **Colleen Munro** was disgusted. She said having the Lions in Wellington was such great fun; they were spending millions of dollars in the city; and she was already counting down the days to the next tour. She planned to publish the names of "all the greedy councillors who voted for this" - her words - "so that the voice of the people can be heard and they can be voted out of office come the 2018 elections." She for one wouldn't forget, let alone forgive. This was after photobombing a shot I was taking of Motor-mouth Scott, The Millers and their mates in fancy suits on the day of the second test. A feisty one for sure, I wouldn't bet against Colleen influencing the election outcome.

I was ready for a break by this time, eased my way through the crowd to the bar, and spotted **Andy Morley**, one of the guys I'd first encountered in The Quadrant in Hamilton, chatting to the **Lions in Pink**. I'd wrongly concluded he was part of **Bello's** group. Over a beer together, Andy corrected me, saying that mostly as a result of encouragement from his kids, he decided at the last minute to join the tour, was here on his own, going with the flow and just joining in when it seemed people wouldn't mind him doing so. He's a really nice guy, so I could understand how people were happy to let him into their gangs.

This group – surprisingly perhaps – proved not to be Lions fans. They were part of a local corporate team building event that just happened to end up at Mac's Brewbar for their post event tucker and booze.

The Establishment fights back: The constant noise was starting to get to me, so I took a little walk in the open air along the waterfront for 30 minutes or so. The sea breeze was getting pretty cold by then, so I turned back to the city, ending up in Courtenay Place. I called in at The Tasting Room – heaving – to see if we could be squeezed in. We were lucky. A table for two would be available about 6.30pm. I texted Val and resumed my stroll. I only just recognised The Establishment pub on the corner of Courtenay and Blair, where we'd had a beer with the Berry Hill RFC boys after coming down from Mount Victoria. How different can a pub be? We thought it soulless on the quiet lunchtime the day before, completely lacking in character. It was now heaving with bodies, louder than Mac's Brewbar and felt a real fun place to be. I checked the manager was okay with me taking pictures as well as handing out and leaving flyers. She was. Back to work.

It was just too loud to even think about getting a sensible recording on the voice recorders, so I just enjoyed the atmosphere, chatted (shouted to be more accurate) to a few people and took some pictures of the good fun Flame Heads on Tour. It's fair to say they were attracting a lot of attention.

Sam Gibbons emailed me after the tour and had this to say about The Establishment:

Having been on 3 previous Lions tours with my Gibbo family, it was only me and my partner in crime - my twin brother - for NZ 2017. What carnage it was.

Wellington, the second stop of Gibbo Twins On Tour, was immense. The Establishment bar, Wellington was by far the best atmospheric place in the capital and what a welcome we received. The gaffer (also known as a Gibbo) and his team was what rugby touring is all about. Singing until the late early morning hours and one or two jars were had for sure, lol - the rugby family as one.

What also made it ultra special was the heroics and history made from the 2nd Test.

Twin brother **Jack** added this a couple of days later:

Jaded, but full of excitement for what was to follow when we landed in Auckland prior to the 1st test. A battle that was lost, and fair play, the All Blacks did their homework. However, the turnaround for the final test was immense! We are both in agreement it was the best rugby match we had EVER witnessed - let alone the series. Part of history!

You may recall Sam and Jack from the first image in the book, which got picked up and used by a lot of UK and New Zealand newspapers. They are the veteran tourist flameheads wrapped in the Union Flag above. The picture above is courtesy of Sam.

"Sometimes you just shouldn't go back": Val had texted that she was on her way, so I wandered along the road to meet her off the bus. We were both really looking forward to our Beef Wellingtons. There was never a question that we would order a different dish. It truly had been one of the great meals we have ever eaten in a restaurant.

I'm so glad Rory couldn't make it. Apologies to all the fans I met that I told to enjoy a Beef Wellington in Wellington at The Tasting Room restaurant. As you already know, in 2015 I raved about it in an article about great meals I'd had in New Zealand, but the chef had changed. My Beef Wellington this time was a huge disappointment. I must say however, there were plenty of happy diners eating other dishes, and the waitress and manager dealt with things brilliantly, although it was the latter who made the comment about not going back to places!

Move over darling: Two weeks earlier we thought we'd found the youngest Lions tourist at Waitomo caves.

Sorry Josie, your reign was short.

In The Tasting Room we spotted an 11-week-old sporting an Ireland mini-kit. Sure enough, mum **Caoimhe** (pronounced Kee-va) **Sheehan** already knew young **Tadhg** (pronounced like Tiger without the 'r') was on the way when she and dad **Tim** (pronounced Tim) had booked to come here.

They live in Abu Dhabi but weren't going to let a trifle such as pregnancy and new infant get in the way of their Lions tour aspirations.

A bus home and an early-ish night after chatting with Jo and Mike for a while saw the end of a day I'd thoroughly enjoyed. Next day would prove even better.

July 1st, Match Day 9: Lions v New Zealand All Blacks, 2nd Test

Lions fans knew only too well that this day would make or break their tour. If the All Blacks wrapped up the series with a win that evening there could be a massive slump in mood for the final week. Conversely, a Lions win would be the perfect script to maintain excitement and anticipation of what would undoubtedly be one of the all-time most momentous of Lions triumphs – winning a series against one of the strongest All Blacks teams ever.

Another text from Jo to say a Welsh Male Voice Choir was performing at the supermarket she was in sent us scurrying to try and catch them. It was all over by the time we got there, but this chap was one of the participants. I can't help wondering what he's got on the front of his shirt to warrant the disdainful look he's getting?

By the time we got into the city the bars were already filling. The tension amongst Lions fans was palpable. Optimism and fearing the worst were two states of mind clearly in as much of a competitive struggle as the rugby teams. We were to get a strong sense that optimists on the Lions side were not quite convinced themselves. Hope would be a better description of what they expressed. Those articulating their fear for the night's result seemed to be steeling themselves to make the most of the coming week anyway, in an attempt to mitigate the disappointment they anticipated.

It didn't stop any of them partying though. Neither did the rain.

We started our afternoon in the München Fan Zone. Even during the walk from the bus stop it was obvious there were a huge number more fans on the streets of Wellington than there had been anywhere before. **Keith Duffy and Pauline Baxter** were the first people we met on the way in to the Fan Zone, now carrying a giant soft toy lion they'd bought, as well as Martin's picture.

Wellington pubs were full again from early on Saturday

Someone had planned ahead well - additional bars and food outlets had been set up in the square to serve the much bigger crowd than the previous day. There was a full programme of very high class entertainment lined up for the stage, but in all honesty, even with their huge amplifiers, performers were going to face an uphill struggle to be heard above the noise of the assembled fans.

About half past midday a queue started forming outside the TSB Bank Arena, the venue for the official Lions tour reception that afternoon between 1pm and 4pm. Too good an opportunity to miss handing out flyers, we stationed ourselves at the entrance point, trying to explain to as many as possible what FOCUS ON THE FANS was all about – principally them. A few wanted photos taken. The Beefeaters were **Geoff Collenso and Gary Plucker**.

I didn't get names of the rest below, although you may recognise the group with the Rhondda flag as they were sporting their gold T-shirts the day before. My thanks to a young man called **Sam Mathews**, (below, top left) who took a wodge of flyers and began passing them down the part of the queue we couldn't access.

After the doors opened we recognised that later arrivals would only be interested in getting in and getting their money's worth of booze, food, rugby anecdotes from ex-players and patriotic sing-songs, so retired under the dripping canopy for a well earned beer. Or two. We met **Lloyd Smith** who had been run over by a taxi in Auckland, which resulted in a fractured fibia. He was going to be allowed to fly home on schedule.

Dewi Jones told us a great **small world story – number 7**. Like many other fans, he'd visited the historic Petone RFC in Wellington. Chatting to the Welsh ex-pat bloke next to him at the bar, the guy mentioned he'd been at Barry College from 1966-1969. The rest of their exchange started with Dewi:

"Well you must know a bloke called Alan Partridge then."

"Alan – he was my best mate in college. I haven't seen him for more than 30 years since I came out here."

"Would you like to speak to him?" asked Dewi. "He's married to my sister."

Dewi promptly called his sister in Coventry. Alan was out, but Sis was flabbergasted to be chatting with him.

Dewi had to grab the phone back after 10 minutes as it was costing him a fortune.

The arrival of **Lions in Pink** caused their usual uplift to an already very lively and spirited atmosphere. They had bred since we last saw them, and now numbered five. Friends **David Johnston**, **Ian Davies and Heath Byron** had now joined them. **Jason Dempsey** would make up the final member later.

Wandering over to München to say Hello to Andy, Stu and their additions to the pride, we could hardly get past the entrance, but got chatting with **Darrell Cooper and Lisa Clemmett**, Kiwis who had caught the spirit and were in full Panda fancy dress, with Lions fans **Lloyd Collier and James Leckenby**. I'm not sure who the Jon Richardson lookalike is.

Stu and Andy emerged and told us they were off to meet with and pay their tribute to **Adam Gilshnan** at a bar in the city.

You'll remember Adam is the founder of the Adopt-A-Lions-Fan Facebook page that had meant so much to so many travelling fans. I wanted to talk with him for my blog, so accompanied the guys to their rendezvous at Café Browns.

On the way we crossed paths with another group of lads who had been high profile in the New Zealand press during the tour.

The Scooter Boys, as they became collectively known amongst Lions fans, had ridden 850km on backroads from Auckland to Wellington on 50cc scooters, with a support driver (**South African, Neil Oliver**) in a van. **Breffni O'Reilly (Ireland)** had recruited **Gary Speak (England) and Adam Barclay (Scotland)** to join him and **Kiwis William Petersen, Ryan Toki and George McMahon** on the three days of wet, cold and slow journey (average speed 40km/hour), which Breffni described as the best of his life. They'd been welcomed with open arms every step of the way – even by the curious policeman who stopped them on the outskirts of Wellington and at first disbelieved the response of "Auckland" to his question: "Where have you guys come from?"

Mid-way through the journey, Breffni got an email from the reporter at The New Zealand Herald who had interviewed him previously. A man in Hawkes Bay had contacted the paper to say he thought he and Breffni might be related and wanted to meet. Breffni rang the guy, who came over to Wellington the day before the 2nd Test and took him and his mates to a funeral – promising them the best day ever! Which Breffni says it was too. Weird but true.

Only the Irish!

Arriving in Wellington on the day of the Hurricanes match, their first night stay was arranged through Adopt-A-Lions-Fan, but they had accommodation booked and paid for the rest of the week. Their first night host said if they wanted to stay with him all week he'd lend them a car and they could have the run of the place. They stayed, had a fantastic time with their host and all around town.

Oh! I nearly forgot. They raised over NZ$5000 for a New Zealand based children's charity. Nice one boys.

I'm not sure what's going on at the rear of this bull!

Redbeard contest! I finish a distant third.

The Lions in Pink and I salute Adopt-A-Lions-Fan founder Adam Gilshnan (maybe I should have had both hands on the camera – that's my water in the foreground)

We were all stoked to meet **Adam Gilshnan**. He's a humble guy.

Just listening to him describe how Adopt-A-Lions-Fan came about was fascinating, inspiring and a lesson in humility, all at once. It was pleasing to hear that one of the Lions' major sponsors had tracked him down and donated tickets for the 2nd test. He wasn't sure if he should disclose who, so chose not to.

During the conversation **Paul Roles** appeared – he'd spotted Stu and felt it was necessary to compare beards. While Stu's is of course naturally red/ginger, Paul's clearly wasn't. But he had enough paint left after colouring his own copious growth to offer to spray my rather less impressive facial hair. When the group he was with heard that, it was inevitable I was going to have to let him. It felt I was getting a serious amount of paint on me but I couldn't see the fruits of his labour until finding a mirror later. I think I was right to be a tad disappointed in your effort Paul. ☺

Paul's tour story didn't end with the tour itself. He swapped his personalised Lions shirt for a Chiefs fan's shirt in Hamilton towards the end of the tour. One of his Adopt-A-Lions-Fan hosts, **Mark Wakefield,** then spotted Paul's shirt for sale on TradeMe, a New Zealand e-bay equivalent. Mark bought the shirt for NZ$90, and is giving it more experiences of New Zealand as he shows it the sights of his home town Taupo and watches All Blacks games while wearing it. He's created a Facebook page for the shirt to show off its extended journey as well. Mark intends to return the shirt to Paul, when he's had his fun.

Paul Roles and Stu James

Above picture courtesy of Annelise Kerr

Annelise Kerr on Franz Josef Glacier, South Island

All pictures on this page courtesy of Annelise Kerr

Malcolm Kerr, Michael Todd and Paul Roles in Hobbiton

Annelise the Lioness, before the first test in Auckland

Back in the Fan Zone, Scott and his crew had dressed for the occasion, and were in fine voice.

When I met **Stuart Rundell and Bob Marks** they had just taken a little stick from **Scott Quinnell** in the fan event they'd just left. He'd admired their blazers, but when they'd responded to Scott's "Where are you from?" with "Ashby-de-la-Zouch, Leicestershire", it was their use of **'...shire'** that Scott decided made them posh, not the town of Ashby's full grand monicker or the blazers.

Matthew Nightingale, Ed Howard, Jamie Flood and Blair McMurray are the four wearing inflatable suits who would later attract the attention of the Kiwi TV director a good deal throughout the match.

Just as they had around the city during the day, having posed in hundreds of selfie requests.

When I found Val again the earlybird fans were beginning to drift off to the stadium. We were ready for some grub, and I grabbed this photo on our way to find somewhere quiet to sit and eat after the hustle and bustle all day. The **Otago Tartan Trekkers (OTTs) are Ivor and Carol Menzies, with friends David and Isabel Halliday**. All in berets made from distinctive yellow and blue Otago Tartan, created to commemorate early settlers to the province, who were mostly Scottish crofters and shepherds.

Papparich on Grey St fitted the bill for our food, Malaysian, in a bright, nicely decorated room mostly occupied by Asians. The food was pretty good, the service a bit haphazard, but not dramatically enough to bother us. Next task was to find a pub we'd enjoy watching the game in. Bars were mostly empty of Lions fans by this time – with less than 40 minutes to kick off even the diehard drinkers had left for the stadium. Kiwi fans hadn't yet replaced them.

The match: We had a look in The George, which earlier was brimful of red jerseys, but now its cavernous space seemed lifeless.

Across the road we were tempted to look in **The General Practitioner (GP)**. We were very glad we did.

It's small inside, with an instantly cosy feel as you walk in – despite there being virtually nobody in at that stage. The place itself has an ambiance that draws you in. Then you notice the array of antique medical instruments beautifully displayed around the room. Most importantly on that night though; what were the tellies like?

They are small, and the one by the bar had a terrible picture. The only other one was also small by pub standards, but the picture was better, although the viewing range was limited by the pillars in the building. Despite the small screens, we liked the feel of the place, and with few people around we could get a decent seat with a good view, so decided we'd stay. By the time we'd got a beer and wine the best table was occupied by a single man – but shifting chairs around the next best table to be able to see better, the man invited us to share his table.

The McGrath Brothers – Peter, John and Danny　　**John with Sophie Freestone**　　**Random Revellers – post match**

A lovely atmosphere in a great old fashioned pub with modern standards

The man, **John McGrath,** turned out to be a brother of the **landlord of The General Practitioner, Danny**. John and **another brother, Peter**, would be watching the game here – and he told us Danny might make an appearance if work permitted. John is a great character.

He described himself as an "itinerant chef". He worked in insurance, finance and merchant banking before opening a ski and surf shop in Wellington. A horse riding school, an event management company and a plethora of restaurants, cafés and bars followed. He has been a film critic for sixteen years and wrote a book titled "Watch this Movie" containing reviews of 1,100 of his favourite films. John was New Zealand's accredited press representative at seven Cannes Film Festivals. He's a freelance writer about wine and lifestyle. He works as an executive chef in the Alps in the winter and on luxury super yachts in the Mediterranean during the summer. You get the sense he's enjoyed life and continues to do so.

He didn't bore us with his life story during the evening. All the previous paragraph is a summary of the blurb about John on the website that sells the books he's written. Unusually for a published author, he urges people not to buy his books. He says he's never been paid the royalties he's owed.

John's very wry and dry sense of humour kept us entertained with banter throughout the early game.

Until the 25th minute.

Sonny Bill Williams didn't so much tackle Anthony Watson as shoulder charge him while he was already being tackled. John and Peter thought it warranted no more than a warning before the slow-mo replay for the benefit of the TMO (Television Match Official). After that, they thought it might just about get Williams a yellow card, and vehemently pooh-poohed my observation that in the northern hemisphere a lot of referees would view Williams' transgression as worthy of a red.

John was apoplectic when the red card was finally produced.

He soon recovered his easy going banter, especially as the All Blacks proved they are nearly as big a challenge with 14 players as they are with 15. In truth, for an awful long time the Lions didn't execute their game plan well, with far too much indiscipline and many errors providing the All Blacks with ten very kickable penalties. Beauden Barrett very surprisingly missed three of the easier of them. The All Blacks would surely have been too far out of sight for the Lions to pull back if those nine points hadn't been squandered.

Nonetheless, it's never over until it's over, and in the latter stages the Lions began to turn the tables, converting their numeric advantage into just about enough points to level the series. Lions fans wouldn't care about the means, just the end.

The GP is far from the nearest pub to the ground, so I was surprised to see fans filling the bar within minutes of the final whistle. It never quite got too packed, and the McGrath brothers - Danny had joined us mid way through the first half - were all excellent company as we celebrated while they drowned their sorrows with wine and some of the very fine whisky Danny stocks. We left the pub in the early hours exchanging mutual wishes that the third test would be everything we hoped for in a game of rugby, and a fitting decider to a series that had already written its prominent place in history.

Of course we both really hoped the other would be stuffed out of sight, but believed it would be much tighter that that in reality. Who knew?

Our best night on the town of the tour. Very tame by most fans' standards, but we had an early start next day.

2nd July: Wellington to Rotorua

Because we'd cut short our first stay in Rotorua, and because we liked Allison and Dave very much, we wanted to take them for a meal. They'd already offered us the opportunity to break our trip back to Auckland by staying overnight with them again. We thought it was a good idea, and that if we did, as I've said, we'd be slightly less imposing on Jo and Mike than we already had been. We arranged to head off early on Sunday morning. I'm fairly sure I was sober enough to drive.

We stopped after an hour or so for brekkie at a café just before Otaki. This **River Cottage** must be as famous for its food as the Fearnley-Whittingstall one in the UK. The small car park was packed, the queue to order long, but the aromas from the kitchen and the display of their home made breads, pastries and cakes just made the wait more enticing than irritating. Our food took a long time to come as well, but you are warned about the wait time when ordering, and there was a ready supply of Sunday newspapers to read or people to watch, whichever your preference. Regular glimpses of the high quality fare to come when plates of food were carried to their eager recipients meant everyone in the place looked very chilled. Well worth a stop if you are headed along State Highway 1 in that area.

Full of Bull: The road was busy with camper vans sporting Lions colours all the way to the curious town of Bulls. With so much signage pertaining to the animal, we thought it must be named after some kind of cattle related activity prevalent in the town – an insemination centre perhaps?

But no, Mr. Google tells us it was named after James Bull, an Englishman who opened the town's first general store way back when. There are some mildly amusing puns on display through the town to describe its amenities: look out for Consta-bull (Police Station), Forgive-a-bull (Anglican Church), Cure-a-bull (Medical Centre) and if you need a comfort break, 'Relieve-a-bull'.

Corny, but perhaps 'Predict-a-bull'.

A little surprised, and grateful, that more traffic headed up State Highway 3 from Bulls than SH 1, we enjoyed the scenic route through the hills alongside Rangitikei River, along Desert Road on the eastern side of Tongariro National Park and on to Lake Taupo. An hour later the familiar sulfur smell welcomed us to Rotorua.

Desert Road

I quickly finished my Telegraph Online blog I'd started before the game, and discovered **Paul Roles** had emailed me a picture of him celebrating the Lions vistory – a Lion on a Lion statue he found in Wellington, right.

Then we had a lovely evening with Allison and Dave, sharing more of our respective histories and a curry in their second favourite Indian restaurant (the #1 was closed for refurbishment).

3rd July: Rotorua to Auckland – the long way round

Next morning dawned bright and breezy. Rather than hack straight back to Auckland we decided on a day by the seaside. The journey to Tauranga on the Bay of Plenty coast was only an hour. It's a city of 125,000, and the approach from the road we took brings you in on the industrial side, so at first sight it doesn't appear that attractive. Track round to the coast and it's a wholly different story. Fabulous beaches are fringed with what looks like high quality holiday accommodation, all leading towards the dominant feature, the extinct volcano Mt Maunganui, standing imperiously above the harbour and city.

It's a lovely place for a good walk round the base of the mountain to spend an hour or more witnessing big waves crashing on the rocks. The trail wasn't fully open so we couldn't get round to see ships carefully navigating the narrow harbour entrance. We decided against the trek up to the summit – for time reasons rather than stamina.

Sandy beaches and rocky shoreline both feature on the coast at Tauranga

Heading north, State Highway 2 hugs the coast before turning inland towards Waihi, from where we went back to the sea along Highway 25, heading towards Coromandel Peninsula. We'd been round the peninsula last time we were in New Zealand, knew it was a long haul with a good deal of untarmacked road, so cut across the bottom end of it on SH25A to a road which really does hug the west coast of the Firth of Thames. We avoided the main road for as long as we could carry on around the coast, eventually reaching Auckland around 6pm.

The sort of five-hour drive where you get out of the car and say: "That was nice."

I hope you have the impression that we adore Shirin. For this third visit to her home she'd arranged to stay with a friend who runs a little B&B. In case you're thinking she'd had enough of us and wanted to escape, I should add that we'd been told of this arrangement months before we'd arrived in New Zealand. Shirin thought the dual benefit would be to give Val and I a little space on our own, and Mairie, her friend, a little extra income after she'd suffered a minor stroke. See why we love her?

Dinner 'at home', a few glasses of Otago's finest and we were ready for an early night.

4th – 8th July: Auckland – History In The Making

America's Independence Day also dawned bright and breezy, so we decided to make a day-trip to Waiheke Island. Ferries from Auckland run every half-hour and we avoided any wait at all by running to board with seconds to spare. Amazingly, we discovered as we boarded that the woman with a pushchair who ran ahead of us to the ferry had given birth just six hours earlier. I asked what time she was due to start work that day and got a severe look before she realised it was meant as a joke.

The forty-minute trip drops you at Matiatia Bay ferry terminal, from where we thought we'd take the Scenic Bush Walk into the main settlement Oneroa. After not too many squelchy steps through the standing water on the grass we reconsidered our plan and walked the twenty minutes or so to Oneroa along Oceanview Road. We thought this road was rather misnamed. Once you've turned the first bend from the ferry after about 200 yards, the ocean isn't visible from Oceanview Road in any direction for most of its length.

As you reach the centre there's a little complex on Korora Road with a community art gallery that's worth a look in. There are some really nice works amongst the paintings, photographs, ceramics and sculptures on show, all by local people. The adjacent library is a very modern building that apparently split the community when constructed. Personally I love its box design with vertical wood planking and large expanses of glass.

Oneroa is a pleasant little town with a steep descent down to its large bay, itself overlooked by a variety of lovely properties. There are a few shops and cafés to while away an hour or so, but most people visit the island for its wineries. There are many vineyards that also have restaurants bookable for lunch. My experience of vineyards in Australia earlier in 2017 was that the wine was more expensive where it was made than in supermarkets down the road. It seems to be the same in New Zealand. The French and Italian concept of selling from the cellar door at more favourable prices seems to have lost something in translation for Aussie and Kiwi producers. With no middle men, no end retailer mark up and no transport costs to pay, I struggle to be persuaded that I should pay extra for the privilege of drinking from the premises where the contents were produced. Their food is usually ridiculously more expensive than high class local restaurants too. NZ$50 for a plate of bread, cheese and ham doesn't rate as good value in my book.

We opted instead to jump on a bus and visit the famous **Charlie Farley's** beachfront restaurant and bar at Onetangi Bay. We rather preferred the look of the menu in **The Boathouse Café and Bar** a few yards along though. Either is a stunning place to have lunch, especially when the temperature on a sunny winter's day means sitting on the deck in tee shirts and listening to the ocean not five yards across the road. Until the sun went in and the breeze got up sufficiently for the few Lions fans to don their heavy waterproof jackets they'd earlier discarded.

We had a marvellous, languid and not a little indulgent lunch in The Boathouse, with three courses of super food, very good wine and great service.

As we were leaving I got chatting to a couple of fans relaxing at an oceanfront table, and was taking a photo of **Andrew Ward and Ewen Johnstone** when I realised I'd left my flash in the bag Val was carrying. I needed it to fill in the dark shadows the bright sun was creating. Val was in conversation with a couple of blokes at the table on the level above us. Apparently my request to pass the flash down to me was quite abrupt according to **Nick Hillyard and Roger Meadows**, as when I made my way back to Val, they took the mickey out of me royally for treating her like a lackey. They were jesting of course, and we got into conversation about our respective trips.

Nick and Roger are lifelong school friends from the UK who have both lived in a variety of countries, but have made the effort to keep in touch. Roger still lives in the UK (Chichester) but has a house on Waiheke so that he and his wife can meet up with their daughter, who lives in Auckland. Nick and his wife live in Sydney. They have got together at all of the Rugby World Cups since 1991, combining their rugby with another shared passion, playing as much golf as they can possibly fit in. Which is what they were also doing on this tour.

The day after playing at St. Andrews (in Hamilton, not THE St. Andrews) they went to the surf beaches at Raglan on the west coast. Whilst driving, they spotted a beautiful golf course with ravines, water, sea views… and hundreds of sheep on the fairway, although only a few are in the photo below. Nick and Roger stopped at the clubhouse to find out more. The sheep help to keep the grass short, but also cause a few issues, illustrated well in some of the local rules, which include:

i.   Always clean your ball but don't lick your fingers

ii. If your ball lodges in a sheep's arse, you can take a drop within two club lengths, without penalty

We spent a very agreeable afternoon in the excellent company of inveterate golfers and epicureans Nick Hillyard and Roger Meadows. Clearly no dress code at Raglan GC!

They spotted another course on their way back from New Plymouth also inhabited by hundreds of sheep. On this course though, greenkeepers on quad bikes cleared the sheep from fairways and greens at the holes where people were playing. It struck me that more than a few sheep and lambs must be hit on the head by golf balls. I imagine mutton and lamb dishes feature heavily on the clubhouse menus.

They had played some high quality golf courses, including the Jack Nicklaus designed one at Kinloch on Lake Taupo. At $235 a round it's extraordinarily expensive by New Zealand standards, although the guys describe it as a very challenging, beautiful course – and far too difficult for them!

Roger plans his trips meticulously. His philosophy is that **"Life is too short to ever have a bad meal"**. Therefore he researches cafes and restaurants, looking at menus and wine lists, then creates an Excel spreadsheet recording the plan for each day of his trip. This will include where they'll have breakfast, lunch and supper, along with times and locations for coffee breaks inbetween. They book restaurants ahead so there is no possibility of turning up to find their destination without a table for them, and potentially having a bad meal in an alternative eaterie. He also includes accommodation, expected kilometres travelled and anticipated costs for each event. Before Nick departed, his wife - knowing Roger well and surveying the spreadsheet he'd sent across - wryly observed that on day 13 of their trip, they would – shock, horror! - only have a 30 minute stop for coffee! Whilst Roger admits this level of planning might seem a bit anal to some, for him it is part of his pleasure of coming away and ensures he enjoys exactly the trip he expects. Can't argue with that.

Pictures on this page courtesy of Roger Meadows

Such forward planning has its advantages. They didn't want to miss out on the Lions NZ 2017 tour, so both became members of Auckland Blues two years earlier to take advantage of getting preferential rights to buy tickets. Knowing they had tickets guaranteed, they were also able to book accommodation well in advance.

Nick told us that in previous world cups and Lions tours, fans and players come to Waiheke Island largely because it has several world class restaurants as well as its forty vineyards. The Fullers ferry we'd travelled on was the one Manu Tuilangi had infamously jumped off after England's exit from the RWC 2011. Roger was horrified that we hadn't visited any of the vineyards, and promptly offered to drive us to a couple of his favourites, after a whistlestop tour around the island's best viewing spots.

A generous offer we had no intention of refusing.

After we'd stopped at a few viewpoints Roger headed for Mudbrick Winery, above right, where we greeted Andy and Ewen again, then enjoyed a very fine if not very generous glass of shiraz. The beautifully crafted terraced gardens offer superb views that extend across the harbour to the city. It was nearly dusk so Roger suggested we squeeze in one more vineyard, where if the sunset was to be as dramatic as it seemed it might be that evening, this would be the place to capture it on camera.

Batch Winery was pretty much closing down for the evening by the time we reached it. I suspect Roger is well known there though, as the manager was very happy for us to while away time chatting over another glass of fine red. Nick told us he'd won a competition in 'Duty Free' magazine, the main trade publication for the industry he used to work in. They ran a worldwide sweepstake inviting readers to guess the correct result of the second test score in Wellington. The prize for this was three bottles of very good whisky. Which led us to the conclusion that the best way to finish our day would be with a quick snifter of a single malt until the rather less than hoped for sunset finally fizzled away.

Roger raced us back to the ferry terminal where once again we timed our run to the just-about-to-depart boat to perfection. On the way, having talked up the sunsets, he promised to send me some of his favourite sunset pictures – no doubt taken while sipping fine wine.

I think he might just have wanted to make me a teeny bit jealous.

You succeeded my friend.

On the ferry I saw that Rory had emailed to say he'd been so tied up in Wellington with the friends putting him up and work that he hadn't been able to fit in meeting with me. We agreed to have lunch the next day.

Wednesday 5th July started with a mix of showers and sunshine. Val and Shirin went to the art gallery we'd tried to visit during our earlier stay, then on to lunch in the city. I did some work until it was time for me to leave for North Harbour and collect Rory from the wonderfully located but reasonably budget hotel he was staying in right on the harbour. From there we went round to Devonport to a café he knew.

A private audience with Rory Underwood: After the preliminaries of how we both came to know Robert Taylor, and Rory describing the work he was doing with NZRU on the tour, I told him about Al Pearce's Civil Service story and my 'audience' with Warren Gatland, as he hadn't seen the article. That led to discussing the Lions future viability. You'll recall that Warren's case for their continuance was passionately emotional, so it was really interesting to hear a more dispassionate view from an Aviva Premiership club non-executive director – Rory's on the board of Leicester Tigers.

It's an undeniable fact that in these days of Rugby Premiership, clubs invest much greater sums into their players. Rugby clubs don't enjoy the astonishing income from broadcasters their soccer club counterparts do, and rugby players may not enjoy the stupefying riches of even average footballers these days, but they are paid pretty well by their employers. (Interesting aside: The Football Supporters Federation pointed out that after receiving the latest hike in broadcast fees, all twenty Premier League clubs could have let fans in for free all season, and would still have received more revenue than they did the previous season. They didn't do any such thing of course).

With increasing demands on squads from European competitions, there are many more pressures on the elite rugby clubs to manage their commercial and playing resources over a much longer season than in the past. Rory recalled that his domestic season in 1993 had ended on 1st May with a Pilkington Cup win over Quins. He joined the Lions squad with almost three weeks to prepare for the tour to New Zealand, which comprised thirteen matches. The final fixture of the 2017 club season, the Premiership play-off final, took place on 27 May, only one week before the first of the ten Lions games arranged for the tour of 2017.

The 1993 Lions tour finished earlier than this year's too, leaving players with more time to recover and prepare for the approaching new club season, which started later then as well. Rory expects Lions players of 2017 are unlikely to be available to start at least the first two matches of the new season for their clubs. Those with injuries picked up on tour could miss considerably more. As a businessman himself, Rory understands the desire for owners and chairmen of Premiership clubs to maximise the return on their investment. Club Rugby is undoubtedly a business.

Pictures on this page courtesy of Roger Meadows

With his former player's hat on, like Phil Vickery, Rory also feels that there should be a place and a future for the Lions. A balance must be found that allows for players and fans from four nations to produce and enjoy the highest level of elite rugby that can be brought together internationally. If the commercial necessities of professional club rugby and international unions dictate that has to be in the form of shorter tours, so be it.

I really enjoyed hearing the views of someone with huge experience of and passion for the game, who also has to take into account the commercial realities of professional sport. It made for great, balanced insight, that I hope will prevail amongst those charged with determining international rugby schedules. Like any situation where there is potential for conflict, we agreed there should be a willingness from both sides to find a solution that best serves the players and fans.

As we left the café Rory said to me: "What is it about New Zealand houses? Why don't they have bloody central heating?"

Thursday 6th July: My late Mum was a forgiving soul who always tried to see the best in people. She'd never have dreamed of raining on anyone's parade. Her birthday, though, brought rain with a vengeance to the Americas Cup victory parade through Auckland. The fickle mistress I talked about earlier – Auckland's weather – was up to her malevolent tricks. Bright enough to tempt tens of thousands on to the streets in the hours leading up to the commencement of the country's greatest national celebration in years; once we were all jammed into place with virtually nowhere to seek refuge, the heavens opened. And stayed open for hours.

Just before the downpour started, on our way past an obvious outside broadcast radio van on the waterfront, I stopped to ask the woman standing by the van, **Belinda Hanley**, who she worked for. It was a part of New Zealand Media, who own the national newspaper The New Zealand Herald. I had my Auckland media badge on from the previous visit, so when she asked, I explained about FOCUS ON THE FANS. Belinda liked the story, so asked if I would like to do a piece to camera for the newspaper's online streaming channel, Focus TV, and an interview for Radio Sport with Tony Veitch, the guy covering the parade. Tony came out for a chat as he wasn't on air at the time, was also very enthusiastic, and said we'd talk the next morning to set it up.

Despite the downpour, virtually every boat behind the security fences of the marina had a party in full swing onboard. I figured someone might take pity and let a member of the press aboard, where I could take shelter, something Val had very wisely decided to do for at least a while. I managed to catch the eye of **Alexis Reeves** on **Darleen**, a small, rather old looking boat amongst the gin palaces all around. There were a dozen or so people around and on Darleen, all supping beer from the numerous bottles piled into cool boxes on the slip. Alexis came up to the gate, listened to my plea to be allowed access so that I could get better shots when the boat parade started and welcomed me through with the insistence that I join the party and took a beer. I discovered that many of the assembled group worked with a company called Southern Spars, and had built part of the Kiwis' winning yacht. No wonder they all looked and sounded pleased as Punch. A slight easing of the rain for a while allowed me to take a shot of these history-makers aboard Darleen, who I learned is well over 100 years old. She looks good for her age.

Talking of ages, it was taking an age for the heroes to transfer from their bus parade to their boat parade. There were speeches to be made. In the meantime, two former Americas Cup winning yachts sailed past us, one carrying a group of Lions fans, who had booked it especially from the company who now operate the yachts as a tourist attraction offering pleasure trips.

Thinking there might be an even better vantage point further down the marina, I ventured nearer to where the parade boat would depart. With very narrow views from the rear of the massive boats, I thought I'd see if I could see more from the end of a slipway. The owner of **Dock Holiday, Dave Horsburgh**, spotted me and invited me to join him, his fiancée Juliet and her two children aboard his wonderful boat. Dave was enthusiastically waving a large US flag, which he saw as irony, but I suspect many of the thousands around the harbour who didn't know any better might have interpreted it as defiance from a defeated Yank. Finally, speeches over, the crew and Americas Cup appeared and set off on a very slow tour of the harbour amidst a cacophony of cheers and boat horns, creating a spirit that no amount of rain could dampen.

Dave is an Air New Zealand pilot on the Heathrow run via Los Angeles. We've been in touch and he intends to drop by on one of his layovers soon so we can catch up. Here's a selection of images on the day New Zealand turned out to honour its latest sporting heroes, mostly taken from Dave's deck (top left).

Alexis, kneeling, and his Southern Spars heroes

I felt so sorry for the Māori canoeists. They were sitting out on the water in the very worst of the weather for at least two hours. Even if it's as cold as the conoeists must have been, skin is waterproof; unfortunately cameras aren't. With the downpour strengthening I decided the better part of valour was to go find Val and get home to a change of clothes. She too was soaked, despite taking refuge in the waterfront's book-swap tent along with as many others who could squeeze in.

It continued to pour down all afternoon so we stayed tucked up at Shirin's until taking her and Mairie out for a meal. Shirin had chosen her favourite Italian restaurant, Bosco Verde in Manukau Road, Epsom. It's a cosy little place that very much reminded Val and I of the Italian restaurant within walking distance of our first house in Slough, the main reason we frequented La Fontana far too often for our own good, but couldn't resist. The food here was very similar – authentic and very delicious. It's BYO with no corkage charge too – a good idea when local wines are so expensive. Mairie proved a hoot as well, with that admirable lack of inhibition and disregard for protocol that often makes the aged with sound faculties so amusing. Despite her stroke, Mairie's faculties were definitely sound.

Friday 7 July. I hadn't heard from Tony Veitch by mid-morning so emailed Belinda. On the bus into the city I got a reply suggesting we meet at their offices at 3pm. We filled the time before that by walking round the waterfront bars to drop off more flyers ahead of the game on Saturday.

At 3pm I did a single-take video interview with **Tristram Clayton** for Focus TV to go online, before recording a single-take fifteen minute interview with Tony for broadcast on Saturday morning. On the way out, passing The Hits studio, **Stace and Flynny** were on air, and started waving wildly to me as I walked past the glass wall of their studio. I was surprised, but I suppose they have to be good at remembering people in their walk of life. I was also touched.

Jason Tikao, their producer, called me into the studio to see how things had been going. I told him the story I'd just told Tony about **Robbie Regan**, a guy I'd bumped into walking to the studios. He was staring at my tabard and realised I might be interested in his tale. Unable to commit to coming on the tour because of work, he'd watched the second test the Saturday before at home in Wales. As soon as the Lions had clinched the game he went to the travel agent, booked an extremely expensive flight to New Zealand that arrived in Auckland at 11am that very Friday morning, would be watching the match on Saturday and flying home on Sunday. Over sixty hours of flying for eighty minutes of rugby. He rationalised his actions as: **"In any other circumstances nobody would ever fly to New Zealand for 2 days. Once the series was level I felt there was no option but to be here. What choice did I have?"**

Jason thought it nuts but nice, and fed it to Stace and Flynny for broadcast straight away. Three media moments in one day. No wonder I got recognised twice on the streets next day!

Robbie was more in need of a reviving beer than being immortalised in camera. He'd quickly disappeared into one of the crammed bars where I'd already left flyers.

In my last drop-off before going to the studios, O'Hagan's, these guys stopped me in the tented area before the pub itself to ask about The Telegraph.

After telling me their names: from left, **Steve Thompson, Stephen Thompson, Simon Richards (aka 'Tart') and Will Thompson (aka 'H'),** Simon delivered a very deliberate and succinct summary of their tour, that spoke volumes more than the words themselves.

"We've had a fantastic time."

8th July, Match Day 10 – Lions v New Zealand All Blacks, 3rd test

On that Saturday morning Auckland was undeniably the mass of red that Rory speaks of in his foreword.

It's still a small world: It once again seemed remarkable that within the multitude of red shirts, inside the first hour we would encounter four lots of fans we already knew. I couldn't have been more delighted that the very first Lions fan we crossed paths with after stepping from the bus was **Roy Powell from Berry Hill RFC**. Who was with him? **Derrick Symonds**, the absentee from Mount Victoria in Wellington. So now I had met the full Berry Hill crew.

Do you remember I said to remember Derrick's man-flu?

After I got home, their mate **Spike Powles** sent me a picture. When I asked him to remind me of Derrick's surname, Spike told me via a Facebook message a somewhat different story to the man-flu one we'd heard:

"We'd had a late drink till 4.30am after the Hurricanes game on Tuesday. We got home as the dust carts were going through the middle of Wellington. We've never seen him from then till the Saturday of the second test. Derrick locked himself in his room telling roommate Roy Powell that he had serious man flu - nothing to do with the 2 bottles of scotch he had drunk on Tuesday."

You can decide which version you believe.

The picture Spike sent me is below left – happy with the result in Wellington.

A couple of seconds after leaving Roy and Derrick, we took the chance to chat with **Robin Harrison**, right, who swears that drink had nothing to do with him stepping off a kerb in Auckland and breaking his ankle.

His pal **Andrew Palmer** (the first of two further APs I'd meet that day) is a born and bred Kiwi, but Robin emigrated here 22 years ago. Ordinarily an All Blacks fan now, he swaps back to his homeland roots and supports the Lions when they're in town.

It was a lovely sunny morning to be wandering round the streets of central Auckland amongst the thousands of fans.

For this group on the left it's just as well that the weather was as benign as we'd witnessed on the whole tour. Three of them - **Holly Redfern, her dad, Colin Thornewill, and Holly's boyfriend, Jordan Lovatt,** had been skydiving that morning.

Holly's mum, **Louise Redfern,** had passed on the opportunity.

I'd stopped them because of their big bow ties I'd spotted coming towards me from a distance.

Colin Thornewill, Louise Redfern, Jordan Lovatt and Holly Redfern

It was a pleasure to meet Lions Rugby COO Charlie McEwen's very engaging godchild **Barney Tibbatts and his dad, Shaun,** in Auckland for the game with Barney's equally engaging best friend **Thomas Grafton and his dad, James**. They were keen to be photographed not just with their dads but also with a couple of guys who happened to be walking past riding their lions. A couple of days later I received this message from them (written by Thomas).

Hi!

Our names are Thomas Grafton and Barnaby Tibbatts. We are both from England and have been best friends since day 1. We both grew up in Hong Kong and then Thomas moved to Singapore in 2017.

We both have a deep deep passion for rugby and Barney also loves to swim. Thomas also loves to fix cars. We have a funny story to share to you guys during our experience in New Zealand.

So yesterday 7/07/17 we went to this place called the fun zone where there was a bouncy castle which was rugby related. During playing at the place this reporter came along who told us that this was going on TV so obviously we had to join in. During his report he told the camera that he was going to race us two on the obstacle course and since we were the only kids there we realised it was us. So the reporter did a countdown from 3 2 1 and we were off.

Everybody got past the tyres easily, and a tube which we got through - not easily but we managed. We were all tied at that point and we had to get through this hole with some kind of Long ball at the TOP. So Barney got through with ease and so did the reporter (surprisingly) but Thomas got stuck. He pushed, he pulled, but he was not moving.

At that point Barney had already finished and won the race (no surprise). The reporter finished second and then there was Thomas who was still stuck halfway on the course.

Everyone thought it was hysterical.

I asked for some help and Barney came and pulled me out. But there was one problem, Thomas's jeans have ripped in the most uncomfortable place (you probably know where). And the camera just had to zoom in on where my jeans have ripped.

That's our funny story of our tour so far.

Thank you.

Thank you so much boys. Brilliant. I hope the rest of your stay was as much fun.

Outside **The Occidental** pub on Vulcan Lane we met **the Leighton family** once again. Their bad news had continued – their hire car had been broken into the previous evening. The children's rucksacks containing all their work while away had been stolen, together with Max's camera gear. Once again, they all looked remarkably upbeat in the face of adversity. That was partly due to the fact that Max, convinced his luck must turn, had won a sizeable bet he'd made and put the proceeds towards tickets for the final test. I'm very pleased to report Max emailed a couple of weeks later to say that the rucksacks had been recovered with their contents intact. The camera gear wasn't.

Just moments later, while photographing the splendour of the Household Cavalry Regiment Blues and Royals blazers sported by **Jim Evans, Alan Rose and Nick Flynn,** the Scottish pair we'd enjoyed meeting at Auckland airport, **Sandy Geddes and Norrie Flowers,** emerged from the pub. They'd found soft toy Kiwis to replace the defeated Wallabies, and were confident they would bring the Lions the same sort of luck that evening.

We elected to make a quick sojourn into the pub for a single beer – honest.

While Val sipped hers I made a quick round of the fans inside. **Sam Lawrence** was with a group of his mates. He's forgotten to email me their names.

Andy Beller didn't forget to email. In fact he sent me the background to him being there with **Kelly Brennan-Kleyn and Lee Donald**, along with a sort of explanation of how he had summarised a typical week during his trip as: **"2 days rugby; 2 days travelling and 3 days doing what I'm told."**

As a forty something single bloke, and on the advice of my mother, I thought I'd indulge the dream of taking myself on a full Lions tour. Somewhere between booking the trip and departing, a friend that I'd met through work became more than a friend. Whilst broaching the subject of buggering off around to the other side of the World to follow "some rugby team" (Kelly is an American; "I don't need to understand rugby, we've got proper sports") she asked two questions: "Does the motor home have heating?" and "Will we be going to Cloudy Bay?" (more statement than question I feel). An additional flight was booked and my mid-life crisis had been gate crashed!

What an amazing trip, as most of us Lions fans this year will probably say, as most Lions fans probably say every four years.

We hiked trails, cycled old railway lines, drank wine, ate great food, more booze was consumed and then every few days I'd bugger off from the campsite to go watch The Lions.

When we first arrived in Auckland at the end of May there had just been an extra release of tickets for the first test. Our host, Lee, who we were staying with for the first few days wanted to get some but was stuck in a meeting at work so Kelly jumped to the rescue and clicked refresh until tickets were confirmed for herself and Lee.

The First Test against the All Blacks and Kelly's first ever rugby match.

It was decided by the missus that I'd stay sitting with the same people I'd watched all the matches with rather than swap my ticket for Lee's.

The reports back from Lee after the match.

"Can I drink?" was the first question Kelly had uttered; then "Can I shout 'Punch him in the face!'" was the next question.....

We met at the stadium after the game and I had an almost mute girlfriend. I think she enjoyed herself.

During the second test, about 50 minutes in, I received a text message:

"Why are you giving away so many penalties away.......?"

Hooked!!

It's beginning to sound like love to me. Great.

Kelly, Andy and Lee thrill-seeking at Lost World Adventure Caving, who have given permission to reproduce this picture

The Novocastrians were a sizeable and fun group. Professor Andrew Walton embarrassed his elder daughter Ciara by mentioning his professorial status when furnishing me with his name. Ciara's been living in Australia for a year, and had travelled to meet her dad and little sister Colette, who had just graduated from Leeds Uni.

Sir Colin Chater (as he introduced himself, perhaps a friendly dig at Prof Walton?) is a director of Novos RFC, and proudly told me the club boasts the very lovely (my words, not his, but I'm sure he'd agree) England Ladies Captain and 2016 World Player of the Year, Sarah Hunter, amongst their former players. I'm indebted to Sir Colin for the names of the rest of the entourage: Holding Flag: Shaun Stewart; Back Row Left to right: Deborah Baird-Palmer, Prof Andrew Walton, Gillian Chater, (Sir) Colin Chater; Front Row: Rachael Yost, Nadia Rokan; Right side back to front: Rachael Bass, James Bass, Andrew Palmer, Ciara Walton, Colette Walton.

Mike Cutt with sons Frasier and Toby – smelling good

On the way out we discovered some fellow Northumbrians. **Martin and Karen Armstrong's** Lions tour was part of the celebration of their 25th wedding anniversary and Martin's 50th.

Then we exchanged brief greetings with **Jordan Howes and his grandad** on Queen Street on our way to meet Mike Cutt and his boys in the Fan Zone.

If it all sounds whirlwind and whistle-stop, that's because it all felt that way that day. We got a sense of urgency in fans everywhere for the daytime to pass so the rugby could begin and the pre-match tension finally be eased.

Consequently it was very pleasant to sit down for an hour or so while all around was still frenetic, catching up with Mike on what's happening in our lives and on mutual friends (particularly the love life of mutual friend **Ralph Peters),** and picking Mike's brains on Lions tour destinations. South Africa was his favourite.

Mike then had his NZRU hospitality to go to, which that day would feature Rory as a speaker. We were peckish and decided we rather liked The Occidental, so would return there for some lunch.

As we were leaving the Fan Zone, we met sisters **Rosie and Patricia Cray,** left. Having completed their own make-up and that of boyfriends **Peter Nash and Andrew Pointon**, they were merrily painting the faces of anyone who asked them to…

… while their dad **Steve Cray** pranced around nearby in a blow up rampant lion, right.

After eating in the pub my eye was drawn to **Francesca Padley's** clearly self-made Lions cap. She and partner, **George Collins,** explained they have been living in Auckland on a working holiday visa, trying to earn sufficient to tour the rest of the country before returning home. They don't have much saved yet, but the fever pitch atmosphere when Lions fans hit town for the third time in 5 weeks made them want to be a part of what was going on around them. They decided to spend the little savings they had on third test tickets, bought through a reseller. They figured it was the opportunity to take away a very special memory of their time in New Zealand.

George told me recently that they were called to the box office when they tried to get into Eden Park as the gate attendant said there was 'an issue' with their tickets. Fearing the worst, that they had wasted their precious savings on fake tickets and wouldn't be able to get into the ground, it actually ended up that they were moved to prime seats five rows back from the touch line. He also reports that they were very glad they spent the money – it was truly a night they will remember for ever, and one that has made them dream of returning to experience a full series in twelve years time.

Just as we were leaving, **Neil England,** left, looked very happy to be wedged in the doorway with four lovely blondes who readily accepted his invitation to be photographed with him.

Daren Parsons, Steve Pitts and Chris Baker, his three mates outside the pub, were glad he'd just got the beers in rather than being on his way to get them.

Lion glove puppets **Llew and Leo,** right, had been on the whole tour in a camper van, had met Scott Quinnell in the Sky fan van, had flown in a helicopter to the top of a glacier, and now introduced me to their friend **Ceri** and her friends outside the pub. One of Ceri's friends had heard my radio interview with Tony Veitch that morning.

They showed me some brilliant pictures they'd taken on their phones. It was suggested they make a Christmas card of one on top of Franz Josef Glacier, but they weren't sure how to do it. I offered to do it for them but haven't heard from Ceri or her friends, or been able to trace them.

The Final Fan Trail: It was nearing 5pm so we figured people would be starting along the 4.2km Fan Trail from Queen's Wharf on the city centre waterfront to Eden Park.

This would be our last chance to hand out flyers. People were obviously intent on getting to the ground so we didn't ask anybody to stop for photos, just walked alongside and chatted briefly where we could. It was impossible not to feel the excitement and sense of expectation. The vast majority of Lions fans seemed to feel a victory tonight was written in the stars.

We hadn't walked the Fan Trail previously, so enjoyed seeing the entertainment that had been laid on along its entire length. As well as food and drink outlets, street performers, roller skaters, bagpipers, cheerleaders, light installations, a DJ, drag artistes, hip hop and fire dancers, the Clan Celtica Drummers and Celtic Flyers band provided ample distraction for fans, adding very much to the wonderful party mood.

Outside a busy bar along the way we were greeted with cheers as my flash drew the attention of those squeezing in a last beer before going to the ground.

In a final tribute to the romance of rugby, on the edge of that throng were newly engaged couple **Orna Nicholl and Conor Manning**. Conor had popped the question on tour.

With a good sized diamond by the look of it. (Proper Preparation...)

Orna's sister **Keara Nicholl,** below, wouldn't be drawn on whether she expected her partner **Julian Shaw** to follow suit. Neither would Julian.

In the same bar, Val called me across to say hello to another Gatland. **Warren's sister, Kim Petersen, was with her partner Geoff and nephew Tim**

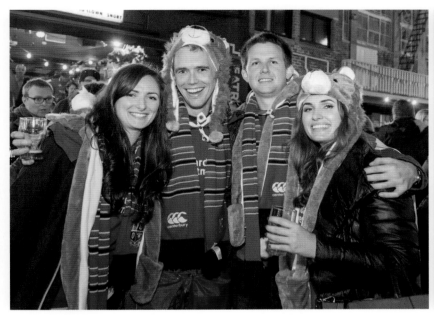 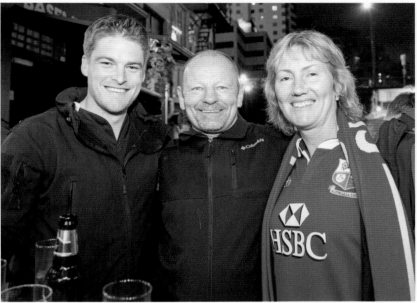

On Karangahape Road and the Great North Road I couldn't resist snapping some of the throng excitedly making their way towards the ground. Numbers and noise had swelled greatly as fans converged in the urgency to reach the ground before kick off. Lions fans easily outnumbered and outsang All Blacks supporters.

Holly Foreman was very excited just before the game - and apparently loves Neil Jenkins (as she told me many times ☺)

Lions fans dominated the streets to the stadium

Plenty of fancy dress along the fan trail

That's what you call a real Lions flag - fans on the way to the stadium

One should dress appropriately for such an important match - perhaps one should have shaved too

The final match: Without tickets, we opted to watch in the same pub where I'd enjoyed the Blues game 5½ weeks earlier, The Dominion. The match was intense – the All Blacks constantly hammering on the Lions door, looking for a breach, mostly repelled by incredibly committed defence. With the Lions always chasing the game, two moments stood out for me. Elliot Daly's monster penalty from well inside his own half, and Owen Farrell's 47 metre penalty in the 78th minute to level the scores. The first provided a monumental boost to the spirit in the stadium for the remainder of the match - both for his side and for the watching Lions fans. Farrell's kick was executed by a player whose all round game hadn't on that day been up to his usual standards, yet he was able to channel any nerves or anxiety, summoning the composure to do what he's proved over many years to be one of the very best in the world at.

Of course, they nearly blew it by not securing the restart after Farrell's successful kick, which led to the remarkable turnover of a penalty award that would otherwise have handed the All Blacks victory on a plate. Sam Warburton's intervention with referee Romain Poite was an object lesson in captaincy. It gave the official time to reflect, perhaps on the whole series rather than the moment, but who will ever know? Only him. Perhaps it was Jérôme Garcès, the line judge, who used the time to reflect. Most credit him with the intervention that prompted Poite's turnabout. Either way, nobody can really deny that under the laws of the game the All Blacks were robbed. However, most of the many fans from both sides I spoke with afterwards and since, accepted Poite had probably reached the right conclusion for the series by the wrong route.

It led to the curious and unusual situation of players at the finale of a tumultuous and most enjoyable series of rugby matches wandering around the field wondering what to do, and an eerie silence in the stands. It brought to my mind the scene that Bob Geldof described after the Wembley end of Live Aid finished, and which became the title of his autobiography; a youth outside the stadium asked him: **"Is that it?"**

Fans would have relished the prospect of extra time, or a decider. But perhaps M. Poite inadvertantly got it just right. The subsequent intermingling of the players on the podium epitomised the great sportsmanship and respect for the opponent that exists in this toughest of sports. The joint raising of the trophy symbolised the respective strengths of the squads and coaches cancelling each other out on and off the field.

We walked home through the rain hand in hand, very happy to have been in New Zealand again, having thoroughly enjoyed what I am certain will not be our last Lions tour.

9th July - 12th July: Full Circle

A fond farewell: Val definitely had tears in her eyes bidding Shirin farewell. I understood completely. Shirin had proved a generous, delightful host and fascinating person to come to know. We very much enjoyed trying to reciprocate and learning even more about her when she spent a week at our house in September. We will definitely remain in regular contact.

We closed the loop on our journey within New Zealand by returning to its starting point, Mike and Colleen's lovely Whangarei house.

I spent the rest of Sunday writing the last blog for Telegraph Online and catching up with necessary admin. I was rather pleased with the opening to my final blog.

"And now, the end is near..."

...and for the Lions, the final curtain was definitely drawn.

On the Monday we enjoyed a last magical mystery tour, starting with the long way round on the fabulously scenic coastal road to Russell, the first capital of New Zealand. It's a nice little place to while away a morning. We took the tiny car ferry back to Opua, then headed all the way across to sample the west coast scenery on our way back south, traversing back to the east coast along SH14 to Whangarei.

A long circular journey that left us wanting no more than a meal, some wine and to crash out. All three easily accomplished in a very relaxed end to our trip in the home that had seen such a marvellous start to it. Here's a little of the scenery we encountered on each coast.

East coastal route from Whangarei to Russell

Omapere Bay on the west coastal route

On Tuesday 11th July we returned to Auckland at a leisurely pace, checked in to the airport hotel we'd booked and had a slobbish day, ready to be up long before dawn for our flights home next day.

Post Script

The vast majority of commentators and writers about rugby have hailed the Lions of 2017 as valiant warriors who defied the expectations of the majority of the rugby world and so nearly achieved what no other team has done for 23 years; defeat the All Blacks in consecutive test matches on their own turf. (France in 1994 in case you're wondering).

That they did so in the most challenging and gruelling of tours has rightly written their place in Lions history as one of the finest squads ever to wear the shirt, shorts and socks that symbolise the parts this group of players far exceeded the sum of.

We fans were proud to be there to witness their achievements on the field, wonder at the marvel of nature that is the host country and celebrate together the unique sporting entity that is The British & Irish Lions.

Val fell in love on this tour. With the culture and game of rugby. So much so that she wanted to go to a live match when we got home. Her anniversary present a month later had to be tickets for the new Aviva Premiership season's curtain raiser, Gloucester taking on champions Exeter at Kingsholm. What a game at which to be introduced to live rugby. Seven tries on the scoreboard in a feast of running rugby, the decider coming in the last seconds of overtime in favour of the home team. Cue wild celebrations from most of the 15,500 present.

When you're amongst more than 20,000 people congregated in a far corner of the world, you can only speak to so many of them. In trying to portray the experience of being a Lions fan on tour, this book has, by definition in one sense, only scratched the surface. That holds true just as much for every other fan as it does for us; our unique experience will have been different to the unique experience of every individual who travelled to New Zealand and donned the red jersey. We hope, though, it's given a flavour of the millions of conversations and stories that will have been shared amongst the thousands who made the trip we didn't get to meet.

We all have a common bond though. We were there. I'd like to end with a few accounts from fans who reached out after hearing about FOCUS ON THE FANS on tour, on social media or by word of mouth. Each tells their own story; why they embarked on their Lions tour; what was important and memorable about it to them.

I'll start with a telephone conversation I had with Colin Picton – friend of the brilliant Motormouth Scott I met in Wellington. Colin gave me the names of the rest of the group just before the book went to print, and told me another couple of stories.

The guys - against the strong advice of a local who told them not to be tempted because of treacherous conditions - went the shorter route over the mountains to Queenstown from Wanaka without tyre chains. The pass we didn't take because we didn't have snow chains. By the time the guys went over it was considerably colder than when we were there and there was plenty of snow and ice. Colin hated driving up the mountain. When they stopped to stretch their legs on the peak of the pass they all got out – to see their people carrier slide off on its own as Colin had unwittingly parked on black ice. It was a desperate (and I imagine hilarious) struggle for the six of them to manhandle the car across the ice back to the road rather than it fall off the edge of the mountain.

I've driven in mountains a lot in France. When it's icy and snowy, driving down them is a far more hair-raising and much riskier challenge than going up. Colin agrees. He was scared out of his wits nursing the van down to Queenstown at a snail's pace, with his foot almost permanently on the brake rather than the gas. He swears the brake discs were all so hot by the time they got to Queenstown they were glowing orange.

The fellas nearly extended their time in New Zealand by an extra day. Walking into a bar in Auckland the night before they were leaving they happened upon a table of six ex-All Blacks, among them Andrew Mehrtens. Apparently the Kiwi legends were generously buying food for anyone in the bar to share. When Colin and his mates reciprocated with jugs of beer for the ABs, they were invited to pull up chairs and join them. A very messy and enjoyable night was enjoyed by all well into the early hours, when the Kiwis began to encourage the guys to stay another day. Apparently missing their flights was seriously considered, but somehow through the haze of booze and bonhomie with their new found friends, good sense prevailed and they went straight from the bar to the airport to suffer their hangovers.

All the words in the following emails and the related pictures sent to me are courtesy of, and copyright, the sender. I'm enormously grateful for both. Apart from highlighting names I have largely left the messages exactly as they were delivered to me – in their own words.

Hi Ken,

I saw your post on FB via the Unofficial B&I Lions Tour page and I wanted to share my experience of the NZ Lions tour.

Around 2 years ago my husband (then fiancé) and I decided that we wanted to go to New Zealand for the 2017 Lions tour for our honeymoon (we were due to get married in Sept 2016). Around the same time that we had decided this, my parents and mother-in-law also declared that they wanted to go to New Zealand. My dad had recently retired and had always wanted to do a Lions tour. So we all decided to go together - my husband and I staying in a motor home and our parents staying in hotels.

In June 2016 I found out I was pregnant with our first child - a little unexpected but not unwanted. So our honeymoon would now be with the addition of a 4-month-old baby. Thankfully the fact that we had arranged for a motor home whilst out in NZ meant that we would have a "home-from-home" and we wouldn't need to keep packing every few days to change hotels. It was also now an added bonus that all his grandparents would be out there too!

We got married on 17th Sept 2016 at Llanerch Vineyard and it was a perfect day (apart from the fact that I couldn't drink). We asked our guests to contribute to our honeymoon fund if they wanted to give us gifts, and they were incredibly generous. Their contributions helped us enormously in affording the trip of a lifetime for us.

On 20th February 2017 Joseff James Hubert Esposti was born. After a couple of months he was already attending Cardiff Blues rugby games at the Arms Park and away in Caerphilly, so whether he likes it or not he will be a rugby fan!

On the 19th June we flew out to New Zealand. Joseff was great on the flights and slept most of the way, with only the occasional wobble. After a couple of sleepless nights once out there he settled into a routine quite quickly and was brilliant - he took it all in his stride.

We had tickets for all three test matches. We'd bought a baby-carrier and ear defenders for him, so the noise at the games didn't upset him. He was fantastic. He slept through the first test (who can blame him?), and he was awake for most of the second and third tests. He attracted a lot of attention at the games. I don't know whether people thought we were brave, cool or just mad! I'm not sure I even know.

It was definitely challenging bringing a four-month-old baby to the other side of the world and living out of a motor home for three weeks, but neither of us regret it. We had such a wonderful honeymoon and I wouldn't change a thing (well, maybe the score of the final test...). Having Joseff there made it even more special, even if he won't remember a thing about it! We'd like to go back in 12 years with him so he can experience it properly.

I've attached a photo of the three of us at the second test and one of just Joseff. I hope this is the sort of thing you are looking for. Let me know if you have any further questions or want more information/pictures at all.

Thanks,

Jo, Tony and Joseff Esposti

Pictures on this page courtesy of Jo Esposti

A chap called **Simon-James Smith** contacted me in mid-August after getting wind of what I was doing. He is completing a similar project, but over a longer period. It's focusing on fans attending international rugby on a wider scale than just the Lions. However, Simon-James was in New Zealand for the tour and has kindly allowed me to reproduce some of his images here. Thanks.

The picture on this page courtesy of Simon-James Smith

Pictures on this page courtesy of Simon-James Smith

Honours even

Picture on this page courtesy of Simon-James Smith

A dream can come true – if you wait long enough

My personal Lions journey began in 1972, when, as a young teenage boy, I attended a presentation by Carwyn James** at Ystrad Mynach in the Rhymney Valley. The school hall was packed to listen to Carwyn's take on the victorious '71 Tour, which already had mythical status in the world of rugby.

My own interest in rugby was fuelled by the success of the Welsh team of that era, along with the daily sight of one of John Dawes' Welsh rugby shirts in our school presentation cabinet. John Sydney Dawes was a former pupil of Lewis' School, Pengam and revered captain of Wales and the '71 Lions team. As a 14-year-old, it's not difficult supporting a team that wins so often with such a fast and flowing style. For their time, the Welsh team were on a par with the All Blacks of today.

I recall Carwyn describing his coaching style, based on adopting the right approach for each player. Some would need a fire and brimstone lecture, others a nod and a wink. This appreciation of the individual's needs within the team was an important lesson for this 14-year-old to learn. So was the potential for a team of people being greater than the sum of their individual strengths. (Another lesson I learned later as a Welsh and Leicester Tigers rugby fan was how much more I valued victory after experiencing many years of defeats!). These lessons have resonance in so many parts of our lives.

Of course, back in 1972 the prospect of actually following a Lions tour to the other side of the world was the sort of impossible dream that only a starry-eyed youth could dare to consider. At that point in my life I had rarely left Wales, never mind crossed the equator. 45 years on and I have achieved that impossible dream, helped along the way with some significant doses of luck in my life. Not least of which was my wife **Sheila** taking an interest in my rugby passion! It was she who declared that the 2017 Lions trip should be our joint 60th birthday present.

And what a present! How many sports teams can muster 20,000 fans willing to travel half way around the world? And not just for a one-off match, but for several weeks of matches. All those red Lions jackets, shirts and flags certainly made their presence felt around the country. To experience a Lions Tour in New Zealand is to participate in a nationwide festival of rugby. The Kiwi public and the superb Lions Tour organisation played their part in making this such a memorable trip.

And I will never forget the feelings of joy, relief and wonder when that final whistle blew in the Wellington test. (It surpassed even those of the 2005 Welsh victory over England, with Gavin Henson's late 44 metre touchline penalty. Any Welshman will know that's saying something.) We went mental! This Lions team had beaten the mighty All Blacks in their own backyard and I was there….

Suddenly our presence on this Tour took on a new meaning. The hype around being the '16th man' could actually be true and our investments in travel, clothing and vocal support had really made a difference. How wonderful it was to see a group of individual players work so hard for and with each other; and with so little time for preparation. Hats off to Warren Gatland and the whole back-room team in making it happen.

** Carwyn James was coach of the victorious 1971 Lions

Pictures on this and the following page courtesy of Andy Toy

Whilst so much of the world has changed since 1971 – such as professional rugby, cheap air travel and the internet – I find the ethos of the Lions remains the same. In their bid to achieve a sporting miracle the Lions players combine to deliver a performance so much greater than sum of the individuals.

Andy Toy 25th July 2017

Hi Ken

Our tour was an amazing experience in a country where Rugby is at home. Got to meet some of the past and present national rugby stars also there for the series. Unforgettable experience and a privilege to be part off. Celebrated at best with your friends - Martin & Helen!

Kind Regards

Caroline Mc Glone

A Munster fan, Caroline is secretary of Perth Irish RFC, for whom she also plays. That's Perth Australia, not in Scotland. Caroline sent me the following pictures, featuring her friends **Martin Downey** and **Helen Sheridan** as well as herself.

Pictures on this page courtesy of Caroline McGlone

Left: Caroline with Helen – note 'EDIT & SEND' is the wrong way around. I flipped the picture Caroline sent so you could read the shirt logos the right way around!

Below: I thought this must be a famous ex-All Black prop, but it turns out he's Taniel Palu, a bouncer at the hotel next to Eden Park.

Pictures on this page courtesy of Caroline McGlone

*My wife, **Claire**, and myself travelled for the full six weeks and attended every match. We were accompanied to most of them by our son, **Liam**, who was spending his Gap Year working in New Zealand at King's College, Auckland. Great meeting you in Dunedin, Wellington, and Auckland. What a fantastic tour. Best wishes with the publication.*

Graeme Cook

The Cooks also took in some scenery and experiences amongst the rugby.

The picture on this page courtesy of Graeme Cook

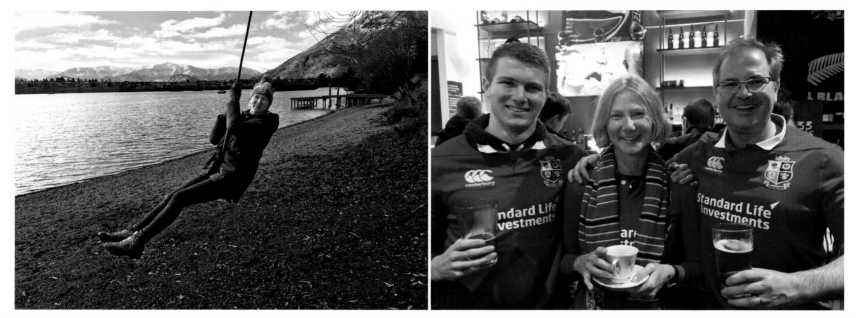

Pictures on this page courtesy of Graeme Cook

Hi Ken

My sister and I were both born and bred in Great Britain. My sister born in Cardiff and me in Solihull England. 22 years ago my sister married a Scot and moved to Hong Kong. 19 years ago I married a Kiwi and moved to New Zealand.

My sister and her family have come over for the Lions Tour – we make an interesting crowd. When we stopped at the Big Cow pub in Te Poi on our way to Hamilton from Te Puke (pronounced pookie not puke ☺) my husband led the way in to the pub wearing his All Blacks top followed by us in our Lions and the people there thought he was our tour guide!

We got group photos in the Anann bar in Te Puke on the way to the game. I've attached my fave one of me and my sister... and one where my daughter photo bombed us with an all blacks scarf.... And a group one - although I'm a bit cut off that one it's the best group one we have.

My cousin Jon and his son Murray were also going to the Chiefs game – making their way up from the Dunedin game in a campervan - typical tourists. I hadn't seen them for 15 years when Murray was just a toddler. We arranged to meet at the stadium (we started at the Speights Ale House but it got too mobbed) ... we went inside to the food and drinks area then found out Jon and Murray were on the opposite side of the ground and security wouldn't let us move to each other. So we watched the game knowing we were all there and looking forward to the big reunion after! I think one of us has a group photo of that event but am still trying to track it down.

I'm sure there are more exciting tales than these to be included in your book but it's nice to share them. Looking forward to seeing the book when it's published.

Cheers

Pam

Pictures on this page courtesy of Pam Tod

Hi! So many great memories, but a moment which summed up the atmosphere for us was arriving in Wellington to see all the airport ground staff wearing "Lion Tamer" high vis jackets. Not only did they pose for pics with us (in our lion onesies) but they gave us our own jacket to keep!!

Our group would all agree that the Kiwis were the most hospitable hosts you could ask for. Nothing was too much trouble and our trip was full of fantastic experiences with both old friends and new. After the Lions beat the All Blacks in the second test, we weren't too sure how the atmosphere would be in the bars afterwards but it was still great and more than one All Black supporter remarked "A win's a win, mate". ***Emma Francis***

Emma Francis, Sara Vesey-Holt, Steven Francis and Kelly George

Emma and Sarah

Emma, Kelly and Sara

Emma and hubby Steven

Pictures on this page courtesy of Emma Francis

Maggie Lord sent some pics and this response to my enquiries about them – with a remarkable story of how they travelled to the third test.

Hi Ken

The stadium was Westpac in Wellington, the atmosphere was electric, especially with the score, although the last few minutes were uber stressful. The walk back into town in the pouring rain was an absolute scream, a sea of red with Lions supporters singing and dancing in the rain, splodging in puddles and chanting 'Lions, Lions' all the way.

The second pic is outside the Novotel at Ellerslie, Auckland. We were waiting for the coach to take us into town for the 3rd Test, it was late and stuck in traffic. So we decided to dress the Lion up in suitable kit while we were waiting. Then guess what turned up? Only the Lions Team bus for us! The driver had taken it upon himself to pick us up as he was in the vicinity. So we travelled to the match in style. Brilliant. We did have some quizzical looks en route though!

We met some fabulous people in NZ. Lions supporters and natives, all with tales to tell, such good company and we had lots of laughs along the way. We loved NZ, we only managed to travel around the North Island but will happily go again to visit the South but in their summer months.

Kind Regards

Maggie

Yorkie and Maggie Lord from Morpeth, Northumberland

Pictures on this page courtesy of Maggie Lord

Pete Jones emailed to send me some pics, but like I often do, forgot to attach them. When I contacted him to let him know, we had a brief exchange of emails in which I explained I'd brought back a bit of e-coli from New Zealand and was laid up for a while after we got home. Here are his comments on the tour.

Hi Ken,

E-Coli that's bad nasty stuff ...... there were plenty of us that went down with the flu and sickness bug and it managed to wipe me out for about 4 weeks in total. Hope you fully recovered. **(NB: the second petri-dish proved negative 3 weeks after the first bred a colony– Ken)**

I don't know exactly what you are looking for Ken but I have just put a few lines together to see if it helps ..... I'm sure you can reword things and make it sound a lot better than I have put down. **(NB: I haven't reworded – Ken)**

*Fantastic 3 weeks spent travelling around the North Island in a Motor Home with **Phil Miles** and **Mick Payne**. We were also joined for the 3 Tests by **Ash Barker** (Ex Pat from Wellington), all of us mates from our RAF days.*

*Like many other touring Lions fans we wanted to make the most of our time on the island and managed to visit many of the recommended tourist hotspots between the Test matches. From visiting friends **Chris & Leon Shouksmith in Army Bay, Whangaparaoa**, walking the Treaty Grounds in Paihia & Bay of Islands, then on to Taupo, Wellington, Rotorua, and a quick stop off to see **Auntie Christine** in Tauranga & Mount Maunganui as we headed back for the final test, a brilliant time was had by all. Everywhere we went we were made to feel more than welcome and the locals couldn't do more for you.*

Again, like probably many we had the pleasure of bumping in to friends that we hadn't seen for many, many years as well as making many new friends amongst the thousands of touring Lions fans and New Zealanders along the way. The memories, the country and the wonderful people of New Zealand will stay with us forever, but the one thing that will stay will me the most was the brilliant atmosphere, friendly rivalry and banter throughout the whole tour - especially on game day .... it was electric!!

Best regards

Pete J

Mick Payne, Ash Barker, Phil Miles & Pete Jones – Auckland
1st Test Fan Zone just after their appearance on NZ TV News
Pictures on this page and following page courtesy of Pete Jones

The guys with 'a lovely local lady' (Pete's caption)
1st Test morning in a very wet Auckland

The very dapper Mick Payne

Mick, Phil & Pete - Auckland, night prior to 3rd test having been to watch RNZ Navy v RAF Vultures played in horrendous conditions at RNZ Naval Base Devonport

On 18 October 2017, just after I announced the availability of the online version of the book, I received a message from Gerard Geenty (aka Gersh, aka 'Arold to his Richmond Good Old Boys (GOBS) mates. **"Is it too late?"** Well the printer hadn't yet been instructed, and Gersh had a reasonable excuse for being tardy - he'd only just got back from the tour. Hence this becoming the 2nd online edition already. Let him explain.

For the Lions tours of 2009 and 2013 I flew the 27 miles from Saba, in the Dutch West Indies where I live, to St Maarten to watch each of the test matches in a sports bar (no TV rugby on Saba), having to stay overnight for the South Africa games because of the time difference. Not ideal. So in July 2013, I decided that for the 2017 tour I'd fly the 8,500 miles to New Zealand instead and watch all the games live. By the end of August my other half, Emilie, was coming too and an 8 week tour had become a 5 month world trip.

Four years in the planning; four years of anticipation; four seemingly endless years of waiting; and then we were off. A bit like the Lions Tour itself.

*On 16th May 2017 we left Saba on the last flight to St Maarten; the following day we flew to LA for a week; then Fiji for a week; finally arriving in Auckland on 30th May. We were based in Auckland with very old friends, **David and Tammy Muir**, who had organised the whole tour for us: match tickets, flights, rental cars, hotels – everything - our own 'South Pacific Tours'!*

Auckland was already filling up with red shirts and there was a buzz in O'Hagan's pub even on 31st May. We drove up to Ruakaka and celebrated David's birthday on 2nd June, having celebrated mine the day before, and on the Saturday we got into Whangerei sensibly early to soak up the atmosphere in the pubs before walking to the ground. Maybe 2,000 Lions fans; a shaky start to the tour; but a win.

Back down to Auckland on Monday and a couple of visits to O'Hagan's before preparing for the Blues game in the Portland pub. Not enough beers to prepare us for the disappointment of the first loss of the tour though and against the supposedly weakest of the Super Rugby teams – as David kept on reminding me.

Flew down to Christchurch on Friday and we were shocked and saddened to see a city still very scarred by the earthquake of 2011; we visited the Wall of Remembrance, erected in tribute to the 185 who lost their lives on that February day; then we started to meet the people of the South Island – and they had not been cowed by nature's wrath.

It was difficult to buy beer or wine in Christchurch – it seemed that wherever we went the locals wanted to buy us drinks and to talk about where we came from, the tour to date and the matches to come. Wahoo, Christine, Brian et al – we thank you for your hospitality. And Lions supporters too, like Sen, an Indian Scot, who on first meeting we couldn't understand a word he said – perhaps we hadn't hydrated sufficiently.

The following evening, we were in uncovered seating in the West Stand at the AMI, warming our hands on the famous 'Brat Dogs' as the Lions' aggressive defence and fast line speed suffocated the Crusaders. The final whistle saw a 12-3 victory over the strongest Super Rugby franchise (as I would point out to David later) and the tour was off and running again; a crunch night, pivotal in the run-up to the Tests.

*We drove down to Dunedin, overnighting in a freezing Tekapo, with our own Billy mascot sat proudly on the dashboard. Our accommodation in Dunedin was run by the friendliest management we were to come across; the pubs and restaurants were awash with red; we ran into Sen again, bedecked in Tam-o-shanter, Lions shirt and kilt – and this time we could understand him! I think the Guinness helped. The weather, however, was less friendly with lashing rain and Antarctic wind-chill: thank God the match was indoors. In the ground we sat next to **Wayne Tacon** from Poneke Rugby Club in Wellington, who invited us to a seniors' tournament at his club on the Friday before the second test. The match provided some great attacking play by the Lions and produced 3 tries but unfortunately the 23-22 loss reflected a lack of killer instinct at vital moments. At least Wayne was happy with the score line.*

A drive to Queenstown provided us with 3 days 'off', as it would the Lions squad later in the tour. After a quiet night with David and family back in Auckland, we drove down to Rotorua on Saturday 17th June for the Maori All Blacks game – another defining moment. We stayed at Cozy Cottages – I'll not elaborate – and had General Admission tickets which allowed for standing on the steep banks of the stadium – great for goats, less so for Lions. A heavy drizzle which soaked to the skin did not dampen the spirits nor quell the "Oh Maro Itoje" chants as the Lions triumphed 32-10. The evening was further enhanced by Warren Gatland signing the Saban flag that we were taking to every game – and indeed on our whole trip.

One week to go before the First Test: a Saturday 'test' side seemed to be emerging; they were playing expansive running rugby in attack; the fast line speed in defence had suffocated the Crusaders and the Maori; we had Jenkins-esque kickers in Farrell and Halfpenny; could we win the series? Or was I becoming delusional?

On to Waikato and a convincing 6-34 victory over the Chiefs. More significant than the victory were the performances of Lawes, Daly, Williams and Nowell: one wondered whether they had done enough to leapfrog their Saturday-side oppo's.

Thursday's announcement of the Test squad left me surprised to say the least: Warburton and Itoje on the bench; O'Mahoney captain; Kruis and Alan Wyn locking; Halfpenny and Sexton on the bench; Williams and Teo starting; and George North not even in the 23. It wasn't so much the picks and absentees that surprised; it was more the unexpected pragmatism of Gatland and the ruthlessness with which he dropped his faithful Welsh stalwarts, giving preference to players who'd shown real form. Perhaps after the dropping of O'Driscoll in Australia I shouldn't have been surprised.

The day before the First Test, we attended a QBE Lions Charity Luncheon at the North Harbour Club with John Spencer, Bryn Gatland and James Parsons as guest speakers (more signatures to add to the Saba flag). As we mingled and chatted with other guests prior to sitting down, it became clear that we were a rare breed: we were in fact the only Lions supporters present amongst the 300 or so that sat down to lunch, John Spencer excepted. However, once again the hospitality and friendliness shown was exceptional and at the end of the lunch we were invited to join a large party of club members at a local hostelry; needless to say it was a most enjoyable but messy evening.

Match day, First Test: we took David along for lunch at The Lone Star, North Shore to catch up with old buddies from Richmond Good Old Boys – the GOBs – Fat Tony, Shagger, Damo et al plus another dozen or so friends and family. A well lubricated lunch ended at 4pm, from whence Emilie and I headed to O'Hagan's to ensure we stayed hydrated for the game. Can't begin to remember how many times the band played Delilah and Sweet Caroline – but that's what Lions touring is all about. Train to the ground (more singing) and met up with David – the ground at least 30% red. The game was difficult to explain: we only had about 40% possession; we played well without dominating; we scored perhaps the greatest test try since Saint Andre's in 1991; the All Blacks didn't look unbeatable; and yet we lost by 15 points. A typical test match against the AB's – as David frequently pointed out - and a hangover of downcast despondency. Perhaps I had been delusional.

I refused to be depressed though, as win or lose I was living the dream that I'd had since 1971 of following a Lions tour in New Zealand; so what if it wasn't a winning tour. With that in mind, on Monday we drove down to Wellington for the match against the Hurricanes before the all-important Second Test. We had a great stopover in Taupo on the way down, contributing significantly to the local economy, before arriving late afternoon on Tuesday with time only to drop our bags and head off for the game.

A coldish, though dry evening brought outstanding performances from Lawes and Henderson which helped the Lions to a 14 point lead; however Hendo's yellow card led to the Lions drawing the game 31-31 with Biggar missing a last minute drop-goal opportunity. Had Lawes done enough? Had Hendo? We'd have to wait and see.

Some Richmond GOBs were in town and we made the Leuven Bar on Featherston our HQ. Evening drinks with Fat Tony and Tom Stokes, a GOB and also Operations Manager for the Lions, afforded the opportunity to drop the Saban flag off with him in the hope of getting some players to sign it. At the Leuven, as throughout our New Zealand odyssey, we were to meet and get to know a complete cross-section of very friendly and knowledgeable locals: from current and ex-players to parliamentary lobbyists, not forgetting the fantastic bar staff.

Thursday's team announcements were another bold move from Gats. The long talked of pairing of Sexton and Farrell in the 10-12 slot – which in our opinion was a gamble he had to take in a test we had to win; the return of Warburton (though at 6 not 7 – how could you leave O'Brien out?); inclusion of Itoje at the expense of Kruis; and Lawes making the bench. The AB's had two enforced changes. We were generally happy, though the consensus was that we'd have paired Itoje with Kruis.

We tried to fill days with visits to museums, art galleries and rides up the cable car – anything to delay getting on the 'pop'; but ultimately we found ourselves back at the Leuven Bar. On Friday lunchtime we joined several hundred locals and Lions supporters at Poneke Rugby Club for a seniors' tournament which featured Gavin Hastings as MC and player; a Lions supporters side did so well that at times the opposition had more than 20 players on the field – perhaps the test side could learn something from this. A big thank you to Wayne and his club for their marvellous hospitality.

Inevitably, Saturday 1st July found us brunching at the Leuven; by 2pm it was a heaving mass of red and black with animated conversations only interrupted by orders for more rounds and choruses of the old favourites. The weather was abysmal: cold and grey with constant rain and heavier showers. The locals told us we were lucky that an Antarctic Southerly wasn't blowing. It was in this 'lucky' weather that we set off for the short walk to the Cake Tin at 6pm.

On the streets all you could see was red and black; but this time there was more red than black. It was the same story in the stadium: there were more Lions than All Blacks in an AB's home test. Chants of 'All Blacks' were completely drowned out by 'Lions' and the occasional chant of 'Waisake Naholo' immediately became 'Oh Maro Itoje'.

Category D seats meant 14 rows above pitch level, immediately behind the posts with no cover whatsoever. Waterproofs meant nothing, rain just soaked through. But I didn't care: I was at the Cake Tin; the Second Test Match of a Lions series against New Zealand; and I had a feeling it was our day. Even sat here writing this I can feel the tears welling up because the moment was so big.

Everyone knows the headlines; but the 'Silly Bill' sending off led to the Lions losing their shape and forgetting their game plan; not until Mako got yellow carded and it was fourteen against fourteen did we regain control; however regain it we did; and with 3 minutes left on the clock, Farrell provided the cherry on top. 21-24 and a win in New Zealand against the AB's. The stadium went crazy – it was like the Telstra in 2003.

The walk back into town was one big sing-song; Wellington had turned red and was ready to party. Naturally we returned to the Leuven where we found red and black partying together. The kiwis were shell-shocked but, to a man, they acknowledged the defeat with a grudging respect. Amongst the packed throng I ran into an ex-Harlequins Kiwi who I'd shared a few beers with earlier and as he left, he threw me his All Black beanie hat shouting "You deserve the scalp". We 'closed' the Leuven at 2am and headed to the Green Man to party 'til dawn. A few hours sleep, bloodies at the Leuven, then off to a harbourside restaurant to meet up with Chris 'Colin' Ritchie, another GOB and former Rozzer to continue the celebrations.

Things had quietened down by Monday, with most Lions having left town; we had to stay until Tuesday to collect visas for China before heading back to Auckland to prepare for the decider. That week, David was a worried man - and not just because of Wellington: he and Tammy were expecting their first grandchild and Charlotte's baby was due next Saturday. In 1987, David had tickets for the first RWC Final but didn't make it because Charlotte chose that day to be born. Was 2017 to be déjà vu?

The pre-test excesses of Wellington were not repeated and a nervous build-up to Saturday was filled with tourist visits, quiet dinners and filling in time with prep for the next leg of our journey.

Finally Saturday arrived, cold, grey, miserable and drizzly – I was anything but. Echoing the afternoon of the First test, we took part in 'choir practice' at O'Hagan's, drinking copious quantities of Guinness purely to lubricate the vocal chords. Another raucous and comedic train ride to Eden Park to meet David (unless Charlotte had done it again) and watch the final act of this 8 week adventure. He was there – with his cellphone switched off we joked – and we drank toasts to our adventure and the memories that we would share forever (and also to the late arrival of Charlotte's 'bump'!).

Everyone who knows the game of rugby also knows how that match unfolded but it is difficult to describe to anyone who wasn't there the feeling of emptiness at the final whistle. Whilst we may have escaped the bullet of a last minute AB's penalty which could have won them the game by 3 points, the scoreboard read 15-15. No one knew whether to celebrate or not; no one knew how to behave; no one knew what to do. The tour was over and the series was drawn. David and I looked at each other, shrugged, hugged and shook hands. Then he started whingeing about the referee and I knew he saw it as a loss. With that in mind I knew what every Lions supporter began to realise: that to go to New Zealand with a scratch side and virtually no preparation time and walk away with a drawn series is a magnificent achievement, rarely equalled. It had to be enjoyed and it had to be celebrated – and where better to do it? O'Hagan's of course. Partying as only the Lions can.

Emilie and I left New Zealand the following Wednesday knowing that we were now part of a small club: a group of rugby mad supporters who had followed a complete Lions tour in New Zealand and attended every match. The dream of a lifetime made possible by David, Tammy and their family. Thank you to them; thank you to the wonderful people of New Zealand; and of course thank you to the British and Irish Lions. Long may the tours prosper; never let them die.

"Gerard 'Gersh' Geenty (aka 'Arold) and Emilie Declippeleir"

PS Our 'world tour' continued through Australia, Japan, China, Hong Kong, Macau, Thailand, Canada, USA and St Kitts before we arrived home on 5th October 2017. 12 countries; 20 flights; 3 sea voyages; 1 river voyage; almost 50 abodes; countless trains, buses and coaches; and many car rentals. Also, whilst we were away our island was hit by two Category 5 hurricanes within 2 weeks of each other – house and businesses undamaged; no one on island seriously hurt. And our Saban flag was signed by more than 50 people during the tour. Roll on 2021.

Whangarei

Christchurch

Undercover in Dunedin

Rotorua

Hamilton

Eden Park 1st Test

Wellington 2nd Test

Eden Park 3rd Test

Eden Park 3rd Test

Pictures on this page and following 3 pages courtesy of Gerard Geenty

Besides the rugby, which Gersh clearly enjoyed, the very evident subtext to his and Emi's story is about friends.

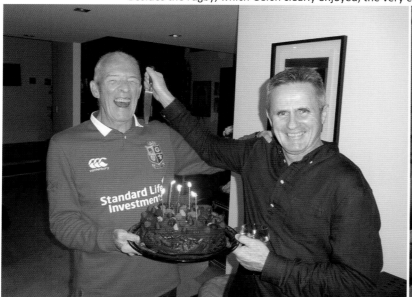

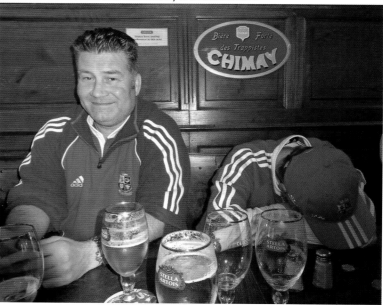

Top: Birthday Boys, Gersh and David
Bottom: Friends from Saba who now live in NZ. Gersh, Curtis, Daniella, Damien and Sharron

Top: Second Test, Wellington, Leuven Bar. Fat Tony and son Hugo
Bottom Gersh's Birthday Dinner at the Malthouse, Greenhithe, Auckland. June 1st

Gersh's caption didn't mention whether Emi was greeting an old friend in the
Green Man, Wellington or had found a new one

Top: Charlotte Muir's Birthday Party
Bottom: 'Arold, Emi and Fat Tony at the Green Man, Wellington

Top: Emi makes another new friend - and meets a bloke in red
Bottom: Will Emi ever forgive Gersh for this 'morning after the night before' shot?

Top: Christchurch. Wahoo, Emi, Christine, Gersh and Brian
Bottom: O'Hagan's Pub, The Viaduct, Auckland. A little quieter than a few days earlier. Gersh and Emi write postcards and enjoy a few Guinness before leaving NZ for Australia

I rather liked the simplicity of the message received from **Paul Wallace** the day after the third test.

I liked the content even more!

"Your book sounds fantastic! Going to buy it regardless. Thank you!"

Paul's boys are Sam, the elder one on the left, and Logan.

We'll finish with a tale that, for me, encapsulates how even the most thrilling of sport (which all who witnessed this series would agree the ten matches delivered in spades) can still be surpassed by the emotions it so often acts as the catalyst for. In this case, very much satisfying a long dreamed of rugby wanderlust Stephen Jones talked about and so much more besides, as the last line of **Tom Davies'** email self-evidently demonstrates.

Hello

I would love to share a story or two with you. It's not really about me, more about my dad and it all really started with a perfect storm that began at the start of the year. Although already I'm getting ahead of myself.

I moved over to New Zealand in 2011 after the Rugby World Cup and to be honest it was not a difficult decision to make. During that world cup a group of family and friends shared three camper vans, a few stories and one or two beers. My brother and sister both eventually left New Zealand, but after 6 years here I settled down with my now wife. I always knew my dad (the 'Nurse Doctor' to his NZ friend's family**) wanted to see a rugby tour. He brought us up watching Welsh rugby club games and national matches but he never made the trip across for an overseas event.

Late 2016 he was partially convinced to come to NZ with my mum, but her lack of love for the cold and rugby threatened to add a handbrake to the tour. The perfect storm came in the form of a new addition to our family in NZ. With a due date in September it meant a delay for my mother's flight freeing up the Nurse Doctor to make the trip alone at the tender age of just 62.

Before packing his bags Nurse Doctor got caught up in the excitement and went out to buy himself official Lions merchandise. He arrived on the 9th of June in Christchurch wearing the full noise. His first day he came to our Christchurch house which we had offered out on the Adopt-a-Lions-Fan Facebook page, which became such an integral part of his tour.

Within 24hrs myself and the Nurse Doctor were geared up in matching Lions gear and I realised more than ever how similar we are - in looks, humour and general interaction with Lions and Kiwis.

The tour took us down to Dunedin where we stayed with locals Jonny and Chrissy, who not only fed us their own lamb, but watered us and drove us into town in between sharing photos of their unique way to castrate sheep.

The tour followed similar veins of sharing lost evenings with new friends and drinking companions, but the highlight of the trip was the week in the Coromandel in the north island, after the Māori All Blacks game. We stopped up in Whitianga for the night where we went to a local bar to watch the Lions v Chiefs game. Within two minutes of being in the bar we were greeted by a giant of a man who identified us by our matching jackets. He spoke very knowledgeably about rugby for around ten minutes, and then casually mentioned 'It was very different when I played them in 1983'. Our humble host sat us down with his wife and we enjoyed the match together and drunkenly promised we would be in touch.

Aside from going to 6 of the games the one thing I wanted to do was take the Nurse Doctor fishing for something of a decent size. We timed this during our Coromandel trip, but the weather got the better of the whole event. All trips were cancelled for the week as a weather bomb hit - the flooded road and a landslide the reasons. But we never gave up hope.

My last ditch effort was a call to Buster from the Snapper Express near Thames the day before we were due to fly back to Christchurch. Buster laughed when I asked if he was going out as the rain was hammering it down and wind was blowing. I explained that my dad was here for the Lions and in Wales a big fish was 20cm, so I'd love to see him land something decent. He paused for a moment and said 'The Lions eh? Aahhh, I love people from Wales. There may be an early weather window tomorrow morning. What time is your flight?'. Within four hours Buster had agreed to get us out on the ocean at sunrise and back to shore to give us enough time to make our 2pm flight. In true Kiwi style Buster came through.

My now obviously pregnant wife, Seryna***, was slaying the snapper and the Nurse Doctor did not stop smiling. Buster talked about Wales and rugby, constantly ribbing at our chances of a win. He got us back to shore, snapper bagged, and we hit the road. Two landslides and a reroute of an extra half an hour meant we managed to make our gate with minutes to spare.

I could write for hours about the Lions tour. It's more than rugby. It's a global event that brings people together. Whilst the moment that we beat the All Blacks in Wellington will live long in my memory as the greatest rugby match I have ever attended, it is the pre-match interaction with fans (now friends), as well as our amazing hosts that I will look back and smile and laugh about.

I could never have thought it, but myself and the Nurse Doctor are even closer now, despite living as far away as possible.

Kind regards

Tom

** Why Nurse Doctor? Tom's dad Wayne befriended a New Zealander working over here many years ago. One weekend they threw a fancy-dress party. Kelly the Kiwi told Wayne he looked like Nursie from Blackadder, and has called him that ever since. Years later when visiting from New Zealand with young children of his own, Kelly introduced Wayne to his kids as Nursie. When Tom met Kelly's son Toby in New Zealand as an adult, Toby told Tom he'd always referred to his dad as Nurse Doctor.   *** On 3 October 2017 Seryna and Tom became a family of three with the arrival of Gruffydd Cai Davies. Congratulations.

Tom and Nurse Doctor reunited

The Davies' on Hot Water Beach, Coromandel

Snapper Express certainly delivered on a promise

After the Hurricanes match in Wellington

In a Rotorua Geothermal Park

Pictures on this page courtesy of Tom Davies

Thanks Tom. Proof positive that a Lions tour really is never just about the rugby.